The Practical Renaissance

The Practical Renaissance

Information Culture and the Quest for Knowledge in Early Modern England, 1500–1640

Donna A. Seger

BLOOMSBURY ACADEMIC
LONDON • NEW YORK • OXFORD • NEW DELHI • SYDNEY

BLOOMSBURY ACADEMIC
Bloomsbury Publishing Plc
50 Bedford Square, London, WC1B 3DP, UK
1385 Broadway, New York, NY 10018, USA
29 Earlsfort Terrace, Dublin 2, Ireland

BLOOMSBURY, BLOOMSBURY ACADEMIC and the Diana logo are trademarks of
Bloomsbury Publishing Plc

First published in Great Britain 2022

Copyright © Donna Amelia Seger, 2022

Donna Amelia Seger has asserted her right under the Copyright, Designs and Patents Act, 1988, to be identified as Author of this work.

For legal purposes the Acknowledgments on p. xi constitute an extension of this copyright page.

Cover design: Graham Robert Ward
Cover image: Plate from *The Expert Gardener*, London, 1640. Folger Shakespeare Library.

All rights reserved. No part of this publication may be reproduced or transmitted in any form or by any means, electronic or mechanical, including photocopying, recording, or any information storage or retrieval system, without prior permission in writing from the publishers.

Bloomsbury Publishing Plc does not have any control over, or responsibility for, any third-party websites referred to or in this book. All internet addresses given in this book were correct at the time of going to press. The author and publisher regret any inconvenience caused if addresses have changed or sites have ceased to exist, but can accept no responsibility for any such changes.

A catalogue record for this book is available from the British Library.

Library of Congress Cataloging-in-Publication Data
Names: Seger, Donna A., author.
Title: The practical Renaissance : information culture and the quest for knowledge in early modern England / Donna A. Seger.
Description: London ; New York : Bloomsbury Academic, [2022] | Includes bibliographical references and index.
Identifiers: LCCN 2021037611 (print) | LCCN 2021037612 (ebook) | ISBN 9781350200241 (paperback) | ISBN 9781350200203 (hardback) | ISBN 9781350200210 (pdf) | ISBN 9781350200227 (ebook)
Subjects: LCSH: English literature—Early modern, 1500–1700—History and criticism. | Knowledge, Theory of—England—History—16th century. | Knowledge, Theory of—England—History—17th century. | Literature and society—England—History—16th century. | Literature and society—England—History—17th century. | England—Intellectual life—16th century. | England—Intellectual life—17th century.
Classification: LCC PR428.K66 S44 2022 (print) | LCC PR428.K66 (ebook) | DDC 820.9/355—dc23
LC record available at https://lccn.loc.gov/2021037611
LC ebook record available at https://lccn.loc.gov/2021037612

ISBN: HB: 978-1-3502-0020-3
PB: 978-1-3502-0024-1
ePDF: 978-1-3502-0021-0
eBook: 978-1-3502-0022-7

Typeset by RefineCatch Limited, Bungay, Suffolk

To find out more about our authors and books visit www.bloomsbury.com and sign up for our newsletters.

My bookes and instruments shall be my companie,
On them to looke, and practise by my selfe.

WILLIAM SHAKESPEARE,
THE TAMING OF THE SHREW
i.i. 83

For my husband, father & brother

CONTENTS

List of Figures x
Acknowledgments xi
Conventions xiii

Introduction: Jewels Abound 1

1 Regimens and Rules: The Rudiments of Health and Husbandry 17

2 Measure for Measure: Mensuration and Mathematics 45

3 Elizabethan Alterations: Continuity and Crisis 63

4 Maritime Matters 93

5 Public Discourses; Practical Concerns 117

6 The Knowledge-Mongers 143

Notes 165
Select Bibliography 207
Index 221

FIGURES

1. Sebastian Brant (1485–1521), "Of Useless Books," *Stultifera navis*, Woodcuts (Basel, 1498). ... 5
2. Everard Digby (c. 1550–1605), *De arte natandi libri duo, quorum prior regulas ipsius artis, posterior vero praxin demonstrationemque continet*, (London, 1587). ... 37
3. John Fitzherbert (d. 1531), *New tracte or Treatyse moost profitable for all husbandemen* (London, 1523). ... 42
4. Hans Holbein the Younger (1497–1543), *Jean de Dinteville and Georges de Selve* ("The Ambassadors") (1533). Detail of the arm of Dinteville and scientific instruments. Oil on oak, 207 × 209.5 cm. ... 59
5. William Cunningham (b. 1531), *The cosmographical glasse, conteinyng the pleasant principles of cosmographie, geographie, hydrographie, or nauigation* (London, 1559), folding plate facing folio 8: plan view of Norwich. ... 62
6. William Clowes (1543/4–1604), *A briefe and necessarie treatise, touching the cure of the disease called Morbus Gallicus, or Lues Venerea, by unctions and other approoued waies of curing / newlie corrected and augmented . . .* (London, 1589). ... 71
7. Thomas Dawson (active 1568–1620), *A booke of cookerie, otherwise called the good huswifes handmaid* (London, 1597). ... 90
8. John Davis (d. 1621), *The Seamans Secrets* (London, 1626), sig. C4v. ... 95
9. John Parkinson (1567–1650), *Paradisi in sole paradisus terrestris. Or, a garden of all sorts of pleasant flowers which our English ayre will permit to be noursed vp* (1629), p. 355. ... 134
10. William Bourne (c. 1535–1582), Gabriel Harvey's copy of Bourne's *Regiment for the Sea* (London, 1592), title page. ... 150
11. Cyprian Lucar (1544–1611?), *A Treatise named Lucarsolace* (London, 1590), pp. 156–157. ... 152

ACKNOWLEDGMENTS

As I write this in May of 2021, I am thinking about my students at Salem State University at the end of a long academic/pandemic year: last year's class of graduates is experiencing their delayed graduation while this year's class prepares for their own commencement. These students, and many classes before them, were the essential inspiration for this book, which is derived as much out of teaching as reading. Teaching four courses a semester for over a quarter of a century has compelled me to adopt many of the approaches and techniques utilized by the authors of practical publications in the early modern era, including epitomization, classification and illustration. A professor is a gatherer, a translator, and a facilitator, surveying the field, distilling factors and forces down to their essences, and providing both the rules and the tools for engagement. My students at Salem State, both undergraduates and graduates, have seldom been satisfied with abstract academic ideas, contemporary narratives, or striking images: their curiosity was focused more on connections and consequences, and consequently, so was mine. I am also grateful for the inspiration and support of so many of my colleagues in the History Department: their seemingly effortless balance of teaching, research, administrative, service and myriad other obligations each and every semester has been a constant example and motivation for me.

I have always found the community in which I live, Salem, Massachusetts, to be inspiring as well. I am grateful to my close circle of friends and the wider circle of passionate people (some former students) who make this old city (by American standards) such an interesting place to live and work. Likewise, I am grateful to my immediate family, including my husband John, my father Tom and brother Matthew (precise, stylistic and conceptual editors, respectively), stepson Allen, stepmother Pam, and brother-in-law Brian, for their constant encouragement and support, as well as to members of my network of extended family and friends in New York, New Jersey, Virginia, and North Carolina. Three cats were in close proximity as I was writing this book, casting no criticism (I think) and creating a calming presence: Darcy, Trinity, and Tuck.

As an historian I want to document the time in which this book was written by expressing my gratitude to those institutions that have worked diligently to expand the accessibility of their textual resources through digitization. This work would not have been possible without access to

Early English Books Online (EEBO) through Salem State's Berry Library, a privilege for which I am extremely grateful, every day. The Folger Shakespeare Library, The Newberry Library, and the Wellcome Library have been invaluable resources as well. And finally, many thanks to Mark Fisher, and to Emily Drewe and Abigail Lane of Bloomsbury, who shepherded this text from manuscript to book.

CONVENTIONS

All titles are in their original spelling with capitalization conventions (or lack thereof); complete titles are included in the Notes and short titles in the Bibliography. Quotations from the texts are in modernized spelling, including the substitution of j for i, v for u, and w for vv, as well as all contractions.

Introduction:

Jewels Abound

Writing in 1612, William Sclater remarked that "this age is strangely in love with epitomes, if faith itself shall be drawn to her compendium." Sclater was a Puritan clergyman who was contributing to the ongoing dialogue about the biblical and legal legitimacy of church tithes, but he could just as well have been referencing health, husbandry, navigation, or any other expanding body of knowledge in the early modern era, epitomized and disseminated to a growing audience through successive editions of printed compendia, manuals, or "useful" books. What began in fifteenth-century Italy as essential abstracts of newly-recovered classical texts evolved into more basic reference works in the realms of daily life and work or of "history of nature altered or wrought," in the categorization of Francis Bacon, who both acknowledged their existence and called for their reform in *Of the Proficience and Advancement of Learning, Divine and Human*, according to the rationale that "we see remote and superficial generalities, do but offer knowledge to [the] scorn of practical men, and are no more aiding to practice, than an Ortelius universal map is to direct the way between London and York."[1]

The words of both Bacon and Sclater reflect the emergence of a print culture of information and instruction that developed over the course of the sixteenth century and flourished in the seventeenth: while the word "practical" was limited to actual and active practices in the former century, by the middle of the latter it was employed in a much more general way, as for example in a succession of religious works such as Lewis Bayly's *The practise of pietie* and Henry Hammond's *A practicall catechisme*, popular texts that would seem to confirm Sclater's worst fears about his countrymen's increasing unfamiliarity with scripture.[2] Nearly everything could be epitomized to the essence of its practical character: piety, language, law, measurement, medicine, music, navigation, patience, penmanship, perspective, rhetoric, warfare. Even the *Theatrum orbis terrarum* of Abraham Ortelius was epitomized in 1601 in the form of an octavo with "small maps."³ There were comparisons between the "historical" and the "practical," contrasting impressions of how things were once done or perceived with instructions for the present. Recovered knowledge was key, but both the Renaissance and the Reformation also emphasized self-reliance and self-sufficiency in matters both secular and spiritual. Texts could provide both the path to salvation and *A vvay to get vvealth*, according to the title of Gervase Markham's popular compilation, in which the six major agricultural vocations are referred to as "callings."⁴

Early modern printers and publishers utilized a variety of terms to convey the value of their compendia and compilations as ready reference to prospective readers: increasingly visible from the later sixteenth century and tied almost universally to practical pursuits was *Jewel(l)*, denoting a precious printed (and thus permanent) storehouse of useful information which one could tap into at any time. First to appear were the *Jewels* of health, providing recipes old and new, proactive and preventative, general and plague-specific. The works of Swiss naturalist and Italian surgeon Conrad Gessner and Leonardo Fioravanti were translated into English as *The newe iewell of health* (1576) and *A ioyfull iewell* (1579) respectively; a slim plague tract by Thomas Brasbridge was published repeatedly under the title *The poore mans iewell*. Texts about agriculture began to discern between husbandry and "huswifery" in the later sixteenth century, leading to the emergence of a new genre of household manuals like Thomas Dawson's popular *The good husvvifes ievvell* (1587). In their format and content, *Jewel* books evolved in different ways over time with their utilitarian character always the first consideration: Hugh Plat's *The jewell house of art and nature* (1594) was an updated medieval miscellany, featuring a variety of improving "inventions" for household and husbandry, and *The merchants ievvel* (1628) of Nicolas Hunt contained essential conversion tables for traveling traders. John Blagrave's *The mathematical ievvel* (1585) is the perfect metaphorical title, as it refers both to a book and an instrument (an astrolabe of his own design), "the use of which jewel, is so abundant and ample, that it leads any man practicing thereon, the direct pathway ... through the whole arts of astronomy, cosmography, geography, topography, navigation, longitudes of regions, dialing, spherical triangles, setting figures, and briefly of whatsoever concerns the globe or the sphere, with great and incredible speed, plainness, facility and pleasure."⁵ While instruments were the ways and means of knowledge acquisition in several early modern endeavors, the word covered a spectrum of meanings: medical texts referred to the three "instruments" of health—diet, surgery, and medicine—while William Barlow's *The nauigators supply* (1597) a catalog of his own inventions with instructions for both construction and purchase, featured the "traveler's jewel," for the calculation of time. Instruments and jewels, material or otherwise, were both a pathway towards knowledge and knowledge itself.

And then there was *Cabinet*, an even more visual metaphor for the publication of practical information: many books made the claim of opening up "cabinets" that were previously closed and exposing their secrets, or mysteries, to the world while at the same time serving as veritable cabinets containing essential information. This metaphor gave the impression, correctly, that the information that was being dispensed had been around for quite some time and indeed, the majority of sixteenth-century instructive texts were compilations of repackaged "knowledge" from either classical or continental sources. New "discoveries" began to surface at the end of the century, and the relationship between the practical and the empirical became more apparent, as information—a word used increasingly interchangeably with *knowledge*—was characterized as being the result of experiments and experience rather than just "gathering" from the "approved" ancient authorities. In *The jewell house*, which was a transitional work in more ways than one, Plat highlighted the experimental quality of his recipes, which were "faithfully and familiarly set down, according to the Author's own experience." Several decades later, in his preface to *The mysteryes of nature, and art* (1634), containing instructions for not-so practical waterworks, fireworks, and artworks, John Bate emphasized *practice*: his instructions were "gathered", but also "practiced, or found out by industry and experience."[6] While Bate's technology might have been a bit superfluous, his methodology followed Bacon, and anticipated Thomas Fuller's more prosaic observation that "knowledge is a treasure, but practice is the key to it."[7] Texts that focused on the evolving practice of agriculture, mensuration, navigation, and (with qualifications) medicine represent a popular "scientific" discourse underlying the more magisterial Scientific Revolution in the seventeenth century, and the crucible of technological activity that would produce the Industrial Revolution in the next.

Contemporaries realized that the advent of printing by moveable type increased access to many words, the word of God chief, but not exclusive, among them, but were not so aware of the forces—religious, political, social and cultural—unleashed consequently. It took considerable historical perspective to identify the "permanent Renaissance" of Elizabeth Eisenstein, characterized by the wider dissemination, improved standardization, and fixity of its printed expressions, and connected to the other major culture movements of the early modern era, the Reformation and the Scientific Revolution. In her definitive study, Eisenstein includes the authors of practical publications in her "Commonwealth of Learning," and observes that

> Even a superficial observer of sixteenth-century literature cannot fail to be impressed by the 'avalanche' of treatises which were used to explain, by a variety of 'easy steps', (often supplemented by sharp-edged diagrams) just 'how to' draw a picture, compose a madrigal, mix paints, bake clay, keep accounts, survey a field, handle all manner of tools and instruments, work mines, assay metals, move armies or obelisks, design buildings, bridges and machines.[8]

All these "how-to" books have been the subjects of a succession of studies following Eisenstein, illuminating the genre but topical subsets within it more particularly. This literature is as varied as the texts on which it is focused, encompassing everything from the Italian "guides to good living" of Rudolph Bell's *How to Do It*, the English husbandry manuals examined by Andrew McRae in *God Speed the Plough*, the western European nautical manuals analyzed by Margaret Schotte in *Sailing School* and the "vernacular science" practiced by Hugh Plat and his contemporaries at the turn of the seventeenth century in Deborah Harkness's *The Jewel House: Elizabethan London and the Scientific Revolution*. The close cohort of the technical treatise, compilations of diverse recipes derived from the medieval "secrets" tradition, flourished in the sixteenth century and have received increasing attention in the twenty-first, following the publication of William Eamon's definitive *Science and the Secrets of Nature: Books of Secrets in Medieval and Early Modern Culture*.[9] The histories of medicine, food, agriculture, printing, mechanics, architecture, and nearly every aspect of early modern "everyday life" draw on treatises and recipe collections, both anecdotally and systematically.[10] These works include substantive discussions of the sources, contexts, reception, and audiences of these practical books and recipes, as well as *how* they were read. *Why* they were read is assumed for the most part: these were perceived as "useful" texts after all; the antithesis of those "useless" tomes collected, but not read, by Sebastian Brant's first fool in his widely popular *Ship of Fools* (1494): *For to have plenty it is a pleasant thing in my conceit and to have them ay in honde. But what they mean do I not understand* (see Figure 1).

The books around this "book fool" are not useless, of course, but they are made so by his inability or unwillingness to read them and *apply* their knowledge, in fulfillment of humanist ideals.[11] A collection of beautiful object-books was one Renaissance ideal, but so too was the idea of knowledge utilized to improve and perfect one's person, city, or society: learning. Self-fashioning was self-improvement, and "useful books" became a key way to achieve both in the early modern era. Given the comparatively late, literary, and secular characteristics of the English Renaissance, the role of informative and instructive texts deserves at least as much attention as its more creative expressions in terms of reflecting and shaping English culture. Grounding these texts—jewels, cabinets, closets, compendia, manuals, handbooks and *vade mecums*—in the general context of culture and society in early modern England is the essential task of this book, and in doing so, establishing their connections, both topically and universally, to the dynamic trends and events of the sixteenth and early seventeenth centuries. Our understanding of the culture and society of early modern England is increasingly nuanced and layered, but knowledge of personal, political and polemical structures is greater than that of arguably its most essential layer: practical information and its demand.

FIGURE 1 *Sebastian Brant (1485–1521), "Of Useless Books," Stultifera navis, Woodcuts (Basel, 1498). Special Collections, University of Houston Libraries.*

Parameters must be established as practical publications do indeed represent an "avalanche" of texts, by both contemporary and modern standards, and my aim is that of a surveyor rather than a forager, or in the words of Emmanuel Le Roy Ladurie, a parachutist rather than a truffle hunter. Prior to the later twentieth century, almost all discussions of English didactic literature in the early modern era were focused on courtesy or conduct books of instruction aimed at the "rising" gentry. Perhaps courtesy books could be perceived as very practical for an aspiring courtier, but I have excluded most of them for the most part, unless they advocate an *active* practice: manners are not enough; one must be instructed to *do* something. Even *The boke of keruynge* (1508), an early book of (great) household instruction in the production and presentation of feasts, can be seen as practical even though it was not appealing to the wider audience of the *The good husvvifes ievvell*, which also included the "order of meats" and "how they must be served at the table, with their sauces for flesh days at dinner." The most popular—and arguably most useful or used—books of the early modern era were almanacs: as I am focused on examining knowledge diffusion within specific pursuits I am excluding this particular genre, though it certainly informed many practical texts.

What I will be examining are printed treatises, manuals, and recipe/receipt books: texts that offer information and advice about medical, agricultural, domestic, navigational, mathematical and mercantile *processes* and problems. In large part these are medieval genres transformed over the early modern era, by print and its attendant tools: "tables" of content, indexes, illustrations. For most of the sixteenth century, the format of these books belied the fact that the information within was still primarily medieval: they are forms of disclosure and compilation from earlier authorities such as Aristotle, Euclid, Pliny the Elder, Albertus Magnus, Roger Bacon, and Petrus Hispanus, as well as contemporaries Paracelsus, Leonardo Fioravanti, and the very prolific "Master Alexis of Piedmont," the pseudonym of cartographer Girolamo Ruscelli (1500–1566), the founder of the "Academy of Secrets," the first experimental scientific society.[12] The development of both process and authority is evident from the title pages of these texts, as words and phrases such as gathered, collected, long hidden and "newly drawn out" give way to collection, experimentation, and experience. Increasingly we see the words approved, augmented, and corrected utilized separately or all together, perhaps with "purged," as well as more authors publishing under their own authority like Hugh Plat, John Davis, and Gervase Markham. These authors published texts containing information "never heretofore printed" and "their" books continued to be published even after their deaths, as "diverse choice receipts, found in the author's closet since his decease" were uncovered periodically. Words evolved as well as phrases: different authors played with *receipt*, coming up with "conceipt" and "conceit," before the term was replaced altogether by seemingly-original *experiments*. There are two underlying subtexts inherent in many of these early modern works, one constant and the other emerging and both reflective of Renaissance culture: the mastery of nature, which was the keeper of all the secrets, and the discovery of "new" materials, approaches and challenges. Medical texts were grounded in traditional Galenic theory throughout our period, but they had to confront new diseases and new approaches if they were to remain relevant, as did any text offering information and instruction. It took a while to embrace the "new": information had to be ordered before it could be evaluated. The process of reception took time: there were separate but overlapping phases of translation, compilation, verification, correction, and invention. Certain new things could not be ignored—chiefly the New World, the *ars nova*, and new diseases that brought forth new cures—but the Renaissance inclination to look back and find authority in classical texts was just as manifest in England as it was elsewhere. When there was not an ancient source there was generally a contemporary continental one for the English: Italian books of secrets and mathematics, medical tracts from Germany and France, Spanish and Dutch navigational texts. Depending on the period, the subject, and the text, "Englishing" was not necessarily mere translation: it might involve more accommodation of English "style," measurements, dating, and place names. As the sixteenth century progressed, compilation gave way to critique, and ultimately to more discoveries.

The general framework of *The Practical Renaissance* is structured around three chronological eras and their central approaches towards both information and instruction: as matters of dissemination, discovery, and discourse. During the first half of the sixteenth century, the focus was primarily on the dissemination of information that was "gathered" from ancient and continental authors, translated, compiled, summarized and presented to a rather limited English audience. There was some innovation in presentation, but content was essentially derivative with the exception of some agricultural texts: a comparison of texts on health and husbandry in Chapter One highlights the differing approaches of one field that was entirely theoretical and another more rooted in contemporary practice, as was the emerging profession of surveying, one of the various means of "taking measure" examined in Chapter Two. Chapter Three examines these pursuits in the Elizabethan era when the compendia continued but the critiques and exposures of "errors" emerged, along with a pre-Baconian focus on the alteration of nature fostered by the diffusion of alchemical theory and distillation practice, particularly as applied to medicine. The ability to manipulate nature was dependent on an enhanced knowledge of *its* nature, however, and so a new empirical botany emerged in this era, ushered in by the first English herbal of William Turner and successive texts on horticulture and husbandry. The textual emergence of the English "housewife" dates to the beginning of the Elizabethan era, and a more experimental and responsive agriculture emerged in response to the famine conditions at its end. The second half of the sixteenth century was also characterized by a navigational "awakening" following the foundation of the Merchant Adventurers, later known as the Muscovy Company, in 1551.[13] The Northeast Passage did not provide access to the Indies, but it did open England up to long-distance open-sea navigation, and the acquisition of the knowledge and tools necessary to assume some measure of sovereignty over the seas. This is the central focus of Chapter Four, which also considers other maritime matters such as shipbuilding and cartography. With the beginning of the Stuart era, an enhanced dynamic of discourse is evident and explored in Chapters Five and Six: between members of London's "medical marketplace," around issues of cultivation and forestation, and as advocacy for commercial and industrial policies and practices. These were public "conversations" in terms of their conduct and rationale, with arguments made in defense of public health, the public good, and the enterprise of England, and so standards of expertise and authority became part of the dialogue.

Within these broad themes, the development of particular pursuits over the entire 1500–1640 period is explored with an underlying emphasis on reception, authority, content and context. In some fields an increasing trend towards specialization is apparent, coincidental with assertive expertise, but there were also many blurry lines among and within genres. John Partridge's *The widowes treasure* (1586), for example, which included "sundry precious and approved secrets in physic and surgery" as well as "sundry pretty practices and conclusions" of cookery, and "many profitable and wholesome medicines for sundry diseases in cattle" is simultaneously a book of medical (both human and veterinary), household and culinary recipes, with little attempt at a systematic presentation. A survey of the two most common genres of vernacular medical texts, preventative health regimens and plague tracts, will illustrate the more conservative contours of early modern medical practice. Two works a century apart, Thomas Elyot's timely and popular *The castel of helth* (1539) and James Hart's *Klinikē, or, The diet of the diseased* (1633), were both grounded in the Hippocratic-Galenic theory and doctrine of the "non-naturals," the environmental and extra-corporeal factors that affect bodily health: climate, nourishment through food and drink, sleep, exercise, evacuation and emotions. Both works sought to provide their readers with the information necessary to monitor and regulate these factors in order to preserve their health, as well as offer advice to achieve this goal. There is similarity and continuity of opinion, even though Elyot was a Tudor courtier and Hart was a Stuart practicing physician, but these are still very different books as they reflect the different backgrounds and contexts of their authors. *The castel of helth* merged the late medieval medical regimen tradition with the humanist mandate of recovering and presenting classical information in a clear, accessible, vernacular format while *The diet of the diseased* sought to provide a "professional" perspective culled from Hart's own practice as well as the "labors of learned men both ancient and modern" and at the same time correct the pervasive errors flowing from "the lawless intrusion of many ignorant persons upon the profession of Physic." Elyot was slightly defensive about his layman status but still resolute in his belief that he was providing a much-needed service; Hart was equally resolute in his desire to drive "ignorant Empirics" with no formal training out of his profession, offering insights into the crowded and competitive medical marketplace of the early seventeenth century.[14] Both men presented "Hygiene", that branch of classical medical theory focused on the regulation of the non-naturals (as opposed to Physiology and Pathology, concerned with the innate and anatomical aspects of the body and diseases) as a practical course of action that could enable anyone and everyone, well-advised and well-armed with a useful *regimen*, to preserve their health.

The century that divided Elyot and Hart witnessed not only an expansion of medical practitioners due to the inability of the College of Physicians to enforce the national monopoly granted to its licensees in 1523 but also an expansion of medical texts, which also formed part of this increasingly-crowded marketplace. As with medical practitioners, there was a hierarchy of medical publications, with comprehensive and "learned" physiological texts at the top and sparse collections of well-worn recipes or remedies at the bottom. Every epidemic increased the dissemination of the latter, with Thomas Moulton's *This is the myrour or glasse of helth*, a plague treatise with appended assorted remedies, *An hospitall, for the diseased* (authored by T.C. but widely attributed to Thomas Cartwright), and *A rich store-house or treasury for the diseased* (by "A.T. Practitioner in Physic") being the most popular titles.[15] The preface to the *Hospital* includes an earnest appeal addressed to its readers which is representative of the genre's appeal:

> *Art thou diseased in thy head? Art thou grieved in thy heart? Art thou pained with aches? Art thou tormented with a fever? Art thou wounded? Art thou troubled with any irksome sore? Doth thy sight fail? Doth thy hearing wax weak? Doth thy youth wear away? Doth age creep on a pace? Finally, do thy feel thyself infected with the poison of the plague and pestilence? Then delay no time, but with a small price buy a gem worth gold (this book I mean) which though it be little in quantity yet is great in quality and virtue.*[16]

Recipes were everywhere in early modern Europe: in medical pamphlets, in larger collections of household advice, in commonplace manuscripts. Along with regimens, they anticipated the "Everyman his own Doctor" publications of the later seventeenth and eighteenth centuries: while Elyot maintained that his book would enable its readers to know "how to instruct well his physician in sickness that he be not deceived," the *Storehouse* was "set forth for the benefit and comfort of the poorer sort of people that are not of the ability to go to the physicians."[17]

The equally fundamental endeavor of husbandry and its practice is examined throughout *The Practical Renaissance* in its broadest sense: all forms of farming as well as gardening, for pleasure, profit and physic. This is an even broader category than that of health: it is almost all-encompassing as the vast majority of English men and women lived and worked in an agricultural world. Agriculture for sustenance or for economic gain in an era of "improving landlords" was obviously a different pursuit than gardening for pleasure, but there is overlapping territory in the realms of kitchen and urban market gardening, and ultimately my focus will be on changing attitudes towards the *land*: its use and value. Given that early modern practical publications were prescriptive in character, the division between husbandry texts and their spin-off sub-genre, manuals for (always-Good) "hus-wifes" is more idealistic than realistic, but the latter will also be discussed in Chapter Three. Texts concerned with working the land, and extracting value from it, were among the most popular publications in early modern England: over 20 editions of John Fitzherbert's *Boke of Husbandry* were published between 1523 and 1598, nearly thirty of Thomas Tusser's *A hundreth/ Five hundreth Pointes of husbandry* after 1557 and well over 100 of Gervase Markham's assertively English texts, covering every aspect of life and work on the farm, were published over the seventeenth century—many well after Markham's death.[18] Books about husbandry were inherently "vendible", to use the adjective employed by northern bookseller William London in his invaluable *Catalogue of the most vendible books in England* (1657). London classified both husbandry and gardening as "mechanicks": husbandry is "no less profitable than very necessary, but the pleasantest part thereof be *gardening*, an Art so courted with delightful contemplation that though a man be in a willful sweat, he will not feel it."[19]

England's early modern gardening literature was also varied but followed a recognizable pattern: compiled classical and/or continental materials in the sixteenth century, increasing emphasis on experience and empiricism, and seventeenth-manuals that were comparatively more original and "English." *A most briefe and pleasaunte treatyse, teachynge how to dresse, sowe, and set a garden* (1563), *The profitable Arte of Gardening* and *The gardeners labyrinth* (1577), the "gathered" works of the first English garden writer, Thomas Hyll (a prolific compiler and translator by profession), reads very differently than the detailed, joyful, and personal instructions in William Lawson's *Nevv orchard and garden* (1618). Gardening in early modern England was not exclusively a pursuit for pleasure or profit: it was also characterized by an experimental drive that was manifested during the famine of the 1590s when authors like Hugh Plat and Richard Gardiner advocated for various forms of "alternative agriculture."[20] Plat was in many ways the Renaissance Man of late Elizabethan England and the exemplar of the "practical" author, publishing popular texts on gardening, distillation, cookery, and a range of inventions for personal and national use. His publishing life represents the challenges and opportunities of the era—as well as the transition from general knowledge to specialization and the overlapping jurisdiction of the artisan and the "scientist."[21] Much less well known than Plat, but just as prolific and protean, was his contemporary Leonard Mascall, who is probably most distinguished by his popular publications on tree-grafting and animal husbandry, but who also published texts on fishing, vermin eradication, medicine, and stain removal.[22] Mascall, who served as a clerk of the kitchen in the household of Archbishop Matthew Parker and later owned his own Sussex manor house, was both a practitioner and a compiler, but was generally careful to acknowledge whether his information and advice was derived from continental sources or his own experience.

The myriad roles associated with maintaining the ideal household that were assigned to women in the prescriptive literature of the sixteenth and seventeenth centuries as the role of "huswifery" was invented, defined, and expanded in a variety of publications. It is notable that England, where popular books like those of Tusser and Markham were reissued repeatedly with special sections devoted to the demarcated roles of the housewife, was the only country in Europe where printed recipe books were directed exclusively at women, and where the best-selling author of domestic manuals in the later seventeenth century was a woman: Hannah Woolley. Here again we have extremely popular publications, with at least eleven editions of John Partridge's *The treasurie of commodious conceits, & hidden secrets. and may be called, the huswiues closet, of healthfull prouision* published between 1573 and 1653, and seventeen editions of Hugh Plat's *Delights for ladies, to adorn their persons, tables, closets, and distillatories with beauties, banquets, perfumes, and waters* issued in the first half of the seventeenth century. There are titles with shorter runs offering additional information for the long list of feminine responsibilities: still-room secrets liberated through print out of some long-locked closet and put back into the family cabinet for whom only the housewife had the keys, culinary recipes for every occasion and household, instructions for how to preserve and clean anything and everything, and all things provisioning. Of course, our English housewives also had to maintain their kitchen gardens, the foundation of "kitchen physic." Though Hugh Plat offered some creams and waters in his popular *Delights for ladies*, Englishwomen would have to wait for cosmetic recipes and instructions until after the Revolution: the Puritan disdain towards "paint" is strongly represented by various opinions in Thomas Tuke's *A discourse against painting and tincturing of women* (1619). Cosmetic enhancements were not seen as "the beautifying part of physic" before 1660, but rather as artificial or even deceptive beauty, a "hellish invention" and devilish custom, linked to adultery and witchcraft by Tuke.[23]

In addition to regimens and recipes, a fundamental expression of early modern knowledge acquisition and dissemination was *reckoning*: authors of mathematical texts referred to arithmetic and geometry in particular as the "ground" or "wellspring" of the mechanical arts. Robert Recorde's *The grou[n]d of artes*, first published in 1543 and reissued in over forty editions in the later sixteenth and seventeenth century, emphasized the applications of arithmetic, and John Dee's influential "Mathematicall Praeface" to the first English translation of Euclid's *Elements of geometrie* in 1570 provided a "groundplat" in the form of a "fruitful" tree diagram on which myriad pursuits were derived from these "principles," including geography, perspective, architecture and navigation. In his text, Dee highlighted the practical application of mathematics, as a basis for hydraulics, mechanics, construction, gunnery and surveying, an increasingly important endeavor in an age of increasing land values. Dee demonstrated all the varieties of calculation (and introduced the verb "calculate" to the English vocabulary) but also the more essential task of mensuration: geometry was simply the art of measuring land and all "sensible magnitudes."[24] Mathematicians were by inclination and endeavor "practitioners" in early modern England, and mathematical texts were likewise inherently practical, providing their readers with the tools of surveying, assessment, estimation, and accounting. Such tools—and skills—were necessary for both self-improvement and public improvements in a society and kingdom that were increasingly commercialized, so much so that "ready-reckoners" emerged when the requisite calculations became too complex for the artificers who were dependent on them. This codification of essential information through numerical tables transformed the nature of a text, from the path-towards-knowledge to knowledge itself: ready *reference*. Computational tables increased in number and scope from the later sixteenth century on, principally in texts relating to trade and navigation, but instruction remains the essential focus for most practical texts: addressing his fellow carpenters in *The carpenters rule* (1602), Richard More advised that

> as much as nothing is more fit for Carpenters to make them ready, not only in measure but also in other things, than Geometry: that therefore such as are of reasonable capacity, would spend some part of their spare times to study the same, in some measure at the least. For your furtherance herein, there are special good helps, both by the Lecture at Gresham College every Thursday in the Term times (if you were but a little entered) as also by Euclid's Elements of Geometry, which the right Worshipful Sir Henry Billingsley Knight, to the great good of the Common-wealth, though to his own great travail and charge, has translated and published in our English tongue.[25]

Written at the very end of the Elizabethan era from the perspective of just one craft, More's *Rule* represented several key trends relating to the creation and dissemination of practical knowledge: the ongoing effort to correct "errors," its collaborative nature, and its identification as a "public good." More's primary mission was to correct "errors ordinarily committed in measuring of timber," a rather prosaic example of a central Renaissance endeavor, but still representative of the contemporary discourse between contemporary authors and practitioners, as opposed to authorities of the classical past and present. For More, the problem of mismeasurement was daunting: it affected his own trade but also those of shipwrights and anyone who utilized or purchased timber. Thus, he felt compelled to write, even though he was no scholar and could only do so "rudely," identifying the causes of the errors as "either by means of the Rule or Ruler, with which they measure Timber; or else by the misapplying or using thereof." He was grateful to the man whom he believed was the inventor of the instrument, Leonard Digges, who set forth a "Table of Timber measure" which "stands in the place of a good Ruler, well decked with true measures" in his 1556 mensuration text, *A boke named Tectonicon*, but believed that Digges's true measures had been lost with time, when

> many will take upon them to make Rules, who have not Master Digges his book to make them by; or if they have it, understand it not, neither the ground from whence the Rule is made, by which they might examine the Rules which they make: which ground is set down in the eleventh and twelfth chapters of the second part of this book. But ordinarily men make them one by another, whereof hath grown the former error.[26]

Digges had actually been correcting errors himself, and codifying craft practice with mathematical rules, but it was time to do so again, a half century later. The discourse here was between Digges and More, a scholar and a craftsman, both working to create industry standards of practice which would better serve craft and country. Another half century later, John Darling published *The carpenters rule made easie* (1658) which referred to the title instrument as "common" and dispensed with much of the instruction in More's text, and much text altogether, in preference to tables for ready reference for "carpenters, joiners, masons, glaziers, painters, sawyers. Or any others that have occasion to buy or sell or make use of any such kind of measure for themselves or others."[27]

The last two chapters of *The Practical Renaissance* expand the perspective from the farm, household and workshop to the kingdom and beyond. Most early modern prescriptive texts justified their publication by their contributions to the public good but there was increasing utilization of that term in a *collective* sense in the seventeenth century, as well as an assumption that individual improvement was connected to that of the kingdom, and even the empire. This was the strong subtext of navigation texts in the Elizabethan era, such as the popular works of William Bourne and Thomas Blundeville: *A Regiment for the sea* and *Exercises*.[28] With Bourne and Blundeville we have another contrast between the "mechanic" and the gentleman humanist, both revising and adapting previously published information for their English audiences with knowledge acquired by experience, education and collaboration. Bourne's work was a substantial revision of the first English translation of Martín Cortés de Albacar's *Arte de Navegar*, targeted to his Gravesend neighbors bound for the sea: it was updated and amended with each successive edition, becoming almost as much an "instrument" for seamen as the instruments he referenced in the text, a "necessary book for the simplest sort of Seafaring men." By contrast, Blundeville's *Exercises* on arithmetic, geometry, geography, cosmography, astronomy, and navigation are addressed to "so many of our English Gentlemen, both of the Court and Country in these days so earnestly given to travel as well by sea as land, into strange and unknown countries, and specially into the East and West Indies . . ." although in the course of his very practical instructions he seems to realize that the information he has assembled would also profit "all those that desire to be perfect in Architecture, in the Art of Painting, in Freemasons' craft, in joiners' craft, in carvers' craft, or any such art commodious and serviceable in any Commonwealth." Another Renaissance Man with humanist pursuits (poetry, logic, history) was transformed into a utilitarian author by personal interests and inclinations tempered by the demands of the age. Both works continued to be published in the early seventeenth century, as the "enterprise of England" expanded to include merchant avisos and treatises relating to every aspect of plantations overseas, from surveying to husbandry to health.

Just as the ongoing effort to carve out territory and establish some sovereignty over the seas placed texts relating to navigation in the center of a discourse that was inherently public and increasingly dynamic, so too were medical and agriculture treatises centered on contemporary events and trends: England struggled with a succession of plagues in 1603, 1625, and 1636, and the possibilities of agricultural improvement in an age of transition and crisis were broadcast by one of England's most prolific advisory authors, Gervase Markham, who was particularly focused on equating individual and collective wealth. There were several heated medical debates in the first half of the seventeenth century, involving a discourse that was among colleagues, competitors, and contemporaries rather than moderns and ancients. The varied landscape of practitioners continued to generate dissension between the licensed doctors of the College of Physicians and an array of unlicensed and "irregular practitioners," chiefly more hands-on Barber Surgeons and Apothecaries, as well as between those who viewed the provision of medicine as an ongoing service and profession and those who viewed it as a commodity and trade. This debate was dramatized and publicized by the recurrent plagues: the College's inability to enforce its medical monopoly was no doubt a result of its questionable credibility, given the absence of its members from plague-infested London and their "reactive and reluctant" measures against the plague.[29] Windows of opportunity opened up for surgeons like Thomas Thayre who offered plague preservatives ("ready or speedily made at every good Apothecaries") in the midst of pestilential summers, "and no godly and vertuous minded Physician will be herewith offended, or envy my endeavors, considering it is for the benefit and help of many in this or such like dangerous time, wherein many perish for want of counsel and help in their sickness, at the beginning thereof."[30]

Like plague tracts, treatises about the land, from the perspectives of cultivation, assessment, and "improvements" are touchstones for the flow of information over the entire era surveyed by this book. While they are for the most part aimed at, and reflective of, the steward or landowner, tracts from the early seventeenth century are set in a more national context, and against the backdrop of trade depression, dearth, and mortality, most particularly during the crisis of the 1620s. Even before that intensive crisis, but after the Midland Revolt against enclosure in 1607, Arthur Standish published *The commons complaint* against deforestation and the "extreme dearth of victuals" with general remedies of redress, including intensive tree-planting, including both timber trees and fruit trees, breeding of "fowl and pullen" and extermination of vermin. Even though he was ostensibly speaking on behalf of "commoners," there are few expressions of moral economy in Standish's treatise: it is essentially utiliarian. And as such, enclosure was presented as more a part of the solution than the problem: all those trees should be planted in orderly hedges and even in fields devoted to sheep walks, pasture, and commons. "Good fencing" was beneficial to both the landowner and the Commonwealth.[31] While criticism of enclosure continued in religious tracts like that of Thomas Draxe, who echoed Thomas More in his condemnation of England's great estates, which featured "many Chimneys and little Smoke, fair houses and small hospitality; gallant houses and great enclosures [which], often eat up men, and dispeople the Land,"[32] agricultural tracts of the Jacobean era were focused much more on enrichment of the land and increase in its fruits, endeavors that required significant investment and legal security, both signified by enclosure.

The concluding chapter of the *Practical Renaissance*, "The Knowledge-Mongers," connects the texts and trends discussed throughout the book by looking back and ahead from a mid-seventeenth-century perspective: back to the transmission of practical knowledge from the classical era and the contemporary continent to early Tudor England, where and when it was translated, adapted, and diffused into—or challenged by—more experiential learning and new methodologies and practices in the later sixteenth and seventeenth centuries. Secrets and mysteries were exposed to the light of print; the miscellanies continued but became more "ordered" for ready reference. There was relative progress in some endeavors and their structures of knowledge and practice, and stagnation in others: while the stage was set for the agrarian and commercial "revolutions" of the eighteenth century, germ theory was a long way off. The chapter's title refers to a phrase used by Gabriel Plattes in his 1639 treatise, *A discovery of infinite treasure*, which considers a range of topics, chiefly husbandry but also alchemy, cosmography, geography, and industry, from a perspective that is decidedly not *humanist*: the Renaissance was over. Plattes had been schooled by Nature herself; he referred to no ancient authors but included Thomas Tusser, Hugh Plat, John Bate, and Gervase Markham among his fellow "knowledge-mongers": the latter's spectacular career serves as a constructive contrast to Plattes's less successful one.[33] England in the mid-seventeenth century was, and was *in*, a very vulnerable place in Plattes's view: it was "over-peopled" with an insufficient and an uninventive agricultural foundation. Not even the infinite lands of the New World would sustain its growing population and economic diversification if an agrarian revolution based on enclosure, seed propagation, arboriculture, soil improvements, and new "engines" (including a seed drill more than a half-century before that of Jethro Tull) did not occur. He offered up practical directions in fervent prose, employing medical analogies throughout as well as the not-uncommon observation that the best model for England's improvement is the well-ordered and flourishing commonwealth of bees, all bent to work for the common good. In a very Baconian style, but also echoing calls from the Elizabethan era, he advocated for the creation of a "College for Inventions in Husbandry" to sustain its progressive development once his remedies have been adopted. Plattes was quite aware that knowledge-mongering was not a very logical career choice, as he and others had paid "so dear for our wares and give them away for nothing." Both the *Discovery* and his last work, *The profitable intelligencer* (1644) reference turning swords into ploughshares and "unnatural wars" so he must have been very disappointed to see his beloved Commonwealth plunged into civil war. The man who was so focused on feeding England died an ironic death, on the streets of London, for "mere want" by some accounts and starvation by others, leaving his papers, documents of years of observation and experimentation, to his fellow knowledge-monger Samuel Hartlib, in whose famous circle he was enclosed. The utopian society he had described in *A Description of the famous Kingdom of Macaria* (1641; published by Hartlib but attributed to Plattes) was never realized, but the Restoration fostered both the inventions and the society he had envisioned before the Revolution. As Plattes and his contemporaries provided the inspiration and ideas which fueled an ongoing age of improvement in the eighteenth and nineteenth centuries, so the practical English Renaissance laid the foundation for the British Empire: more *jewels* were published after 1660 than before, but their descriptions are more evocative of *vade mecums*, pocket handbooks designed to "go with" their owners/readers rather than remain home locked in a cabinet, a genre symbolic of the needs of a more mobile society.

1

Regimens and Rules:

The Rudiments of Health and Husbandry

Early Tudor England was a society and a land in recovery: from mortality crises and depopulation with the attendant impact on land utilization, from the civil wars and strife that engendered a desire for a new order in all things at the end of the fifteenth century. The "fresh start" represented by the new Tudor regime, was echoed by an apparent demand for information that could refresh and improve one's body and one's *lot*, the essentials of existence, furnished by the most popular of practical publications in the early sixteenth century: those focused on the preservation of health and the improvement of husbandry. The word "practice" is used in the titles and texts of both types of publications, but in the former it is generally a noun rather than a verb, as medical practice was governed by theory and tradition rather than experience. Texts providing instruction to those working the land, or more aptly, those *overseeing* work on the land, were by contrast purely practical, though prescribed steps were sourced from the classical past as well as the present.

Two authors dominated the market for health and husbandry manuals in the early sixteenth century: Thomas Elyot (c. 1490–1546) and John Fitzherbert (d. 1531).[1] Elyot's *The castel of helth gathered and made by Syr Thomas Elyot knyghte, out of the chiefe authors of physyke, wherby euery manne may knowe the state of his owne body, the preseruatio[n] of helthe, and how to instructe welle his physytion in syckenes that he be not deceyued* was first published in 1534, and reprinted in at least seventeenth editions over the sixteenth century, while Fitzherbert's *Boke of husbandry* and *Boke of surueyeng and improume[n]tes* were issued in twenty and thirteen editions respectively in the same period. Their works were, quite literally, never out of circulation in the mid-sixteenth century, and they were referenced by their peers and successors in acknowledgement of their authority. While both men were of similar background and professed similar aims—to disseminate "profitable" and necessary information to the reading public—they came by that information in different ways: Elyot "gathered" his from a succession of authorities from Galen onward, and Fitzherbert *practiced* husbandry (or likely estate management) for 40 years prior to documenting his own observations and experience in print. These two authors, conveying the most essential of information rather than abstract ideas, represent the conflicting and converging sources of knowledge in the early modern era: the past and the present, the gathered and the experienced. Yet despite the divergent sources of their authority, Elyot and Fitzherbert were both concerned with established *order* in an age of recovery in transition, an order that was more individual than communal. Fitzherbert asserted that his book was "necessary to be known of every degree, that they might do and order them self according to the same," while Elyot presented his readers with a daily regimen to follow, with many "general rules" therein. Both authors also offered their readers prescriptions for action: their utility—and attraction—lay not only in their promises of "ready reference," but also in their ability to direct their readers "how to" achieve the *self*-preservation of their bodies and improvements of their lands.

Self-Preservation in its Setting

From our privileged perspective, it is impossible to comprehend fully either the basic difficulties of daily existence or the threats to daily life represented by sicknesses mundane or dramatic over the early modern era. With the assumption that prescriptive literature was responsive, we can only glean shadows of its inspiration, and we can read about the most conspicuous "epidemics," a word that entered the English vocabulary in the sixteenth century, not before. While plague struck with unprecedented ferocity in the fourteenth century, it was endemic until the eighteenth, a fact of life that was never taken for granted. In the Tudor–Stuart era, there were eleven notable plague epidemics: in 1499–1500, 1509, 1513, 1530s, 1563, 1578–1579, 1589–1593, 1603, 1625, 1636, and 1665, roughly every generation, with a relatively long break between 1636 and 1665, which made the latter epidemic even more cruel. In the first half of the sixteenth century, another generational peril was the mysterious English "Sweat" or sweating sickness, which struck in 1485, 1507–1508, 1517, 1528, and 1551. A "great lask" of dysentery (the "bloody flux") was noted in 1540 as well as a "massive manifestation" of new and "strange agues and fevers" (influenza) in 1557–1559.[2] And then there were the "pocks," smallpox and the French Pox (syphilis), which became additional facts of life. A succession crisis and parliamentary petitions were the public consequences of Queen Elizabeth's private struggle with the former in 1562, when both her vulnerability and that of the kingdom were exposed. This was a conspicuous strike, but every year and every day there were deaths during childbirth for anonymous mothers and infants, rotten teeth, blindness and deafness, headaches, breaks and strains, and blemishes: a relentless struggle against the susceptibility of one's body.

Given this context, it is not difficult to comprehend the popularity of books that offered the promise of better health, or more control over one's health: these varied publications are second—albeit a distant second—only to religious texts in terms of editions published in the sixteenth and seventeenth centuries.[3] Like medical practitioners, medical texts were extremely varied in terms of their content and comprehensiveness: the genre encompasses slim pamphlets with random recipes and larger reference works like Christof Wirsung's *General practice of physick* (1598) and everything in between. A useful classification began emerging with the publication of an influential 1979 article by Paul Slack, who divided Tudor vernacular medical literature into eight categories: 1) anatomy and surgery; 2) reflections on theory and practice; 3) herbals; 4) plague tracts; 5) other specific diseases; 6) single or specialized remedies; 7) explanatory textbooks and regimens; and 8) collections of remedies.[4] The more recent *Early Modern English Text Corpus* adopts a slightly different categorization for its 231 texts, combining several of Slack's categories and omitting herbals altogether.[5] In this chapter, I will be focusing primarily on that part of early modern medicine that was typically classified under the label of "hygiene," pertaining to the environmental factors that were deemed necessary for the "preservation of health" and their proper regulation through a diet or regimen, while later chapters will consider more specialized medical texts. In both its classical and early modern meanings, hygiene was both preventative and therapeutic, and consequently dietary *regimens* were prescribed for both the maintenance of health and treatment in times of crisis. Renaissance regimens were a conservative genre, but also a responsive and reflective one, and as such they offer the opportunity to assess the changing context of health and wellness over the sixteenth and early seventeenth centuries.

Because of the mortality crisis of the late medieval era, the popularity of medical texts preceded printing, and consequently England's early printers had a range of texts on which to draw.[6] The classical tradition was not rediscovered in reference to medicine during the Renaissance (as it was never lost) but it was reinvigorated and epitomized as both physicians and laymen sought to navigate the new demographic regime initiated by the Black Death. The Hippocratic-Galenic corpus, with its environmental concepts of health, was both authoritative and flexible enough to offer both explanations and courses of action: both the "natural" components of health (elements, humoral complexion or temperament, age, region, climate) and the "contra-naturals" (disease) are largely out of the individual's control, but the regulation of the "non-naturals" (air, nourishment, activity, sleep and wakefulness, retentions and evacuations, and emotions or "passions of the mind") offered opportunities for self-help and self-sufficiency in an anxious age. Even before the Black Death, Roger Bacon had identified the importance of the preventative regimen for the prolongation of life in his interpretation and commentary on the Aristotelian *Secretum secretorum*, influencing one regimen tradition in England; another was the *Regimen sanitatis Salernitanum*, a didactic poem containing rules for the preservation of health in rhyming Latin verse, ostensibly addressed to Robert of Normandy, son of William the Conqueror, by the faculty of the School of Salerno, the center of syncretistic medical knowledge in Europe. Both traditions converged in John Lydgate's vernacular "Dietary" (c. 1430), of which fifty-nine manuscripts exist: it was issued by England's first printer, William Caxton, and his successor Wynkyn de Worde as *The Gouernayle of helthe*, and assimilated by Richard Pynson in his 1506 almanac *The kalender of shepherdes*, which was itself reprinted regularly over the sixteenth century and into the seventeenth.[7] The *Gouernayle* set the standard for the vernacular medical treatise of the early modern era in its conservatism and moderation: it assumed classical humoral theory and focused on the more practical regulation of the non-naturals by offering recommendations for daily exercise, food and drink intake, and avoidance of the "noise of evil governance." The Baconian and Salernitan regimens, along with their late medieval derivatives, provided content, format, and inspiration for a succession of popular health manuals over the sixteenth and seventeenth centuries, including Thomas Elyot's *The castel of helth*, Andrew Boorde's *Compendyous regyment or dyetary of helth* and *The Breuiary of helthe*, William Bullein's *A newe booke entituled the gouernement of healthe* and *Bulleins bulwarke of defe[n]ce*, Thomas Cogan's *The hauen of health* and William Vaughan's *Naturall and artificial directions for health*, among others.[8]

These general guides to health are the central focus of this chapter, which will follow their development (or lack thereof) through the sixteenth into the seventeenth century, in response to "new" challenges and information, thus offering a particular perspective into the classic Renaissance interplay of classical and contemporary knowledge as well as the continuity of late medieval didactic knowledge, also present in the foundational agricultural texts of the era. Chapters Three and Five will examine the reception of other types of vernacular medical texts in the later sixteenth and seventeenth centuries, as variety and hierarchy, of both publications and practitioners, emerged as key characteristics of early modern medicine. In addition to regimens—as well as the myriad remedies that were published in singular collections and incorporated into household texts as part of "kitchen physic"—a succession of herbals, texts devoted to the practice of midwifery and to particular diseases (generally plague), texts focused on surgery, anatomy, and the "new" alchemical medicine, and more comprehensive textbooks intended for both lay and professional readers were published in the sixteenth and seventeenth centuries. All of these texts offered both information and advice, derived from both classical and continental sources as well as their authors' experience and "industry," and at the same time contributed to the formation of a "medical marketplace," which must have been more than a bit difficult for the average layperson to navigate. Indeed, given the confusing medical landscape of early modern London, where university-trained physicians competed with incorporated barber-surgeons and apothecaries and myriad "irregular" practitioners, texts were just one more resource for the literate population.

English Medical Regimens 1528–1640

Order in all things was an early modern ideal, expressed in social and political terms through the concept of "governance" over a household, a nation, or one's own body. A regimen, or a diet (words which are used interchangeably until diet was restricted to nourishment in the course of the seventeenth century) was the path towards good governance, which was not only ideal, but also foundational, for *Good diet is a perfect way of curing/ and worthy much regard and health assuring/ A King that cannot rule him in his diet/ Will hardly rule his Realm in peace and quiet* in the words of Sir John Harington.[9] The promise of some measure of order or good governance, combined with the essential accessibility and universality of regimens, assured their popularity throughout the early modern era, even when contemporary experience and expertise were prioritized in the later seventeenth century. No one could argue with the instructions "to use good diet to live temperately [and] to eschew excess of meat and drink" in 1528 or 1628 or 1728—or today. The successive English editions of the *Regimen Sanitatis* published between 1528 and 1649 all featured the essential content of "original" text with the additional commentary attributed to Arnoldus de Villa Nova, but their presentations varied considerably. Austin Friar Thomas Paynell, the first English translator of the *Regimen*, focused exclusively on deriving numerical lists from the commentary, as if numbers could replace verse as an aid to remembrance. Or perhaps he recognized that the *ars nova* had created a culture where information need not be committed to memory, but easily accessed through tables and indexes. So instead of verse, Paynell offers numbered doctrines, commandments, remedies, and "inconveniences" that manifest themselves if the rules are not followed. As the *Regimen* incorporated both mental and physical health, its essential doctrines were to "eschew and void great charges, thought and care" as well as anger as often as possible, to eat and drink soberly, eat light suppers (and larger midday dinners), to "walk after meat" and avoid "sleep incontinent" just after eating, to relieve oneself as needed—and to avoid doing so in an overstrenuous manner. There were three general remedies for preservation: to live joyfully, with tranquility of mind, understanding and thought, and (again) to maintain a moderate diet. Practice was important, and the establishment of wholesome routines: wash your eyes and hands with cold water first thing in the morning, then "run a little hither and thither," stretch, comb your hair "to quicken the spirits of the brain," and brush your teeth. Beware of becoming chilled after washing or too still after dining, no afternoon napping, and holding wind in your body could lead to many "inconveniences." Always eat on an empty stomach, but be careful not only of when you eat, but what: every regimen has recommendations for what to eat and what not to eat depending on complexion or humoral composition. For Paynell, the most wholesome foods for everyone were eggs, red wine, wheat bread (refined white manchet in later editions), broth (chicken soup!), milk, fresh "green" cheese, pork, young fowl, white fish, marrow, sweetmeats, raw eggs, sweet wines, and figs, "no fruit so strong a nourisher." Foods which "engender melancholy" and should be avoided if feeling unwell included peaches, pears, apples, milk, hard cheeses, and all salt meats, including venison, rabbit, goat, and beef. Paynell presented his readers lists of helpful hints in verse: five "proofs" of good wine, seven doctrines for choosing wine, five things that signify good ale, four ways to recognize "wholesome air," five remedies against venom (garlic is key), two remedies against ill drink (sage has "great utility"), best to worst choices for flesh, fowl, and fish (veal, chicken, pike), as well as a remedy for seasickness and a recipe for a good general sauce. The virtues of a variety of fruits, herbs and spices are dispensed, including everything from cherries to chervil to mallows and mint, and the qualities of "savoriness," before the regimen extends into more "medical" territory by describing the four humors and prescribing diets for each disposition, and culminates with the rules for phlebotomy and the exact number of bones, teeth, and veins in the human body.[10]

Successive editions of the Paynell translation in the sixteenth century were issued with the claims that they were *amended, augmented, and diligently imprinted*, but the text was not altered substantially until Sir John Harington, the "witty, saucy" godson of Queen Elizabeth, restored the text to verse in 1607. Harington was an always-aspiring courtier who translated and composed many works, including the very first proposal for a flush toilet, a work that was both practical and political.[11] In his preface, Harington refers to *The Englishmans doctor. Or, The Schoole of Salerne. Or, Physicall obseruations for the perfect Preseruing of the body of Man in continuall health* as "a little Academia, where every man may be a Graduate, and proceed Doctor in the ordering of his own body" and "a Garden, where all things grow that are necessary for thy health."[12] Given his courtly disposition, Harington added all sorts of amusing lines, which accentuated the age-old "rules": he offered up "Physicians' counsel and apothecary's pills (without the summing up of costly bills)," meats for both the Protestant and the Puritan, and the sage wisdom of doctors "quiet, merry-man, and diet." The School of Salerno, as epitomized in Harington's verse, advised those concerned for their health not to "scorn garlic like some that think, it only makes men wink, and drink, and stink," observed that "water-drinkers never make good verses," and offered a concise correlation between the general and particular aspects of humoral medicine: "complexions cannot virtue breed or vice, yet may they unto both give inclination." The last early modern English *Regimen*, and the only one to be published by a physician, was Philemon Holland's *Regimen sanitatis Salerni. The schoole of Salernes most learned and iudicious directorie, or methodicall instructions, for the guide and gouerning the health of man*, which was "perused, and corrected from many great and gross imperfections, committed in former impressions: with the comment, and all the Latin verses reduced into English, and ordered in their apt and due places."[13] Holland returned to Paynell's prose format for the commentary and struck out all of Harington's witticisms and "infinite absurdities" in his "new old book": later editions published by his son, the bookseller Henry Holland, included treatises on fish and "experiments," indicating that the regimen format was losing its utility in the later seventeenth century.

The Salernitan *Regimen*, "Englished" and amended, represents the center of a spectrum of vernacular publications extending from simple recipe books for basic distillations, "precious waters," and wines mixed with "stamped" herbs like *The Treasure of pore men* to more comprehensive manuals, offering advice for the maintenance of overall health rather than remedies for specific ailments.[14] The question of authority was largely avoided in the former, while in the latter we see the beginnings of *personal* responsibility for what is being presented in the sixteenth century, a trend that will evolve into professional responsibility in the next century. Thomas Elyot's *The castel of helth* represents a contemporary attempt to establish authority in the realm of daily life by an author who was well-versed in both moral and natural philosophy and also very well acquainted with the royal courtier/councilor role: advice was natural to him. Elyot adopted the gentle explicatory style he employed in his first book, *The boke named the gouernour*, which he dedicated to King Henry VIII, in *The castel of helth*, dedicated to an ailing Thomas Cromwell. The result is a more systematic and accessible presentation of the traditional Greek medicine and how it can be employed by the reader to maintain health. Elyot bore his status as a non-physician as an asset with which he could better relate to his readers, yet he also maintained that in addition to his own studies, he had been instructed in the works of Hippocrates and Galen by "a worshipful physician and one of the most renowned," namely Thomas Linacre, the personal physician to Henry VIII and founder of the College of Physicians. Whereas Linacre sought to restrict and professionalize the practice of medicine by acquiring letters patent for the College from his powerful patient and translating Galen from Greek to Latin, Elyot sought to popularize medical theory by epitomizing it according to humanist standards. After a brief summary of the naturals, non-naturals, and "things against nature," Elyot proceeded to personalize humoral medicine by giving his readers the tools to determine their own complexions, or temperaments, and corresponding diets. There was nothing new about this approach—there were certainly Sanguine,

Phlegmatic, Choleric and Melancholy Men in late medieval manuscripts—but Elyot's prose and popularity cemented these temperaments in English Renaissance culture. The prototypical Sanguine Man was characterized by his "fleshiness," his ruddy complexion (or I should say *visage* to differentiate the exterior from the interior), and abundant reddish hair (owing to the predominance of blood over the other humors in his body); his tendencies towards sleep and evacuation were "much" and easy, and he should seek to preserve his sovereign heat and moisture by eating foods which are characterized by like qualities. Elyot prescribed a long list of foods with their characteristic qualities as well as suggested diets for each complexion, and further suggestions for every non-natural, from sleep to the "commodity of exercise," to approved digestive and purging foods, to the regulation of various "affects" of the mind, so Sanguine Man or Melancholy Woman could fashion regimens for themselves. In contrast to the Salernitan regimens, there was more "doing" than eschewing, although considerations of complexion, age, strength and weakness always had to be taken into account. Emotions, "the last of the things called not natural, is not the least part to be considered," in Elyot's words, and his discussion of their physiological impact expanded with every edition, encompassing anger, "dolor or heaviness of mind," sorrow and joy. Mental "discomfort" could be remedied by both moral and natural philosophy: regarding the latter, Elyot prescribed herbs and spices both mundane and exotic (including the "bone of the heart of a red deer") as "confortatives" for the "hot heart" and violets, pearls, coral, a unicorn's horn, old apples, roses, sanders, an elephant's tooth, water lilies, and coriander for "cold hearts," while gems and precious metals, along with the ever-present bugloss, were considered "confortatives temperate."[15] In a process that will be played out several times over the early modern era, medicinal confortatives, the key to a therapeutic regimen based on the Galenic principle of cure by contraries, will be transformed into more pleasurable alcoholic *cordials*.

The personal dimensions of temperament were also considered in reference to *time*, not just according to daily or seasonal prescriptions, but also of the effects of age, which Elyot accounts not only by the "council of ancient and approved authors" but also by his "own opinion gathered by diligent marking in daily experience." The stages of life are open to some debate in early modern England, but the preference for systematic integration favored four ages from birth to decrepitude—mirroring the four elements, seasons, and humors—over Shakespeare's seven "stages" of life.[16] Only childhood and old age were excepted in the advice given by most regimens, but there are constant reminders that, as in everything else in creation, people change as moisture and heat decay, requiring compensatory strategies over a lifetime. An apparent trend in the seventeenth-century regimens is an expended focus not only on preserving health but also prolonging life, reflected in the titles of Tobias Venner's *Via recta ad vitam longam* (1620) and Everard Maynwaring's *Tutela sanitatis sive Vita protracta* (1664). The interest in longevity is credited generally to the influence of Luigi Cornaro's *Discourses*, which were summarized and published in England as a translation of the Flemish Jesuit Leonardus Lessius's *Hygiasticon: Or, the right course of preserving life and health unto extream old age together with soundnesse and integritie of the senses, judgement, and memorie* in 1636, and the public interest in the "extreme old age" realized by the late and very great Queen Elizabeth I might have been a factor as well. Yet self-preservation was a natural, universal instinct and medical marketing led the field among early modern instructional texts: *The olde mans dietarie*, providing a regimen for bodies "stooping, doting, and tottering with years" was published in 1586 by Thomas Newton, a prolific translator of classical and continental texts in general and medical texts in particular. Newton stressed the importance not only of translating such works but also of investing them with "English attire."[17] Longevity was also proof of character and the ability to follow a regimen and achieve governance over one's body and one's life.

The equation of complexion with character certainly predated Elyot but his use of the word *distemperance* was influential; its variants appeared in myriad texts—not just of the medical genre—from the mid-sixteenth century onwards. Word choices, format (most particularly the use of "Ramist" branching diagrams), bibliographical apparatus, a pronounced focus on the non-naturals as much of natural physiology is "hard and tedious to understand and requires the reader to have some knowledge of natural philosophy," and an overall emphasis on both the practical and the personal all explain the ongoing popularity and impact of the *The castel of helth*, which set the standard for the early modern "how-to" handbook. Later authors recognized it as such, and extant copies with detailed annotations testify to its use and usefulness.[18] In the preface to one of the books of his own health manual published several decades later, the physician William Bullein asserted that Elyot "has planted such fruitful trees that his grafts do grow in each place in this our commonwealth, and his Castel of health cannot decay."[19]

The castel of helth also served to inspire physicians to impart their wisdom to an audience apart from their peers and patients. Professional titles can never be completely dependable in the early modern era, but it appears that several trained physicians published vernacular medical texts in the sixteenth century, including Andrew Boorde, Levinius Lemnius (through the translation of Thomas Newton), Thomas Cogan, and William Bullein, and more doctors entered the medical marketplace of print in the following century. They all referred to their own authority and experience, but still relied on that of the ancients, presenting preventative, therapeutic, and restorative medical advice in varying formats: Andrew Boorde secularized the use of *breviary* in his alphabetical (by Latin word) compendium of anatomy, illnesses, conditions and remedies, *The breuiary of helthe*, and borrowed Lydgate's term "dietary" for its companion volume *A Compendyous regyment or dyetary of helth*, while William Bullein recalled the semblance of order in his *Gouernement of healthe* and revived the traditional dialogue for *Bulleins bulwarke of defe[n]ce againste all sicknes, sornes, and woundes, that dooe daily assaulte mankind*. Thomas Cogan adopted a conventional treatise format for his *The hauen of health* and even admitted in his preface that he had copied Elyot and the ancient authors *verbatim* in places but also tailored his information and recommendations for his intended audience, students at Oxford University. In another expression of adaptation, Cogan employed a Hippocratic variation on the Galenic rules (*labor, cibus, potio, somnus, venus, omnia mediocria*: labor, food, drink, sleep, sex, moderation) as they were "more evident for the common capacity of men, and more convenient for the diet of our English nation."[20] The nationalization of medical regimens continued in the seventeenth century with publications by physicians Venner (*Via recta ad vitam longam*) and James Hart (*Klinikē, or The diet of the diseased*), as well as Thomas Moffatt's *Healths improvement: or, Rules comprizing and discovering the nature, method, and manner of preparing all sorts of food used in this nation*, which was likely written in the 1590s but published in 1655 as edited and enhanced by Christopher Bennett.

"Englishing" involved more than just translating classical or continental texts: adaptation and amendment "for the English nation" were common processes for all sorts of texts, medical included, over the early modern period. Before he presented his "diet for the English nation," Cogan described the English "complexion," a characterization that was also derived from ancient authorities but updated to incorporate the fact that England was no longer the westernmost country in his post-Columbus world:

> the air of Britain is foul with often storms and clouds, without extremity of cold. But to reconcile these sayings of ancient authors, I think that England may be called temperate in heat in respect of Spain, and temperate in cold in respect of Norway, yet to be reckoned cold notwithstanding & moist, because it declines from the midst of the temperate Zone Northward.

Everything was still relative, and the impact of environment mandated that

> Englishmen eat more, and digest faster than the inhabitants of hotter countries [videlicet] the coldness of air enclosing our bodies. And therefore we provide that our tables may be more plentifully furnished oftentimes, than theirs of other nations.[21]

The well-traveled and very quotable Andrew Boorde opined that "ale is for Englishmen a natural drink" while William Bullein asserted that beer was fine for Englishmen, as long as it was brewed from good hops brought forth from the "fruitful grounds of England" like those of his native county of Suffolk. Comparative dietetic observations—along with comical ones—

were employed frequently by Boorde, who also wrote England's first travel guide, *The fyrst boke of the introduction of knowledge* (1547). It was his opinion that "of all nations and countries, England is best served of fish," both fresh-water and the more wholesome salt-water varieties, "potage (which fills men with wind) is not so much used in all Christendom as it is used in England," and "Englishmen sit too long and stupidly eat heavy dishes first."[22] Bullein favored the provincial anecdote over the national one, but his translation of the Latin names for plants into colloquial English—as well as his references to "strange" plants—evoke a more parochial perspective. The wonderful word "outlandish" was employed increasingly by both medical and agricultural authors to refer to spices and herbs that were not native to England: some were indispensable imports (chiefly spices—although essential saffron was cultivated in England—and sugar, which everyone agreed was nourishing) but there were increasing assertions that native substitutes should be sought whenever possible.

As both Boorde and Bullein were practicing physicians, they had to address their peers, although their willingness to accept non-physicians like Elyot as authorities is an indication of just how loose the practice and provision of medicine was in the sixteenth century. The interpretive idea of a diverse "medical marketplace" first took root in the 1980s, and it is now generally understood that the provision of early modern medicine was largely free from regulation and professionalism until well into the seventeenth century. The notion of a medical hierarchy comprising university-trained physicians who theorized and advised, practicing surgeons who treated outward symptoms, and apothecaries who prepared and supplied medicines, has been revealed as more idealistic than realistic. Instead of this hierarchy, there was a diverse and pluralistic range of practitioners and sources of medical advice, encompassing everyone and everything from charter-wielding physicians and barber-surgeons, to apothecaries, midwives, itinerant healers who called themselves "professors" or "students" of physick, and even booksellers.[23] There are references to both Boorde and Bullein's attendance to Henry VIII, though neither was a member of the College of Physicians, which was chartered in 1518 and acquired a national jurisdiction over the practice of medicine in 1523, but lacked both numbers and sufficient tools of enforcement.[24] Still, it is evident that both practitioner-authors perceived themselves as part of both a continuity and community of medical practitioners, and also as intermediaries between physicians and the (reading) public. In his *Breviary*, Boorde presented prologues to physicians, surgeons and "sick men" even before his preface to the reader and asked that the former "exasperate not yourselves against me, for making of this little volume of physic." He made the commonplace claims that it was for the "common wealth" or good and would serve as a safeguard against those "ignorant persons [who] will enterprise to meddle with the ministrations of medicines" while also asserting the scholarly and practical standards for both physicians and surgeons. To his readers, he explained that the brevity of his remedies (which are a rather miscellaneous mix of classical and contemporary medicine and folklore, disguised as a systematic reference text by the use of alphabetical order utilizing Latin names) was due to his beliefs that "the arcane science of physic should not be manifest and open, for then the eximious science should fall into great detriment, and doctors which have studied the faculty should not be regarded as well as they are" and more substantive descriptions might lead to "every bungler practic[ing] physic upon my book."[25] This sense of a book serving as a middle way between *learned* medical professionals and "bunglers," offering just enough information to transform readers into good patients of the former, is echoed in other sixteenth-century regimens, but the authors of medical treatises will not be able to tread such a fine line in the more competitive marketplace of the next century. William Bullein's more vehement condemnation of unlearned—not necessarily unlicensed—practitioners in the prologue to the second book of his *Bulwark of defence* is a preview of the more heated discussions of the seventeenth century. In the dialogue between "Soreness" and a surgeon (Chirurgi), the former asks *What is then the cause, that so many Surgeons nowadays, be despised, and live so basely, and are counted the abjects of the common people: if the Surgeons should so be honored, as you say that they should be, being repairers of decayed men?* The surgeon (Bullein) replies: *Repairers. No rather destroyers, marrers, and manglers, of the bodies of men, women and children: and these men, lack not only learning and knowledge, but also wit and honesty, through whose wickedness the ancient practitioners, and sober doers in Surgery be greatly abused among the common people.* In his professional character, Bullein goes on to condemn those "dog leeches and tinkers," who "never knew letter of books," find work in every village, and cause immeasurable harm wherever they go.[26]

Bullein's concern for the "common people" was a mainstay of early modern regimens in the sixteenth century, and after: while the sources of medical advice seem multitudinous in London, a book could supplement their more meager resources and arm them against all suspect practitioners. The second generation of regimen writers, following Elyot and his *The castel of helth*, began reaching out to a larger audience and at the same time sought to correct "popular errors" in accordance with the intellectual initiatives of both the Renaissance and the Reformation, a dual mission that explains their efforts to educate both laymen about their bodies and aspiring (or perhaps practicing) physicians and surgeons about the knowledge and skills they should possess.[27] Both the patient and the physician were governed by nature (and God), but ultimately *sickness* draws a (battle) line between their two roles, and between preventative and remedial medicine. In the words of Phillip Moore, once sickness was rooted in the human body, there was

> a strife and battle between nature and them, which shall overcome [each] other. And if sickness overcomes nature, then death ensues: but if nature

do overcome the sickness, then the body by little and little is restored to health again. And note that in this combat, between the disease and nature, the Physician is as it were a minister and aider to nature, to help her to overcome the disease.[28]

A *minister* and *aider* to nature, who was aided by the patient, armed with a regimen and thus the self-knowledge to preserve health and prevent disease.

How to Live a Wholesome Life

The Air You Breathe

Galen's non-naturals provide an organizational structure for early modern medical regimens and also for analyses of such texts. Prescriptions for the air, the first non-natural are effective illustrations of the essentially environmental nature of pre-modern medicine. Nothing can be more fundamental than the air that you breathe, and to sustain health, one must live and work in air that is free from all sources of "stink," both natural and human, including marshes, "putrefied standing waters," pools, ponds, mires, dikes, gutters, canals, dunghills or sinks, "except they be of and diverse times mundified and made clean," according to Andrew Boorde, who also advised his readers to situate their houses upon a foundation of clay or stone, and with a prospect facing east, west or southeast or southwest, rather than *due* south, "for the south wind corrupts and makes evil vapors" in *The boke for to learne a man to be wyse in buyldyng of his howse for the helth of body [and] to holde quyetnes for the helth of his soule, and body*.[29] There were only slight variations and additions to this thinking over the next decades, but in the seventeenth century William Vaughan believed that windows should "look northward or eastward" and added nut and fig trees, coleworts, hemlocks, mines and forges, and churchyards to the list of air-corrupting entities as well as suggestions for adjusting one's residence to the "sundry alterations" of the air brought on by seasons and climate, while Tobias Venner went into considerable more detail about the air in general, and winds in particular, in his *Via recta ad vitam longam*. Venner discarded the "moist and excremental blasts" of the west wind, in favor of a situation

> lying open to the South and East, with hills (which may somewhat hinder and keep back the vaporous West wind, and the sharp North wind in the winter) a little remote on the West and North side, having windows looking not only towards the South and North for the reasons aforesaid, but also, so much as may be, towards the East, because the sun in the beginning of the day, upon arising, does excellently clarify, and purge the air of them, and is all the day after better exposed to the most wholesome blasts of the East wind.[30]

One imagines a busy day of window-opening and closing to achieve the perfect balance of vapors and purgation over the course of the day. Later in the century, nationalism appears to trump empiricism when John Archer, Royal Physician to Charles II, declared that the "most" wholesome" region was England, where "the Air is temperate, the Spring temperate, the heat of Summer sufficient to ripen Corn, and Fruit, Autumn Colder, Winter Cold, yet not offending our bodies with extremes, also a Fruitful Soil, men comely of Body, well-colored in the Face, Laudable in their manners, and joyful in their prosperous health, &c. Ingenious in invention."[31]

Food and Drink

The situation of your house was the first step of an orderly regimen, but consumption was a much more involved path, in both idealistic and prescriptive terms. There is much more information about food and drink in early modern regimens (and other medical and household publications) than any of the other non-naturals by far: food and drink were *materia medica* as well as sustenance, and inherently more engaging than discussions of sleep or secretions. Discussions of diet and drink in the sixteenth and seventeenth centuries also offer insights into changing perceptions of new and "foreign" substances over the early modern era, a constant consideration in an age of expanding travel and trade. It was challenging for dietary authors to remain staunchly Galenic in an age of increasing botanical information, with the publication of major "new" herbals on the Continent and England. More than any other non-natural, foodstuffs intersect with all of the other topics of this book—health, husbandry, household and the collective/common "wealth" of England—but let us focus first on an *individual* prescribed regimen. There were several general rules for diet, which were expressed continually throughout the early modern period: the rule of moderation is first and foremost, with gluttony discouraged at every turn, the rules of humoral balance and correction with respect to complexion, the dictates of time (both age and season), and the rule of *custom*, which was a bit more variable. In addition, there were secondary prescriptions for the time of meals (both when they occur and time spent at the table), and the "order of meats," both over the course of the day and during individual meals. Thomas Moffatt's *Healths improvement* ended with the provision that "if our breakfast be of liquid and supping meats, our dinner moist and of boiled meats, and our supper chiefly of roasted meats, a very good order is observed therein, agreeable both to art and the natures of most men." Here he was using the term "meat" as a general synonym for food, much in the same way that "diet" was used for a complete regimen of life and living (though Moffatt utilized that term more particularly for "nourishment," or "an orderly and due course observed in the use of bodily nourishments, for the preservation, recovery or continuance of the health of mankind").[32] Generally the regimens specified that meals should occur only once the former meal had been digested; this was certainly the case with breakfast, but part of the digestive process included activity, so it was not advised to eat heavily in the morning because one's body was not in need of comprehensive replenishment immediately after waking. The other two concerns about breakfast were Galen's failure to mention the morning meal and the encroaching hour of dinner, the main meal of the day, which generally occurred at midday. Consequently, there were divergent opinions, as well as considerations of age, complexion, and season. A light meal with no flesh seems to be the consensus: milk and butter as a posset, eggs, bread, ale and not much more, even less if you are over the age of forty, and ensuring that at least four hours separate your breakfast and dinner at 11:00 or noon. The complete "English breakfast" did not emerge over the early modern era, but the notion that English men and women should eat *some* breakfast does: Thomas Elyot asserted that the morning meal was "necessary in this realm."[33]

Dinner remained the major meal of the day over the entire early modern era, although its time shifted slightly later into the day. The Salernitan recommendation that midday dinners be larger than evening suppers seems to have been authoritative for much of the period: before the imposition of the discipline of the clock, the sun dictated waking and sleep, and consequently people rose and went to bed relatively early and the midday meal became more important in terms of both hunger and digestion, which was envisioned as more of a compartmentalized than ongoing process. Meat was recommended for dinner, any meat, though the prescribed preferences were for younger and fresher meats over older, salted ones: there are many references to *young*, and *fresh*, reflecting the idealistic nature of prescriptive publications. For ease of digestion as well as nourishment, and following standard Galenic advice, Philip Moore recommended "partridges, pheasants, chickens, capons, hens, small birds (pigeons, turtle doves, blackbirds)" as well as "newly-laid eggs, raw or poached, young pork, veal, new milk, fresh fish [from] gravelly and stony rivers" and "bread made of the flour of good wheat, being well-leavened, sufficiently salted, & well baked in an oven, being two or three days old. And also, pure wine."[34] These were either/or recommendations, as consuming a "diversity of meats" at one sitting was discouraged: according to Thomas Elyot, "sundry meats, being diverse in substance and quality, eaten at one meal, is the greatest enemy to health that may be."[35] The *order* of consumption was also important: foods that mollified and "loosen the belly" should be eaten first and "styptic and binding" foods last: these are primarily fruits and vegetables, which improved their reputation over the early modern era, a trend which Joan Thirsk has characterized as a slow, but nevertheless notable dietary "revolution."[36] William Vaughan, in his *Naturall and artificial directions for health*, asserted that fruits were eaten "more for wantonness than for any nutritive or necessary good," but he praised many vegetables, and included a recipe for the very best "sallet" made of pennyroyal, parsley, lettuce and endive, which "opens the obstruction of the liver and keeps the head in good plight." Moffatt was more open to fruit in *Healths improvement*, but like most of his contemporaries, he preferred his apples, peaches and pears "cunningly preserved" or stewed, baked, roasted, dried and/or candied, yet another indication that the preservation of health was perceived as dependent on the preservation of foods, one of many essential tasks assigned to early modern women.

Vegetables, generally referred to as "garden fruit" or "garden herbs," also required considerable alteration to be transformed into nourishing food: boiling and dressing with butter, vinegar, salt *and* sugar, and pepper. Pickled cucumbers were considered more wholesome than raw, and even the "whitest and tenderest-leafed" coleworts (cabbage and cauliflower) "must first gently be sodden in fair water, then again steeped all night in warm milk; afterwards seethed with fat marrow or fat broth."[37] A combination of factors expanded the realm of vegetables in the later sixteenth and seventeenth centuries: the publication of the first English herbals (William Turner's *A new herball* in three parts from 1551–1568, followed by John Gerard's *The herball* or *Generall historie of plants* in 1597), an increased interest in urban and market gardens, and the famine and dearth of the 1590s. Consequently, artichokes (much loved by Henry VIII and apparently "powerful for the exciting of Venus" according to Tobias Venner), asparagus, and the whole range of root vegetables received increasing attention from regimen writers, including the "potato root" in the seventeenth century. Gerard had included the New World import in his 1597 *Herball* and Thomas Moffatt observed that "potato-roots are now so common among us, that even the husbandman buys them to please his wife. They nourish mightily, being either sod, baked or roasted." The closest comparison seemed to be skirret roots, which could

> be roasted four or five together in a wet paper under embers (as one would roast a Potato) or strained into tart-stuff, and so baked with sugar, butter, and rosewater, they are far more pleasant and of stronger nourishment, agreeing with all complexions, sexes and ages, being also of mild heat and a temperate moisture. Did we know all the strengths and virtues of them, they would be much nourished in our Gardens, and equally esteemed with any Potato root.[38]

Whether this was Moffatt writing in the 1590s, or his corrector/reviver Christopher Bennet writing in the 1650s, it is still quite apparent that sugar made everything more nourishing and native plants were preferable to the "outlandish" varieties. In between, Tobias Venner referred to potatoes as very "restorative" and "surpassing the nourishment of all other roots or fruits," and recommended them for "every age and constitution."[39]

The last meal of the day was supper, which should be a slightly smaller version of dinner held about six hours later and no more: William Bullein gave his representative phlegmatic patient a laundry list of what not to eat in his *Bulwark of defence* and concluded that "late suppers" were worst of all, "especially if they be long, for it causes painful nights to follow." Supper could also serve as a test, according to Bullein, encouraging self-awareness and self-sufficiency: "any other meat that you do eat at supper, although it seems repugnant to a phlegmatic stomach, if you sleep well after it, and feel no pain, you may use it as a *necessary food*."[40] Painful nights will also be avoided if you drink in moderation: the general recommendation is to lessen your ale or beer or wine throughout the meal by taking fewer sips or watering the latter down. All beverages, and most particularly wine and beer, have their medical benefits in several non-natural categories: both diet and "emotions of the mind."[41] Most regimen writers preferred wine to beer and ale, because of its "natural heat and moisture" which was akin to that of man. William Bullein asserted that wine was a divine gift of "comfort" taken moderately, but "makes men into monsters.... dishonors noblemen, and beggars poor men" when consumed in excessive quantities. Still, beer and ale have "no such virtue nor goodness as wine have, and the surfeits which be taken of them through drunkenness be worse than the surfeits taken of wine."[42] The problem with wine was that it was primarily an imported commodity, and consequently subject to dictates of price and spoilage. The former was not a concern of our authors, but the latter was, and consequently they included myriad instructions to restore and refresh wines and make them sweeter to suit the English taste. The "pure wine" of Philip Moore's perfect diet would be hard to find in early modern England, if not impossible. Even though both were native products, there are concerns about beer and ale too, but nearly everyone agreed with William Vaughan that the former "receives a certain property of medicine by the hop."[43]

Vaughan's *Approved directions for health*, which was published in seven editions from 1600 to 1633, in many ways represents the peak of regimen writing in its style and content, as well as one of the last "authoritative" medical publications by a layman. Vaughan was an Oxford-educated Welshman who returned home after the Grand Tour with humanist and humanitarian sensibilities: his solution to the poverty he witnessed in early seventeenth-century Wales was colonization, and he became an avid promoter of a Welsh colony in Newfoundland. "New Cambriol" did not take root, but Vaughan's common touch is in evidence in his *Approved directions*, which abandoned the classical treatise or reference format in favor of a more direct presentation, particularly on display in his section on beverages. He employed a dialogue of sorts, with questions framed as *how shall I know, teach me, and show me*. Vaughan instructed his readers to discern good ale from bad, revive sour ale and beer, and keep wine and beer from "turning," as well as revealing the useful secret of how to sober up drunkards and "tosspots" by turning their cravings into distaste (white wine infused with rye blossoms, eels or green frogs, and fried owl's eggs—but ultimately intemperance was a manifestation of lack of faith and sinfulness, so readers must *dig deeper*). *Show me* prompted instructions for "a speedy drink for travelers, when they want beer or ale at their inn," various wine preservatives, and how to make old wine new and remove its "malicious vapors." Drinks made of heath shrubs, licorice, water and vinegar were offered in response to the query of what poor men should drink "when malt is extremely dear," as well as several "wholesome diet drinks" for those in both sickness and health.[44] These would increase in number over the seventeenth century as prescribed drinks metamorphosed into early forms of patent medicines like the various or *elixirs salutatis* or *vitae* offered up by a succession of "students of physick."

Sleep

"After supper matters," in the words of Thomas Tusser, involved securing the house and its outbuildings against the night-time threats of theft and fire and then retiring to a place of rest for prayers and sleep. Sleep encompassed many realms of experience and understanding in early modern England: spiritual, emotional, material and medical. In her exhaustive study of the subject, Sasha Handley asserts that sleep "was understood as a state of transition between day and night, between degrees of consciousness, between the earthly and spiritual realms, and between life and death. The forces of nature molded its boundaries, as did supernatural agents and human action."[45] Regarding the latter, the regimen rules for sleep were very clear: the "natural" time for sleep is nighttime, during which seven hours should suffice for sanguine and choleric complexions, nine for phlegmatic, and in the words of Andrew Boorde, "melancholy men may take their pleasure, for they be the receptacles and the drags of all the other humors."[46] Too much sleep made one sluggish and oblivious; it obfuscated and clouded memory and quickness of wit. Boorde also referenced two phases of sleep, first and second, with an interval period of "watch" in between, the pre-industrial practice of "segmented sleep" identified by A. Roger Ekirch.[47] After a restorative sleep of four hours or so while on the preferred right side, "when you do wake of your first sleep, make water if you feel your bladder charged and then sleep on the left side; and look, as long as you are awake, so often turn yourself in the bed from one side to another." Boorde does not tell his readers what to do during the watching hour(s) besides tossing and turning (although he discourages "venery" during the first sleep so one wonders if the watching period is suitable for this activity), but he included lots of other rules: never sleep on your stomach or your back, or on an empty or too-full stomach, keep your head, clothed in a "nightcap of scarlet," slightly elevated to aid digestion, and make sure that the rest of your body is covered by the layers of quilted cotton, wool and fustian which should cover your feather bed. The colorful Christopher Langton, one of several sixteenth-century medical practitioners who entered the marketplace of print with texts that were not quite constrained by the regimen format but nevertheless still focused on the Galenic non-naturals as a means to proffer instruction, also elaborated upon sleep. He agreed with Boorde that "side-sleeping" was best, advocated elevating the head and neck during sleep, and believed that early-to-bed was best: youth, in particular, should avoid both studying and "banqueting and drinking till midnight" and go to bed as soon after supper as possible. This was the exemplary practice of those "many noblemen, which being troubled with matters of the Commonwealth, have ever observed this custom, that after supper, they went straight to bed, and in the mornings they did dispatch their business."[48] Langton has quite a bit to say about dreams as well, particularly of the "devilish" variety, but perhaps those theories belong more in the realm of emotions.

A half-century later, advice for sleep was much the same: at night, seven hours or so depending on occupation and age, on your side, covered up. There are a few references to *sleeplessness* in the regimens, but early modern insomniacs were better served by recipe and books of simples like William Langham's *The garden of health*, which prescribed a long list of herbs for the problem, readily retrieved through several indices. Pick henbane from the list, go to its chapter (an alphabetical order is utilized, but Langham provided a Table of Contents as well), and read about the myriad ways, incorporating its leaves, stalks, flowers, seeds, roots, and juice, that this particular herb can be used to prompt sleep and even "see marvels" while under its spell. After every entry in his *Garden*, Langham also provided a numbered list of cures (which are also numbered in the text), so the reader had multiple ways of obtaining the required information.[49]

Exercise

Advice and attitudes towards exercise in the regimens speak to the privilege of their readership more than any other non-natural, even diet. One assumes that the vast majority of the English population got more than enough exercise going about their daily activities so when Thomas Elyot articulates the importance of the "commodity" of exercise, including tennis and "playing with weapons," we know that he was addressing a relatively rarified audience. Thomas Cogan, writing for students at Oxford University, conceded that "Husbandmen and Craftsmen, for the most part do live longer and in better health than Gentlemen and learned men, and such as live in bodily rest" and prescribed "vehement" exercise, or physical labor, for the body as a whole or in parts, including dancing, leaping, ball-throwing, football, bowling, riding, tennis (recommended by Galen!) and for the lungs, vociferation, or singing, crying and reading. From his academic perspective, he considered study to be "exercise of the mind."[50] For all regimen writers, exercise served three principal purposes: strengthening of the body, increasing its heat and consequential ability to digest and acquire nourishment, and general detoxification, through the production of a "violent" breath or wind "whereby the pores are cleaned and the filth of the body naturally expelled."⁵¹ There is little sense of the classical emphasis on gymnastic *training* in the regimens: exercise was clearly viewed as a healthy activity, but more associated with leisure than necessity. Outside of the regimen genre, there was one conspicuous book of athletic instruction published in the later sixteenth century: Everard Digby's *De arte natandi* (1587), a treatise on swimming. The fact that this is a Latin text was compensated considerably in terms of its instructive value by the addition of forty-three woodcut illustrations, demonstrating Digby's directions for diverse swimming strokes, everything from the side to the back to the butterfly and with hands bound, like a dog and a dolphin. Digby's book was published in English by Christopher Middleton in 1595 under the title *A Short introduction for to learne to Swimme*, including the original woodcuts and Middleton's high praise for the original author, whom he placed in the company of Aristotle, Hippocrates, Galen, Euclid, Justinian and ... Mercator.⁵²

English regimens were aimed at a male audience as a general rule, but there was a distinct directive aimed at English gentlewomen in Humphrey Brooke's *Ugieine or A conservatory of health* (1650). This text is a bit outside our timeline but worthy of inclusion as it is representative of the general prescription to *keep busy* evident in instructional texts aimed at women. Generally, the concern about idleness was expressed in moral terms, but Brooke offered a medical perspective in his regimen. By both the standards of their continental peers and their domestic inferiors, Brooke asserted that English women needed to get moving as too much rest and sitting

> begets multiplication of humors and excrements & consequently that they are seldom well at ease and void of infirmities: this is especially the unhappiness of women, who mostly leading a sedentary life, lose their colors, and the vivacity of their countenances, and are thereby forced to use paintings, whence (being unskillfully administered) they contract headaches, pains, and blackness in the teeth, and derive many other maladies both to themselves and their posterities.⁵³

He also noted that the "indigent people have this recompense to their poverty, that their necessitated labor keeps them much in health, and without the need, trouble and Physick" and advised English women, "as they respect their health and beauty," to "accustom themselves from their childhoods to convenient labor or exercise" and follow the example of French gentlewomen in acquiring knowledge and skill of practice in confectionary, herbal medicine, and nursing. Exercise for women was not just a matter of cosmetics or morality for Brooke: he also stressed its utility for lessening "difficulty and danger in childing," observing that "Irish women because of their stirring and active lives are straight, tall, full-grown, quick in delivery; the German women are also observed to be such & here in England also the poor and laboring women in city and country are very quick at their labors, and allow

FIGURE 2 *Everard Digby (c. 1550–1605)*, De arte natandi libri duo, quorum prior regulas ipsius artis, posterior vero praxin demonstrationemque continet *(London, 1587)*. Wellcome Collection (Attribution 4.0 International (CC BY 4.0)).

themselves hardly a week's retirement." This was a matter of national importance, as "they that lead sedentary lives usually bear weak and sickly children, and so beget themselves much sorrow & double care and charge in their education: besides the injury they thereby do the Commonwealth."[54]

Evacuations

The dictates of moderation and balance mandated that after nourishment and repletion occur, substances must be evacuated from the body, either naturally or through "purgations by siege" to use Thomas Elyot's term. Elyot asserted that "he that lives in a good order of diet needs neither purgation not vomit" as the natural excretions by stool, urine, tears, sweat, spit, phlegm will occur as a result of the proper observance of the rules for the other non-naturals but nevertheless offered lists of digestives and purgatives for each complexion in case his readers were in need of evacuation aid. More dramatic measures involved phlebotomy, scarifying, cupping, and leeches, suppositories (glisters or cisters), potions, electuaries, and pills, and somewhere in between natural evacuation and these purgations by siege were hemorrhoids and nosebleeds. Elyot does not mention either menstruation or semen among his evacuated substances; one assumes they constitute the "secret" evacuations to which he alludes in later editions of the *Castel*, and "purposely omits."[55]

A century and a score later, one of the last regimen writers, the physician Everard Maynwaring, did not omit either "monthly purgations" or "Venus," both of which "keep the body soluble." Like everything else, the latter must be approached with moderation, as "immoderate" intercourse "exhausts the strength by effusions of spirits, exsiccates and dries the body, hurts the brain and nerves, causes trembling, dulls the sight, debilitates all the faculties, hastens old age, and shortens life."[56] In general, the seventeenth-century regimens authored by physicians go into much more detail about sexuality with considerations of time (time of life, day, season, frequency), brief notice of health benefits, and discussion of threats, including venereal disease. With his characteristic detail culled from experience, James Hart elaborated upon gonorrhea ("the involuntary efflux of seed in either sense, proceeding also sometimes from the debility of the retentive faculty"), and the "hysterical passions" or "fits of the mother," as well as the "green sickness," obstructions, and palpitations of the heart, etc ... which can affect women exclusively, but also concluded that "in both sexes I wish that moderation which becomes Christians is observed."[57]

Emotions

And how to achieve moderation in the regulation of the last (but not least) non-natural, the "passions of the mind"? There was no medicine for emotional moderation, and oddly enough, our Christian authors do not impose religious cordials on the classical conceptions of love, jealousy, anger, fear, sadness, and joy other than to suggest that while "the sickness of the body must have medicine, the passions of the mind must have good counsel" and the pursuit of "quietness and mirth" should be the chief aim of those that wish to preserve their good health. Once again, as in the case of every non-natural, excess was to be avoided: excessive (lustful, jealous) love, excessive (vengeful) anger, excessive sadness, even "immoderate joy." If the author chose to take on the mind's passions (and not all regimen writers did), this was an opportunity to re-emphasize the morality of moderation, particularly love, which in its lustful or jealous forms could be "the author of so much hurt, of so much mischief to the body of man" in the opinion of James Hart. "Foul lustful love" could literally cause disease, but also deprive "the soul of its chief happiness, and so metamorphosing the whole man unto an inform monster, void of all reason, whereby he runs headlong upon his own ruin."[58] Yes, it was possible to die of love, but not if you had mastered your mind and body.

When one considers the succession and development of English regimens over the sixteenth century and well into the seventeenth (necessarily extending the chronological limits of our first part and period), it is apparent that their authors burst through their classical constraints when they adopted a contemporary, nationalistic, or regional empiricism in regard to the environment in general, the climate in particular, and personal prescriptions for diet and exercise. The general Galenic rules still applied, but new—or alternative—foods, beverages, and customs were taken into consideration, especially as successive editions of popular regimens were updated, amended and "improved." New methodologies and challenges were addressed more assertively in other types of medical publications over the early modern era, but even this most conservative of genres had to adapt in order to remain relevant. "Things apt for medicine," Thomas Elyot wrote in his prologue to the 1541 edition of *The castel of helth*, are "growing in this realm, by conference with the most noble authors may be so known, that we shall have less need of things brought out of far countries."[59] The authority of classical tradition, all those noble authors, was not as forceful a foundation for early modern agricultural practice as in the case of medicine: manifest harvests were far more easily gauged than mysterious bodily diseases. Yet there was still a deference to the past in early English agricultural texts. In his poetical preface to the first edition of the first English printed surveying book, John Fitzherbert's *Boke of surueyeng and improume[n]tes* (1523), the printer's apprentice Thomas Berthelet attempted to raise the status of agricultural knowledge by referring to the ancient authorities in an appeal evocative of Elyot:

The worthy Cato/ that excellent Roman/ Columella/ Varro/ and Vergilius/ Of husbandry to write/ had in no disdain/ Nor many other/ eloquent and famous/ Thought it not a thing inglorious/ Such matter to write/ whereby they might advance/ The common wealth. And their country enhance. But in our days/ some are blinded so with folly/ That they count husbandry/ but a thing right vile/ Some had leaver write of love. Ye of bawdry/ Than to so good a matter turn their style/ Fond pleasure and pride so them so beguile/ That sloth wanders about in every way/ And good business is falling into decay.[60]

Surveying in its early sixteenth-century meaning was less a technical endeavor than a first stage of a larger process of estate management, through which property was assessed to ascertain which general and particular "improvements" should be made to increase the financial value of an estate. As we will see, the practice and profession of surveying will become increasingly technical and skillful over the century, but in 1523 Fitzherbert (and Berthelet) were addressing a first generation of Tudor "improving landlords". Fitzherbert's other publication from that year, *Here begynneth a newe tracte or treatyse moost profytable for all husbandmen and very frutefull for all other persons to rede* (succinctly referred to as the *Boke of husbandry* in successive editions), was more focused on the practice of farming, a field that he largely had to himself in the first half of the sixteenth century and one that was characterized, like the popular health publications of the era, by an association of individual and collective thrift.

Seeds of Discretion

Husbandry was foundational in Tudor England: the word itself is more a synonym for the rural *economy* than agriculture in its contemporary sense. For Fitzherbert, who represents a traditional view based on his own experience and observations rather than gathering from established authorities, husbandry consisted of every activity that was necessary to the cultivation of corn (all grains) and cattle (all livestock) so that the household might "thrive," a word that he used not only to imply sustenance but also profit. Yet just as contemporary health regimens emphasized moderation, a moral imperative passed down through their sources, so did Fitzherbert stress the importance of individual and household *thrift*, reflecting classical and medieval sources and passed down to his successors. The diligent husband was the fulcrum of the household but the "huswife" was essential too, as Fitzherbert anticipated Thomas Tusser's question from later in the century: *take huswife from husbande & what is he than?* Even though Fitzherbert was approaching his readers from the elevated view of a householder/estate manager/property owner, he was dedicated and detailed in his descriptions of the constant labor involved in maintaining a thriving farm, beginning with the plowing, and then proceeding to the sowing, harrowing, fallowing, fertilizing, weeding, mowing, reaping, bundling, and selling processes involved in tillage and extending to the breeding, rearing, and maintenance of livestock, including sheep, cows, oxen, horses, swine (and bees). Fitzherbert included many brief passages on veterinary medicine, particularly those diseases that plagued horses, and a few instructions relative to arboriculture, not quite the focus at this time that it would become later in the century. In an expression of the collective household economy that will characterize all early modern agricultural texts, Fitzherbert laid out the responsibilities of the housewife in detail, including all provisioning as well as the separate, but integral, cultivation of kitchen and physic gardens for cooking and healing and flax and hemp for weaving. Opinions about wealth and thrift, labor, faith, and diligence, are woven into his instruction, and he took a firm stand for practice over theory throughout: "it is better the practice or knowledge of an husband-man well-proved, then the science or cunning of a philosopher not proved, for there is nothing touching husbandry, and other profits contained in this present book, but I have had the experience thereof, and proved the same."[61] The most eloquent statement of the grounding of Fitzherbert's agricultural practice (and philosophy) is contained in a chapter entitled "Seeds of Discretion" in which he asserts that "there is a seed called Discretion, if a husbandman have of that seed and mingle it among his other Corn, they will grow doubtless much the better, for that seed will tell him how many casts of Corn every land ought to have." The seeds of discretion are "but wisdom and reason" and should be shared, for the greater good.[62] The emphasis on husbandry as a practice in which one *husbands* one's resources in an efficient and thrifty way, as both a virtue and a way to achieve wealth was conveyed earlier in the very first agricultural text printed in English, Walter de Henley's *Boke of husbandry* (1508), an imprint of one of a succession of middle English manuscripts produced from the thirteenth through the fifteenth centuries. The two books share a title, similar woodcut illustrations, a few observations (like the preference for oxen over horses as plowing beasts as the latter were too high maintenance and mere carrion at their end) and their mutual emphasis on resourceful husbanding, but Fitzherbert's text was also grounded in its own time, and place.

It is the details that illustrated and confirmed Fitzherbert's authority, or discretion, primarily through his discourse on the diversity of the English agrarian economy: the regional soil types that required different types of plows, manure preferences based on these same regions, (including a general recommendation for *dove's dung*), references to the customs of various counties and districts (the Peak country; the "farther side of Derbyshire"), variant techniques like second or cross-plowing, or "stirrings."[63] While he surveyed both arable and animal husbandry, Fitzherbert acknowledged that some parts of England might suit one or the other better:

> in some countries [counties], if a man plows deep, he shall pass the good ground, and have but little corn: but that country is not for men to keep

FIGURE 3 *John Fitzherbert (d. 1531)*, New tracte or Treatyse moost profitable for all husbandemen *(London, 1523?)*. © *British Library / Bridgeman Images, London.*

husbandry upon, but for to rear and breed cattle or sheep, for else they must go beat their lands with mattocks, as they do in many places of Cornwall, and in some places of Devonshire.[64]

We learn the names of all sorts of English weeds. The agricultural year was ordered on an *English* calendar; weights and measures like the "London bushel" were English standards. Fitzherbert's descriptions in no way conformed to the Roman villas and Mediterranean climate of Palladius or Columella. His book was a *new* text, very conspicuously practical for its era, perhaps even too practical for its intended audience: new gentry and improving landlords investing their city money in land. These men were not actually going to do the labor, which is laid out in detail. Its successive editions point to popularity of purchase, but readership is more difficult to assess. As was evident in his preface a decade before, the printer Thomas Berthelet might have attempted to appeal to both their economic and humanist interests by publishing the classical Greek scholar Xenophon's *Oeconomicus*, a popular Renaissance translation, as *Xenophon's treatise of householde* in 1532, and four other editions followed. A Socratic dialogue about the maintenance of an orderly household set in Athens could hardly be called a practical publication in Tudor England, but this "recovered" text is illustrative of how Renaissance culture could be just as focused on the material and the mundane as the creative and the philosophical.

Pointed contemporary references to the progress of enclosure, the prioritization of pastoral over arable, and the metaphorical menace of "sheep eating people" have informed agricultural history for well over a century, but if Fitzherbert's book is any indication of farming practice in Tudor England, husbandmen must hedge their bets: "the most general living that husbands can have, is by plowing and sowing of their corn, and rearing and breeding of their cattle, and not the one without the other."[65] In yet another expression of moderation and discretion, arable and pastoral agriculture were complementary endeavors in Fitzherbert's traditional view, even symbiotic ones, but perhaps the inexperienced and enterprising gentlemen to whom he addressed his text had other ideas. The concerns expressed about the high prices of grain in official and religious texts of the mid-sixteenth century point to the existence of both a dynamic market in grains and the potential profits to be made through engaged and informed investments in arable enterprises, as does the development of surveying texts over the next century, but texts on husbandry clung to the characterization of the well-ordered household. The problem of food shortages plagued the sixteenth century, but dearth could be a consequence of natural or man-made causes: Tudor proclamations were quite logically focused on the latter, over which they could have some impact. *A proclamation concernynge corne* (1534), issued in the same year that Henry VIII became the Supreme Head of the English church, noted the "sudden" enhancement in price or scarcity of all grains, but especially wheat and rye, due to their purveyance as "common merchandise" as well as the "subtle invention and craft of diverse covetous persons," and put in place a number of corrections, including one stipulating that no person "shall buy or bargain any wheat or rye to sell again, except it to be conveyed by water or land for the provision of the city of London, or other cities and towns having necessity thereof, or to bake in bread to be sold to his subjects, or else for provision of the Iceland fleet."[66] Complaints against "forestallers, regraters, and engrossers" will continue through the century and well into the next, as foodstuffs were indeed transitioning to "common merchandise": one window into this transition is through advice literature on both health *and* husbandry. Thomas Elyot's digression on the dangers of fruit contrasts quite sharply with the advice offered to commercial orchardmen less than a century later. In Elyot's view,

> before that tillage of corn was invented, and that devouring of flesh and fish was of mankind used, men undoubtedly lived by fruits & Nature was therewith contented and satisfied: but by change of the diet of our progenitors, there is caused to be in our bodies such alteration from nature, which was in men at the beginning, that now all fruits generally are noyful [harmful] to man, and do engender ill humors, and be often times the cause of putrefied fevers, if they be much and continually eaten.[67]

After decades of dearth, famine, inflation and the publication of a succession of tracts about tree grafting and fruit cultivation, the author of *The husbandmans fruitfull orchard* (1608) led with profit potential (and practice), and was much more focused on ordering fruits for culling, carrying and conveying than ordering the households that might have produced them. In his brief history of the "revival" of fruit cultivation in England, he credited Henry VIII's royal fruiterer, Richard Harris, with bringing grafts of pippins, cherries and pears from the Continent to establish a model orchard in Kent. A great "increase and plenty of fruit in the land" ensued, and now that both demand and supply were established, it was time to learn all about "gathering": for "there is no need of any foreign fruit, but we are able to serve other places."[68] Changes in diet, changes in the land, changes in economic attitudes: all the result of an evolving awareness among practitioners that classical theories were limited in their application to contemporary challenges and opportunities.

2

Measure for Measure:

Mensuration and Mathematics

In both its abstract and practical approaches, mathematics can hardly be counted among those ancient arts "rediscovered" by the Renaissance: the centrality of Easter on the liturgical calendar necessitated the acquisition and application of computational skills throughout the Medieval era. Arithmetic and geometry (along with two other "mathematical" disciplines, music and astronomy) were among the core fields of the university *quadrivium*, and Leonardo of Pisa liberated (eventually) both Medieval mathematicians and merchants from the constraints of Roman numerals by advocating for the use of the Hindu-Arabic system in his influential *Liber Abacci* very early on in the thirteenth century. Leonardo's *Book of Calculation* generated a cascade of practical mathematics books and schools in later medieval Italy, culminating with Luca Pacioli's *Summa de Arithmetica, Geometria, Proportioni and Proportionalità* in 1494.[1] In England, references to *algorism(e)*, denoting computation with Arabic numbers, appear as early as the thirteenth century, but both the word and the concept are more commonly utilized in the fourteenth, even in such non-practical compositions as Chaucer's *Book of the Duchess* and John Gower's *Confessio Amantis*.

So, mathematics was nothing new in early Tudor England, but over the sixteenth century there would develop both new uses and new demands for quantitative tools, whether "art" or instrument. The drive towards numeracy certainly seems more apparent in the second half of the century, but in the first half two forces were unleashed that would have dramatic consequences for the English economy: the English Reformation, with its royal land grab in the form of the Dissolution of the Monasteries, and the beginning of the transition from regional trade in one commodity to long-distance trade in several commodities. The former force initiated a cascade of land transfers that redefined the economic (and social) relationships on manors across England, while the latter necessitated increasingly complex arrangements among merchant-partners and increasingly sophisticated instruments and procedures for navigation. Furthermore, the ambitious and expensive foreign and military policies of Henry VIII stimulated demand for numerate councilors and military engineers to effect the incompatible tasks of restructuring the vexing royal debt and building a chain of defensive "device forts" in this new artillery age. England's transition from "utter marginality" at the beginning of the sixteenth century to a European and global empire at its end would take both considerable investment and calculation, at both national and individual levels.[2] Apart from these external forces, as arithmetic became more denary it also evolved from a theoretical discipline into a practical *craft*, whether practiced with a pen in hand or with "counters," on a board or table. In its applied forms, it was practiced, in an active or mechanical sense, as opposed to the more passive and theoretical disciplines of natural philosophy. In terms of texts and terminology, while algorism was used as a variant of arithmetic, the *activity* of computation was increasingly referred to as ciphering, although the much older term *reckoning* persisted: John Palsgrave utilized all the accounting terms together in *Lesclarcissement de la langue francoyse*, his French grammar published in 1530: "I cyfer, I acompte or reken by algorism."[3]

Whether craft, "cunning," or "feat," the ability to calculate and cast account was deemed increasingly essential in early modern England to practitioners in a variety of fields: merchants and shopkeepers, military engineers and gunners, navigators and cartographers, builders and surveyors. Both the body of knowledge and the range of practices expanded in response to the needs of these pursuits, from the estimation or assessment of value, to the creation of specialized mathematical instruments that could amplify such efforts—and offer much more. A succession of vernacular publications offering instruction in applied mathematics over the sixteenth and seventeenth centuries traces the evolution of the acquisition of skills, by which one learned how to account and compute, to the onset of textual "ready reckoners" enabling one to simply purchase the desired computations: but in the process a more fundamental numeracy took hold in early modern England, as illustrated by the title of the best-selling mathematical textbook of the era: Robert Recorde's *The grou[n]d of artes teachyng the worke and practise of arithmetike, moch necessary for all states of men*, which was issued in 27 editions from 1543 to 1640.[4] There is ample evidence that mathematics was indeed recognized as the *ground* of arts, the pathway towards an emerging "science," and the gauge of agriculture, trade, and industry.

Taking Stock

Whether it was the counting-house, the workshop, or the manor, proper accounting, the most applied of all the mathematical arts, began with taking stock: assessing possessions, compiling an inventory, or surveying the land.

In evaluating the latter with accurate measurement for size rather than estimation of potential yield, Tudor surveying texts represent the increasing commodification of land in the wake of the Henrician Reformation and the suppression and dissolution of the English monasteries from 1536 to 1541. As much as one-third of England's agricultural land was thrust onto an expansive market that required the tools for comparative evaluation, and thus a new conception of "surveying" emerged: from the general land *management* presented in the first printed English surveying text, John Fitzherbert's *Boke of surueyeng* (1523), to the precise procedure of land *measurement* introduced by Richard Benese in *This boke sheweth the maner of measurynge of all maner of lande as well of woodlande, as of lande in the felde, and comptynge the true nombre of acres of the-same* (1537).[5] Benese was in an extraordinarily informed position: it is difficult to imagine who could be more authoritative in his time. He was the last canon of Merton Priory, and after its confiscation in 1538 he became the Surveyor of Works at Hampton Court Palace and personal chaplain to Henry VIII. As the *Maner of measurynge* was published even before the Priory was suppressed, one wonders if he was called upon to evaluate his own property: and later rewarded for his services. Benese's book instructed its readers in how to measure a variety of manorial assets, including arable and woodland, timber and stone by the square foot, as well as interior boards, tables, panes of glass (a luxury in glazier-poor England), and chamber floors, using both old "instruments" like a perch pole and cord (or rod and line) and arithmetical and geometrical calculations—especially for the "diverse" (valley, mountain, angled) lays of land. Benese included some tables to facilitate the calculation of measurements and laid out rules, of course, as that was expected from all early modern didactic texts, but he also set standards of professional conduct by indicating that the surveyor should not just measure, but also describe and *map* the land, in order to produce a comprehensive appraisal presented to the landowner in the form of a *plat*. All those new Reformation "improving" landlords required economic assessments of their property, but land was also the pathway to gentility for those not born into it: a seventeenth-century surveying text refers to the finished plat as "an ornament for the Lord of the Manor to hang in his study, or other private place, so that at pleasure he may see his Land before him, and the quantity of all or every parcel thereof without any further trouble."[6] It would take a while for arms-adorned manorial maps to grace the library walls of estates across England, but certainly the intensified exchange of land, a result of political, economic, and social forces in mid-sixteenth-century England, created the conditions for the emergence of a surveying profession consisting of quantitative and cartographic practitioners over the next century.

The knowledge and skills required for precise measurement were not confined to estate matters and management, however, and surveying texts published after Benese's *Maner of measurynge* emphasized the wider application of both the art and the craft. A gentleman himself, though a tarnished one due to his participation in Wyatt's Revolt against the "Spanish Marriage" of Mary I, the mathematician and inventor Leonard Digges sought to expand knowledge of the "art of numbering" and the "outward practice" of measuring by addressing surveyors, "landmeaters," joyners, carpenters and masons in particular and artificers in general in his 1556 manual *A boke named Tectonicon*, which was published in sixteen editions by six different printers up to 1692.[7] Like the most popular contemporary texts in health and husbandry, *Tectonicon* is both instructive manual and reference book, providing direction as well as accessible information. In his preface, Digges even instructed his readers how to read—and *use*—his books: first read them through, then again with "more judgement." On the third reading, be mindful of practice: "Note, of diligent reading, joined with ingenious practice causes profitable labor." Digges may have been exaggerating the ability of English joiners and masons to read, but he was more cautious about their ability to calculate and so provided copious examples and illustrations, including computation tables and drawings of the carpenter's rule(r) and the "profitable rod or staff" (cross-staff) used to measure the height and width of buildings. More instruments, practices, and applications were showcased in Digges's other major text, *A geometrical practise, named Pantometria*, which was published posthumously with additions by his son Thomas in 1571.[8] In the *Pantometria*, readers were instructed in the use not only of the quadrant and geometrical square but also of the theodolite, an instrument of Leonard Digges's own invention, along with a "topographical instrument," which seems to have combined all the extant tools of the surveyor into one. The rules, tools and scope of measurement were expanded considerably by both Digges in this manual, with its references to architects, cartographers, chorographers, miners and military engineers: surveying was presented as public service, in the *national* interest, and its practitioners should be able to produce a regional representation, with "the true distance of every notable place from other" as easily as a *plat* of just one estate. It now seemed possible to configure England as the sum of such surveys, an assemblage of "ground plats of cities, towns, forts, castles, palaces, and other edifices" and manors.

Leonard Digges is acclaimed by both contemporaries and historians for his inventiveness: not only of the theodolite (which had continental predecessors) but also, perhaps, of a variant telescope or "proportional glasses" referenced in his son's preface to *Pantometria*:

> my father, by his continual painful practices, assisted with the demonstrations mathematical, was able, and sundry times has, by proportional glasses duly situated in convenient angles, not only discovered things far off, read letters, numbered pieces of money with the very coin and superscription thereof cast by some of his friends on purpose upon downs in open fields but also seven miles off declared what that been done in private places; he has also at sundry times by the sun

fired powder and discharged ordnance half a mile and more distant—which things I am the bolder to report for that there are yet living diverse of his doings *oculati testes*, and many other matters strange and rare which I omit as impertinent to this place. But for invention of these conclusions I have heard him say nothing ever helped him so much as the exquisite knowledge he had, by continual practice, attained in geometrical mensurations.[9]

Obviously this glass, with its almost-magical abilities, enabling its wielder to discover things "far off" and in "private places," along with the long-range firing, was going to capture the attention of readers then and now, as it sounds very much like a pre-seventeenth-century telescope, but Thomas Digges was emphasizing the power of *practice* here, even over its impressive "conclusions": continual practice, even "painful" practice. The methodological "collaboration" of Leonard and Thomas Digges in the *Pantometria* is an early example of the emerging scientific method of experimentation and mathematical analysis in England, with promises of spectacular results.

As the art and practice of surveying was separated from estate management, it became applicable to other endeavors: if one could measure and evaluate area and distance properly, one could appraise the volume of any entity, "superfice" (surface) or vessel as well. The third book of the Digges *Pantometria*, which demonstrates a kind of geometry referred to as "stereometria," emphasized the importance of establishing one rule for the measurement of capacity in all the "sundry kinds of wine vessels, as the tun, the pipe, the puncheon, hogsheads, buts, barrels, &c. every of them differing from another as well in quantity as in fashion" as to teach several rules for each would be "over-tedious."[10] This was the kind of streamlined and applied mathematics that would appeal to those engaged in the dynamic mercantile economy of Tudor England, but the geometrical analysis supporting such evaluation was still beyond the reach of most men: hence the continuing demand for tables for ready reckoning and reference in trade and navigational manuals.

Valentine Leigh's *The moste profitable and commendable science, of surueying of landes, tenementes, and hereditamentes* (1577) is primarily a text about estate *stewardship* rather than surveying in the sense that both Benese and Digges articulated.[11] Leigh did not look beyond the manor geographically or intellectually, but he did present a working agricultural estate as just that: an economic enterprise: consequently we are presented with a merchant's view of a Tudor manor rather than a mathematician's (or a monk's). The word "profitable" in his title was revealing, and Leigh also used the popular word *government*, to preface his intent:

> this present book entreats, which teaches the government of the Manors, lands, and tenements of each person, and how to make a perfect Survey

of the same, to most profit. And also, how to engross your terrors [*terriers*] and Rentals thereof. And finally, how to measure all kinds of land, be it Meadow, Pasture, Arable, Wood, hill or Dale & in what form or figure so ever it is fashioned, or comely lieth, with the form, how to understand the contents thereof, as well by a beneficial Table, already and Plainly made for that behalf, as otherwise by the ordinary Rules to the same appertaining.[12]

In Leigh's view, surveying began with an assessment of the rental value of the land and proceeded to its physical assessment: he includes some instructions for geometrical mensuration but not the full-scale, variable instrumental and mathematical analysis presented by the Digges with their more universal applications. His more specialized approach was in keeping with the diffusion and reception of information in other areas over the sixteenth century: too much information prompted specialization and catering to target audiences, and Leigh was perhaps focused on those first-generation Tudor landlords for whom knowledge of customary tenures was more important than geometrical theorems.

Valentine Leigh was a London mercer, and his surveying work displays an understanding of workplace administration also evident in the first English accounting texts, James Peele's *The maner and fourme how to kepe a perfecte reconyng* (1553), John Weddington's *Breffe instruction, and manner, howe to kepe, marchantes bokes, of accomptes* (1567, published for the English market in the entrepôt of Antwerp), and John Mellis's 1588 "augmentation" of Hugh Oldcastle's *A Briefe instruction and maner hovv to keepe bookes of accompts after the order of debitor and creditor*, which was originally published in 1543 but for which no copy is extant.[13] Luca Pacioli's influence, and that of gold-standard Venetian bookkeeping, is much in evidence in these texts, but they introduced some new, or adapted, concepts as well. All of these works emphasized that the first task of a business was the compilation of an inventory, which James Peele presented as separate from the owner's personal property: a static list of assets or balance sheet, to be analyzed and updated with every bookkeeping period. Peele and Weddington were both bookkeepers, and their manuals testify to the insights and understanding gleaned from their experience, employed as instructive examples for their prospective colleagues.

From Enumeration to Calculation

As the processes of taking stock became more involved, the need for more widespread mathematical knowledge became more apparent. These trends were apparent in Italy centuries before, but in keeping with the rather delayed English Renaissance, apparent in England only in the sixteenth century. The separation, or liberation, of mathematics from the university curriculum and astronomy, is one of the more obvious examples of the practicality of the Renaissance: it was literally brought down to earth and applied to everyday work and life. The craft, or science, of mathematics could be grasped quite easily through illustrations of its utility while the process of learning to reckon was best pursued through proofs and practice. The literature on the history of applied mathematics in England has consistently emphasized the role of the mathematical *practitioner*: even university-educated mathematicians stressed the utilitarian over the theoretical.[14] The famous mathematician, magician, courtier and collector John Dee is perhaps the best example of this: he perceived mathematics as unlimited in its applications, as illustrated by the Ramist table (he called it a "groundplat" and a "mathematical tree") he produced for the preface to the first English translation of Euclid's *Elements* in 1570.[15] According to his categorization and definitions, the "Sciences and Artes Mathematicall" are either principal or derivative: as principles, arithmetic and geometry are classified as both simple and "mixed," but "vulgar" in their applications, or derivatives. Arithmetic is all about numbers, geometry is all about measuring, and from their application a host of subfields would enable practitioners to capture every facet of both the heavenly and elemental parts of the world: astronomy, astrology, cosmography, anthropology (concerning "every divers thing contained in the perfect body of MAN"), music, perspective, architecture, navigation, and many categories that we would now classify as physics, measuring weight, force, and time. All of Dee's categories were active pursuits: teaching, demonstrating, describing, measuring, and as such, "profitable": in the text component of his preface he advocated for the advancement of mathematical knowledge and practice in every segment of society, from the universities to the streets, for "who, nearer at hand, can be a better witness of the fruit received by Arithmetic, then all kind of Merchants?" and

> how many a Common Artificer, is there, in these Realms of England and Ireland, that deals with Numbers, Rule & Compass: Who, with their own Skill and experience, already had, will be able (by these good helps and informations) to find out, and devise new works, strange Engines, and Instruments: for sundry purposes in the Common Wealth? Or for private pleasure? And for the better maintaining of their own estate?[16]

Practical application was also the theme of one of the first texts on arithmetic published in England: *An introduction for to lerne to recken with the pen or with the counters accordynge to the trewe cast of algorysme, in hole nombers or in broken.*[17] Published in eight editions between 1539 and 1629, the text consistently offered all the promises of essential edification characteristic of instructional texts: it asserted its absolute necessity for any endeavor that included all forms of reckoning or accounting, as was the case with "all manner of sciences and artificers," and proceeded to lay out very succinct instructions for the seven processes of arithmetic or algorism: numeration, addition, subtraction, multiplication, partition, progression, and reduction. This would evolve into a standard format for early modern arithmetical texts, including illustrative tables for multiplication and square roots (reduction). The bulk of the book was dedicated to teaching one to reckon with a pen, but the latter section on casting with a counter table asserted that even the illiterate and the "unlearned" could still practice arithmetic.

Another device of instructional texts, the statement of *rules*, was utilized in variant ways: in line with disciplinary standards (the rule of three, the rule of whole numbers, the golden rule) and as a form of inquiry, analysis, and utility. These latter rules were expressed as questions, or scenarios, designed to illustrate the applicability of arithmetic to everyday life. There were "rules" for every possible trading scenario (partnerships, pricing, investment, fraud), rules for builders, shepherds, clothiers, scholars, pilgrims, shoppers and *cats*. Mathematics could even help one reason out testamentary dilemmas: "*A man hath made his testament, the which hath left his wife great, and hath ordained in his testament if she brought forth a son, he should have two parts of his goods, and his wife the other part. And if she brought forth a daughter, then the mother should have two parts and the daughter the other part.*" But what to do if there was a son *and* a daughter? In the last days of Merry Old England before the onset of a more Calvinist culture, a merrymaking couple could also provide an opportunity for calculation: "*a drunkard drinks a barrel of beer in the space of 14 days, and when his wife drinks with him than they drink it all within 10 days. Now I demand in what space that his wife should drink that barrel of beer alone?*"[18]

Robert Recorde, the most important mathematical practitioner and author of the sixteenth century, stressed the essential and universal utility of mathematics in a series of books published from 1542 on: *The ground of artes* (arithmetic), *The pathway to knowledge* (geometry), *The castle of knowledge* (cosmography) and *The whetstone of witte* (arithmetic and algebra).[19] Recorde was a university-educated polymath, comfortable in all of the mathematical disciplines as well as medical theory and practice: his *Urinal of physick* remained in print for over a century, along with *The ground of artes*. Recorde was also an experienced educator, a skill that is on display in all of his books, particularly those that use dialogue as a form of instruction. Dialogue can incorporate "doubts" and examples in the interchange between Master and Scholar, and lead the latter (and the reader) towards understanding. Like all mathematical writers and practitioners, Recorde was evangelical about the necessity of numbering knowledge, the "ground" of all men's affairs and essential for both the Common and private "weals": without it, no tale can be told, no communication long continued, no bargaining ended, no business completed. *The ground of artes* employed the same basic format as the *Introduction for to lerne to reckon with the pen* in terms of the separate branches of arithmetic and the prioritization of pen over counters, but Recorde included a table of "finger-reckoning" taken from Luca Pacioli's 1494 *Summa de Arithmetica* and incorporated illustrative examples into the dialogue. After his death in 1558, editions were published with edits and augmentations by schoolmaster John Mellis and John Dee, as well as diverse "tables and instructions that will bring great profit and delight unto Merchants, Gentlemen, and others." A third part, the "Rule of Practice", was added, as well as reference material for currency exchange, equivalencies of weights and measures in "most places of Christendom for traffic," and some numbering games for sport, pastime, and even divination. This mathematical textbook evolved into a merchant's manual, illustrating the expansion of English trade and the corresponding commercialization of informational culture.

It is clear the Recorde planned an entire *course* in mathematics with his books: while *The ground of arts* continued to be re-issued throughout his life and beyond, he turned his attention to the task of transforming the more abstract mathematical branches into accessible information through a *Knowledge* series, commencing with *The pathway to knowledge* (1551), an introduction to geometry, and proceeding to (or through) a *Gate of knowledge* towards a *Treasure of knowledge* (both focused on practical and applied geometry, but are no longer extant) and ultimately to the final *Castle of knowledge*, through (or in) which the now geometry-fortified reader could apply his learning to the use of cosmographical instruments. Recorde's word choices are interesting: *pathway* had previously been used exclusively as a religious term metaphorically, and Recorde was the first to use it as a way towards information—and knowledge—as opposed to faith and salvation. Many practical pathways will follow as it became a popular title for instructional works in language, military discipline, and medicine. *Castle* of course is reminiscent of the best-selling *The castel of helth*, in which one was armed with essential information for the preservation of health and wellness. Recorde's *Castle* also armed its readers: with the knowledge and equipment that enabled them to master their *external* world. *The Whetstone of witte*, Recorde's last book, returned to the realm of arithmetic as a sequel to *The ground of Artes*, but also introduced "Cossike" practice or algebra. The book was dedicated to the Muscovy Company, and contains practical problems similar to those included in the *Introduction for to lerne to reckon with a pen*. Much of the algebraic description was based on the German mathematician Johannes Scheubel's earlier *Algebrae Compendiosa*, but Recorde introduced a very original contribution in the form of the equals sign: as he began to explain equations, he informed his readers that "to avoid the tedious repetition of these words: is equal to: I will set as I do often in work use, a pair of parallels, or *gemowe* (twin) lines of one length, thus:—— because no 2 things can be more equal."[20] Inspired just as the Digges were to avoid "over-tedious" calculations, Recorde devised an ingenious abbreviation that became a standardized symbol.

Robert Recorde had promised more applications to both the Muscovy Company merchants for whom he consulted and his readers, but the

Whetstone ends abruptly, when a messenger arrives at the door, concluding a dialogue on universal roots between master and scholar. Presumably this was his way of announcing his arrest and imprisonment, relating to his tangles with William Herbert, the First Earl of Pembroke, over his official roles as comptroller of the Bristol Mint and Surveyor of Mines and Monies in Ireland and his accusation of malfeasance cast at Herbert, a royal commissioner. As a result of the judgement in a libel suit brought by Herbert, Robert Recorde died in debtor's prison in 1558, unable to pay the large fine imposed upon him: he was the third major mathematician, along with Richard Benese and Leonard Digges, to bear the consequences (good and bad) of encounters with the Tudor government. Several years later, William Bullein (as was his tendency) provided a poignant eulogy in his *Bulwarke of defence*:

> how well was he seen in tongues, learned in Arts and in Sciences, natural and moral. A father in Phisick, whose learning gave liberty to the ignorant, with his *Whetstone of witte, Castle of knowledge*: and finally, giving place to Aiding nature, died himself in bondage or in prison. By which death he was delivered and made free, and yet lives in the happy land, among the Lauriat learned, his name was Doctor Recorde.[21]

Leonard (and Thomas) Digges and Robert Recorde were referenced in a succession of surveying books in the later sixteenth and early seventeenth centuries, as authorities of their day who supplanted the wisdom of the ancients (except Euclid, who remained the geometrical standard-bearer). As surveying became increasingly professionalized over this period, there was a call to exclude those practitioners who were ignorant of both mathematics and instruments and whose inaccurate estimations and evaluations caused confusion for estate owners, families, and officials. In *A discouerie of sundrie errours and faults daily committed by lande-meaters, ignorant of arithmetike and geometrie, to the damage, and preiudice of many her Maiesties subiects with manifest proofe that none ought to be admitted to that function, but the learned practisioners of those sciences* (1582), Edward Worsop gave thanks for the "extant works in our vulgar tongue as Euclid, the works of Doctor Recorde, of Master Leonard Digges, of Master Thomas Digges and some others," but as the "common sort" could not understand these texts, he had laid out a "good plain and popular discourse" on surveying, for the public good, of course. Rather than a traditional dialogue, he presented his discourse in the form of a conversation between himself and four friends, all of whom were quite ignorant in mathematical theory and terminology and/or had had disastrous experiences with surveyors. As his title indicates, Worsop was quite critical of the state of surveying, primarily because of the ignorance of mathematics among its practitioners, in part due to its unfortunate association with divination and astrology: "certain abusers of Astrology [have] intermingled their false, and vain doctrines with mathematical operations. They make the mathematical cloaks to cover their wicked doctrines, as Papists do the Scriptures to cover theirs."²² Recorde's works were meant to demystify mathematics, but its association with astrology and magic was a common refrain in the sixteenth century and after: the comparison to Catholicism was more circumscribed, but Worsop was very clear in stating his beliefs that "in the time of Popery most singular knowledges were shut up." He does manage to include some lessons about measurement and scale in between his invectives against Catholicism and the current state of surveying, and present the practice as equal parts mathematical, legal, and material: with the plat submitted as a standard deliverable. Later works on surveying, including John Norden's *The surueyors dialogue* (1607), William Folkingham's *Feudigraphia* (1610), and Aaron Rathborne's *The svrveyor in foure bookes* (1616) accepted this tripartite division in large part, and continued to stress the essential role of both arithmetic and geometry (shown as the two pillars of the art on the title page of Rathborne's *Svrveyor*, along with Digges's theodolite) in the surveyor's work, although Norden supplied his readers with more tables than text and Rathborne still expected them to *work it out*. Likewise, Norden slighted the use of surveyor's instruments in his dialogue, while Rathborne included descriptions and operational instructions for an entire arsenal. Folkingham's *Feudigraphia* epitomized the surveyor's craft and expanded the audience beyond lords of the manor to "all under-takers in the plantation of Ireland or Virginia" as surveying was now in service to the expanding British Empire.²³

The methodized mathematics set forth by Recorde and Digges was recognized as both foundational and applicable to the emerging field of gunnery as well: both were credited by Cyprian Lucar in the Appendix to his translation of the first three books of Niccolò Tartaglia's *Quesiti et inventioni diverse* (1546), an enlargement of the latter's groundbreaking *Nova Scientia*, the first printed book on artillery. Lucar's translation introduced Tudor England to the new Italian projectile theories and provided prescriptions for gunnery, the composition of gunpowder, and fortification techniques, and his appendix summarized information from contemporary authors, including Recorde and Digges, about everything artillery.²⁴ He was very clear in his assertion that "skillful shooting" depended on positioning determined by geometrical calculations, which he demonstrated with a succession of colloquies. Lucar set the bar pretty high for a sixteenth-century gunner, not only must he be "quick-spirited" with "good judgement," but also possess the "perfect knowledge" to "plant his Ordinance where he may do [the] most hurt unto the enemies, and be least anoyed by them, and where his Ordinance may not be surprised by the enemy." Experience was helpful in meeting these standards, but the effective gunner also needed information, and must be

> skilfull in Arithmetic, and Geometry, to the end he may be able by his knowledge in those arts to measure heights, depths, breadths, and lengths,

and to draw the plat of any piece of ground, and to make mines, countermines, artificial fireworkes, rampiars, gabbions or baskets of earth, and such like things which are used in time of war to be made for offensive and defensive service.[25]

In addition to surveying and military science, architecture and navigation were the two fields most affected by the applied mathematics introduced into England by Robert Recorde and Leonard Digges. The vast literature related to navigation will be explored in Chapter Four, but publications on architecture in England before the eighteenth century were much more limited, beginning with John Shute's *The first and chief groundes of architecture vsed in all the auncient and famous monymentes: with a farther & more ample defense vppon the same, than hitherto hath been set out by any other* (1563). Shute's *Groundes* was a much more derivative and detached work than Recorde's *Ground*, but he too expressed a pre-Dee appreciation of the integration of the mathematical arts when he noted that the

> certain kindred & affinity is knit unto all the Mathematicals which sciences and knowledges are friends and a maintainer of diverse rational arts: so that without a mean acquaintance or understanding in them neither painters, masons, goldsmiths, embroiderers, carvers, joiners, glaziers, engravers, in all manner of metals and diverse others cannot obtain any worthy praise at all Now all these being branches of that foresaid foundation, stock, or science shall bring forth the fruits of it to their great profits, and the Commodity of the Realm.[26]

Presumably Shute's focus on building inspired him to add even more "rational arts" to the growing list of crafts for which mathematical knowledge was a prerequisite. For all of his prefatory praise for the building trades, however, Shute's approach was more aesthetic than practical: he was more focused on fostering appreciation of the symmetry and construction of classical pillars than anything else. But this was just the beginning of an architectural discourse in early modern England, in which applied mathematics would play a central role.

There was no acknowledgement, but the successor to Recorde's *The ground of artes* is Humfrey Baker's *The welspring of sciences*, first published in 1564.[27] Baker expanded upon Recorde's text with his instructions for calculations with fractions or "broken" numbers, and also included an entire third part devoted to the business of merchants entitled the "Rules of Practice," which was far more detailed than Recorde's *Rules*. Both men had sought the approval of influential merchants as well as courtiers by illustrating how mathematics could aid trade, but while Recorde appealed to the "Company of Merchant Adventurers to New Lands" in *The Whetstone of witte*, Baker dedicated his *Welspring* to the Governor of the other, older

Merchant Adventurers in Antwerp. These two "adventuring" merchant companies represent the future and the past of English overseas trade: the original Merchant Adventurers constituted a chartered trading company licensed to export cloth to the Continent at and through Antwerp, the northern entrepôt in the fifteenth and early sixteenth centuries, while the new Merchant Adventurers to New Lands, better known as the Muscovy Company, was the first of the joint-stock corporations established to open up new markets and avenues in more distant lands. Recorde was appealing to the seekers of the northeast passage to Cathay, while Baker was addressing the established order. Consequently, the latter was a bit more detailed in his *Rules*: for the measurement and pricing of commodities, particularly textiles but also including merchandise sold by weight, and currency and yardage exchange and conversion, as well as for the evaluation of loss and gain. Even though the old Merchant Adventurers was more trade association or guild than corporation, Baker illustrated how mathematics could serve as the basis for the "rules of fellowship" between merchant partners and the "rules of company" between merchants and their factors. This was not completely new territory: earlier in the century the very first mathematical text, *An introduction to lerne to recken with the penne or the counters,* solved similar workplace "problems," and the surveying literature was also increasingly focused on the economic and *social* relationships on the manor. Yet it is interesting to see mathematics presented as an impartial source of order in a dynamic and occasionally disorderly age, when so many of the old rules no longer applied. Just a few years after the publication of *The welspring of sciences,* the Merchant Adventurers' comfortable residence in Antwerp came to an end, and political and religious upheaval on the Continent encouraged the development of new markets by English merchants: in the Mediterranean, in the New World, and in Asia.

Cosmographical Connections

An important part of the *practice* of mathematics in the sixteenth and seventeenth centuries was related to instruments of measurement and calculation. Ancient and medieval instruments, like the armillary sphere, the astrolabe, the compass, the cross-staff, dividers, quadrants large and small, dials, and various astronomical compendia, were explained and (perhaps) adapted, while such new instruments as graphometers, gunners' sights and levels, plane tables, and Leonard Digges's theodolite were introduced, in a manner that might inspire new and more instrumentation: a larger world required tools that were both more powerful and precise. Many of the instruments referenced in early and mid-sixteenth-century texts were associated with the influential Renaissance discipline of Cosmography, which was an all-encompassing and integrative pursuit encompassing the description and measurement of both the universe and the earth, together and in relation to one another, rather than through the separate lenses of astronomy and geography. One of the most popular books of the sixteenth century, the *Cosmographia* of Peter Apian, described its subject as "the description of the world (which consists of four elements, Earth, Water, Air, & Fire), also of the Sun, the Moon, & all the stars, & of the heavens with whatever vault covers them."[28] This description involved measurement, encompassing both mathematical analysis and mechanical means, and also knowledge of all the subsidiary fields, including astrology, astronomy, geography, cartography, navigation *and* instrument-making. The *Cosmographia* was distinguished by its pioneering paper instruments, called *volvelles*, which enabled its readers to engage in their own manipulations and calculations: sometimes it is referred to as a "book—instrument." Apian's former student Gemma Frisius brought out a second, expanded edition in 1529, which became the basis of popular reprints thereafter, and a completely different *Cosmographia*, that of Sebastian Münster, was first published in 1544 and translated (in excerpts) by Richard Eden as 1553 as *A treatyse of the newe India*.[29]

Cosmography is illustrative of the Renaissance preference for the universal over the specific, and the interdisciplinary over specialization: it encompassed so many fields and approaches that it could appeal to anyone: the artist or the "scientist", the astronomer or the navigator, the philosopher or the artificer. In his "Mathematical Praeface," John Dee (who studied with Frisius in Leuven and about whom we will be hearing much more in the next chapter) defined Cosmography as the "matching" of Astronomy and Geography, a term which emphasizes its *connecting* role. He goes on: "which, wholly and perfectly makes description of the Heavenly, and also Elemental part of the World: and of these parts, makes homogall application, and mutual collation necessary."[30] The conception of the cosmographical *world* encompassing heavenly (celestial) and elemental (terrestrial) spheres, was traditional, handed down from Cleomedes and his successors, but the desire to understand the structures and workings of both spheres encouraged empirical documentation and mathematical analysis, as well as the refinement of precise tools of measurement, in later Renaissance Europe. Both the flexibility and the popularity of cosmographical texts inspired their translation and application in England, which was lagging behind the Continent in most of the subsidiary fields in the early sixteenth century. Within the public realm, the practical side prevailed, with Henry VIII appointing the Bavarian emigré Nicholas Kratzer as Royal Astronomer and Horologer in 1519: Kratzer was an innovative instrument-maker, specializing in sundials, who went on to lecture at Oxford. His fellow German and royal appointee, Hans Holbein, painted his portrait in 1528 holding a pair of dividers and surrounded by his instruments: among them a polyhedral dial under construction, a pivoting rule, ruling knife, and scissors. On the shelf to the right behind him is a dismantled universal equinoctial dial. He is the very image of a mechanical man, defined by his

FIGURE 4 *Hans Holbein the Younger (1497–1543), Jean de Dinteville and Georges de Selve ("The Ambassadors") (1533). Detail of the arm of Dinteville and scientific instruments. Oil on oak, 207 × 209.5 cm.* © *National Gallery, London / Art Resource, NY.*

practice and his expertise. Two men who are also defined by their instruments, but as operators (or possessors) rather than makers, are featured in another Holbein painting: the double portrait commonly known as *The Ambassadors* (1533), featuring a pair of Frenchmen at the Tudor court, Jean de Dinteville and Georges de Selve. On the two-tiered table between them, we see a separation of earthly and heavenly objects, with the former on the bottom shelf and the latter on top (see Figure 4). Among the instruments for measuring the universe, there is a celestial globe (sphere), a portable sundial known as a pillar or shepherd's dial, a horary quadrant, a polyhedral dial, a torquetum, and another dismantled equinoctial dial—perhaps the same one as in the Kratzer painting? Might Kratzer have loaned the instruments to Holbein and his ambassadors to lend their depiction the air of mastery and elucidation? The worldly goods on the bottom shelf hint at connections with the top—especially the terrestrial globe and an arithmetic textbook by Peter Apian—but still portray a separate sphere.[31]

English cosmographical texts tend to lean towards one or the other of the two fields that dominate the subject, astronomy or geography, but mathematics could bridge the two disciplines and craft a more integrative perspective. In Recorde's *The castle of knowledge*, the Master asks his student-scholar:

now if the whole circumference of the Heavens be 360 degrees, I demand of you how many miles doth answer to 360 degrees. And the scholar answers: That I may know as in the former work, setting the numbers according to the rule of proportion. Then multiplying 1800 by 360 therewith 64800, which I must divide by 30 and so the quotient will be 21600 whereby I know that 21600 miles doth answer unto 360 degrees in the sky. And so it should seem that those are the just numbers of miles above the earth. The master replies: You need to make no doubt thereof, except you doubt whether they be any part of the Earth without the circuit of Heaven: or else you doubt that the Earth be in the middle of the world.[32]

The scholar replies that the first doubt is foolish and the second needs some proof, which provides the opportunity for Recorde to delve into a more textual description of the world, incorporating the latest discoveries of the "Portingalls" and Spaniards. Description must be augmented by mathematical analysis of distance, climate, and time, all of which are presented in illustrations of the cosmographer's instruments and tables for ready reference. The fourth treatise of the *Castle of knowledge*, a summary with proofs, considers the "forms" of the earth and the Heavens, including "a brief declaration of the motions of the planets" and a reference to the Copernican hypothesis. Recorde does not commit to this new universe, but he does conclude that "the earth is but as a prick in comparison to the sky, which is approved by four diverse arguments." Ever the educator, Recorde used cosmographical theory and inquiry to both introduce and reinforce mathematical practice among his readers.

William Cunningham's *The cosmographical glasse*, published just a few years later than *The Castle of knowledge* and referencing it and other works of Recorde, tilted towards the geographical side of the cosmographical spectrum.[33] Its subtitle declares that it contains the "pleasant" principles of cosmography, geography and hydrography, or navigation, and its preface promises to show its readers "the whole face of all the Earth, withal the corners of the same" from the comfort of a "pleasant house or warm study," thus inspiring English expansion a full thirty years before Richard Hakluyt's *The Principall nauigations, voiages and discoueries of the English nation* (1589). The five books of *The Cosmographical glasse* are earthly-oriented; only the first book references the Cosmographical *world*, encompassing both the heavens and Earth. This book lays out the principal rules of spherical geometry, followed by books on measurement, cartography, navigation, and geographical description, while the second book focuses on measurement, book three on cartography, book four on navigation. Book five engages in geographical description and transports its readers into the realm of natural history, as all of Europe, and parts of Asia, and parts of Africa, Asia and the Americas are described in physical and ethnographical terms.

Each region and city is also given its geographical coordinates, which creating an odd juxtaposition when paired with Cunningham's more subjective descriptions. Ireland, while a land "very fertile" and "subject to the Crown of England" is free from venomous beasts and the source of many medicinal herbs, but its people are "savage, wild, & beastly, they are given to sorcery, superstition & witchcraft: their shirts & smocks are saffroned, they go with long Mantels ... They delight in many coloured things. They are great drinkers of *Aqua vitae* (which is their only medicine.)" He relied on ancient and medieval sources for his brief descriptions of lands in Africa and Asia, but of course America "was to Ptolomaeus, & the Ancient Geographers unknown: as also at this present great part of it is not yet found out." Its name came from its founder, Amerigo Vespucci, "as doeth appear by his owne testimony," and its people were characterized by both childlike immodesty and savage brutality: "They be filthy at meat, & in all secret acts of nature, comparable to brute beasts. Their bread is roots, & their meat mans flesh, for all their enemies, which they overcome, they with great banqueting devour." Cunningham was clearly reliant on Vespucci's sensational accounts of the New World, even though they had not yet been published in England. Though not particularly critical of his contemporary sources, Cunningham came pretty close to the ideal of a Renaissance Man: besides his cosmographical pursuits, he was a professional physician (like Recorde) and a skilled surveyor and cartographer: the map of his native Norwich in *The cosmographical glasse* was the first printed map of an English provincial town, and also an early example of triangulation, as the most prominent church towers in the city were used to fix the location of other city sites (Figure 5). It also brings the surveyor/cartographer (Cunningham himself?) into the space, in the foreground with aide, a plane table, and a (large) magnetic compass: an illustration of both process and product.

Whether more astronomical and geometrical, or geographical and descriptive, English cosmographical texts influenced the authors of navigational texts published in the latter part of the sixteenth century, a time when there was an increasingly influential circle of authors and courtiers who were advocating for the adoption of a more energetic and expansionistic commercial policy on the part of the Tudor government. There is a very notable difference between the sole English navigational text published in the first half of the century, a translation of *Le routier de la mer*, Pierre Garcie's pilot book for the west coast of France, published by the English printers Robert Copland and William Copland in five editions from 1528 to 1557, and the far more comprehensive (and mathematical) texts of the later century. It represents a limited genre, confined to precise sailing directions along a specific coast or route (routier, rutter), and English empirical information was added to the later editions in the form of Richard Proude's directions for the circumnavigation of Britain, but *The rutter of the sea: with the hauens, rodes, soundings, kennings, windes, floods, and ebbes,*

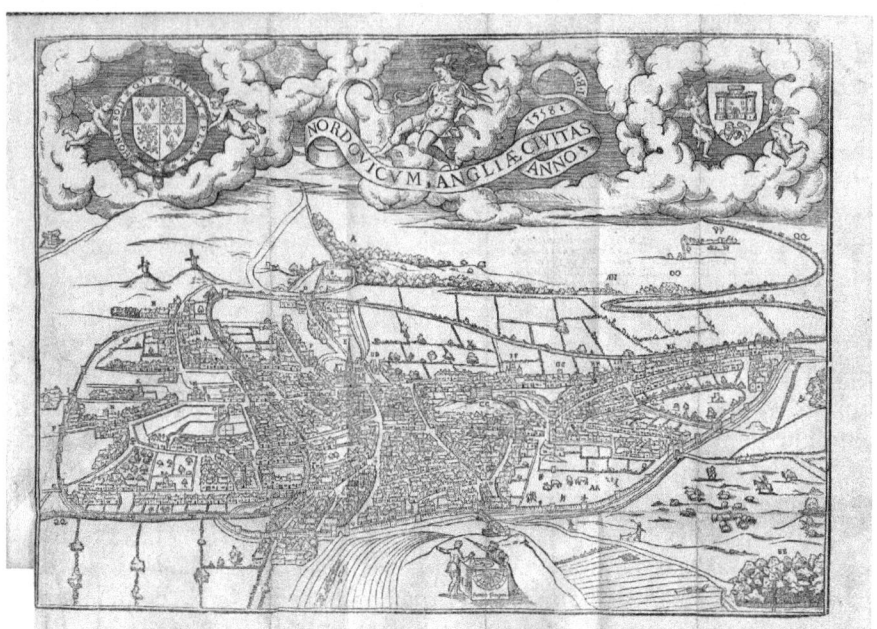

FIGURE 5 *William Cunningham (b. 1531)*, The cosmographical glasse, conteinyng the pleasant principles of cosmographie, geographie, hydrographie, or nauigation *(London, 1559), folding plate facing folio 8: plan view of Norwich. Used by permission of the Folger Shakespeare Library under a Creative Commons Attribution-ShareAlike 4.0 International License.*

daungers and coastes of diuers regions was not only derivative but also purely descriptive. It also represents a *limitation*: pilotage will not enable English mariners and merchants to go very far.[34] Mathematics-based navigation, aided by ever-updated instruments, charts, and information, will be the essential foundation for building the Elizabethan overseas empire.

3

Elizabethan Alterations: Continuity and Crisis

Cultural history seldom falls neatly into dynastic periods, and the Elizabethan era was no exception, for all its "golden" aura. From the perspective of informational and didactic texts as opposed to more creative endeavors, there was an obvious persistence of conservatism: the ancient authorities were still quite authoritative, late medieval medical regimens were still applying humoral medicine to daily life, and Thomas Tusser's customary, cadencing calendar of the agricultural year was expanded to its fullest format. Random recipe books were reprinted, along with those offering "sundry secrets" in printed versions of medieval miscellanies like Thomas Lupton's *A thousand notable things, of sundry sortes. whereof [sic] some are wonderfull, some straunge, some pleasant, diuers necessary, a great sort profitable, and many very precious*, first published in 1579 and reissued multiple times thereafter.[1] It is difficult to discern much thematic or organizational structure in Lupton's vast compendium, with recipes for toothaches, rust-prevention, cat-keeping, "counterfeit Mandrake," and advice for the potentially perilous "threescore and third year" all to be found in the same chapter. So the medieval encyclopedic tradition endured, but there were new elements of Elizabethan information culture that emerged as well, including an emphasis on discovery, not only of newfound lands like Humphrey Gilbert's Newfoundland and Thomas Hariot's Virginia, but of new ideas, new audiences, new crops, new processes, and new devices. Errors in previously published works were discovered as well: of both old and new authors. As in the early Tudor era, translation continued to be an important avenue for information, but there was a shift to translation of near-contemporary continental authors, primarily from France and the Low Countries, and away from a dependence on classical authorities. The empirical, utilitarian, and quantitative approaches that emerged earlier in the century became more commonplace, and a series of authors (and translators) praised the "invention" of *our* age in an explicitly comparative fashion. Richard Surflet, the translator of Charles Estienne's influential husbandry manual *Maison Rustique, or the covntrey farme*, prefaced his text by observing that

> the time doth continually bring some new thing, and that the spirits of the men of this age are so fine and subtle & so full of invention, that no many things which have been liked of heretofore can content them, for either they do alter and change the things, or else the means of doing for those which are better more appropriate, and more beautiful than those of former time.[2]

These are common sentiments, present in texts relating not only to husbandry, which characteristically called for more empirical approaches, but also medicine and domestic pursuits. Such "beautiful" alterations generally involved exposing the essences of things, either through distillation of their composite substances, or the discovery of intrinsic virtues hitherto unknown (or both). This chapter will examine the inventive "spirit" of the Elizabethan age referenced by Surflet with the goal of uncovering just what *was* new in terms of theory and practice in a variety of endeavors, reserving overtly novel navigation for Chapter Four.

The Persistent Plague, the New Pox, and the Indian Weed

The endemic threat of plague encouraged many texts but no innovative remedies as the plague tract continued to be a standard medical reflection and response, particularly during and after the English plague pandemics of 1563, 1593, 1603, 1625 and 1636. Just as the health regimens were contiguous through our period, so were plague tracts, which were even less of a gauge of shifting and responsive medical theory. Such treatises were a significant subgenre of late medieval and early modern medical literature, and their specificity inspired treatises on a range of ailments and conditions over the early modern era. Nancy Siraisi has identified 281 distinct plague tracts dating to the period between the Black Death and 1500, and Paul Slack singles out 23 printed plague treatises published in England between 1485 and 1603, commencing with *A passing gode lityll boke necessarye [and] behouefull ag[e]nst the pestilence*, attributed to Joannes Jacobi and Bengt Knutsson (translator) and printed by William de Machlinia.[3] Plague tracts continued to be published throughout the seventeenth century, most particularly during or after the epidemics of 1603, 1625, 1636 and 1665, and plague "chapters," sections or addenda were also featured in every other type of medical publication over the early modern era. Regimen writers could distinguish their manual by adding a discourse on the plague, as did

Thomas Phayre and Thomas Cogan, particularly as "evil diet" was referenced as one cause of the contagion.[4] Even more so than the regimens, plague tracts possessed a strong moral tone as there was general agreement that the "first cause" of the plague was man's sinfulness, and many works, even those with "medicine" in their titles, were essentially devotional. Nevertheless, even if man had sowed the seeds of his own destruction, there was no clearer articulation of the body under siege, or collective bodies under siege, than those that were expressed in plague writing, in medical, religious, and literary texts. Thomas Dekker's plague pamphlets convey this sense of assault with characteristic fervency:

> for now the Drum of Death is beating up: the cannon of the Pestilence does not yet discharge, but the small shot plays night and day, upon the suburbs: And hath sent seven bullets singing into the City. The arrows fly over our heads and hit some, though they as yet miss us; But none knows how soon the strong Archer, may draw his Bow, and cleave our very hearts: Look forward howsoever, and look up with open eyes, under your shields to receive them as they come flying, lest they pierce you quit through and through, & nail you to destruction.[5]

Despite the focus on the preservation of health in sixteenth-century medical tracts, "shields" remained metaphorical.

And yet, as horrifying as it was, the plague was not perceived as something "new" or altogether different from other diseases in early modern England: rather it was assimilated into existing theories about preventative health. Unlike modern historians of the plague, authors of early modern plague tracts did not spend a lot of time considering its causes. It was acknowledged universally that God was the first cause—of everything. Beyond that, our writers did not have the benefit of hindsight and the knowledge, experience or tools of those observers of the modern third pandemic, who identified the *Yersinia pestis* bacterium and its primary transmission vectors: the fleas fo rodents and rats.[6] The plague appeared contagious to them, but they also noticed that certain people—primarily poor people living in unwholesome conditions—were particularly susceptible while others were less vulnerable. So, while they did not comment on the rats and fleas—which were the agents of transmission (although untethered dogs, cats and pigs are identified as infecting agents)— they did highlight the conditions in which these carriers would flourish. While the language employed to describe the infected and their environment often appears condemnatory, there are also explicit assumptions of both individual and collective responsibility in the plague tracts, derived from both pious and practical impulses. William Bullein's popular *Dialogue against the feuer pestilence*, first published after the "great" plague of 1563 swept away nearly a quarter of London's population, declared that the plague came "most chiefly to them under the place infected, then to sluttish, beastly people, that keep their houses and lodgings unclean, their meat, drink, and clothing most noysome, their labor and travail immoderate" as well as "those which lack provident wisdom to prevent the same by good diet, air, medicine" and Simon Kellwaye's *Defensatiue against the plague* (1593) included not only a personal regimen to follow but also "orders magistrates and rulers of cities and towns should cause to be observed."[7] Indeed, because no effective medical regimen of prevention besides sanitation and social distancing could be found, the burden of "plague management" responsibilities fell on municipal authorities in early modern England and elsewhere, as will be discussed in Chapter Five.

Most plague tracts offered commonsense prescriptions, in accordance with the regimens, humoral theory, and the traditional authorities: there was very little current or comparative advice. Following the dreadful plague of 1563, there was an apparent air of desperation among printer-publishers who wished to present "timely" advice: besides Bullein's contemporary *Dialogue*, several editions of the decades-old *Myrour or glasse of helthe* by Thomas Moulton were published in the 1560s, as well as texts by continental authorities Leonhart Fuchs and Andreas Osiander.[8] The London cloth merchant William Barnard "requested" that another continental authority be consulted and so *The gouerance and preseruation of them that feare the plage* was "set forth" by "John Vandernote, physician and surgeon, admitted by the king his highness." Jan van der Noot, a Flemish émigré and "physician," had actually died back in 1553, after being examined, failed, rejected and fined by the College of Physicians for his "ignorance."[9] Despite the facts of Vandernote's ignorance and death, "his" treatise contains representative plague theory and advice: the plague was caused by evil "vapors and corruptions" of the earth or sky, or both, and once it appeared, the best thing to do was stay in your sweet-smelling home and avoid plague-infested or "stinking" areas. If that was impossible, abstain from anything that could cause putrefaction, or internal corruption of the humors: excessive intercourse, south-facing winds, "superfluity" of anything, all hot foods, fruits and fish. Clean and perfume your home with vinegar, rosewater, bay, juniper, oregano, wormwood, hyssop and aloes, and keep fires burning with logs of oak. Wash your hands frequently with the ever-present and all-powerful vinegar and rosewater and eat well-washed and -salted rue and bread soaked in vinegar first thing in the morning. Strive to drink new, white wine and eat new, white bread as much as possible and never go to bed on a full stomach. "Vandernote" provided a weekly regimen of prepared medicines, including pestilence pills and treacle, and concluded with "A medicine of King Henry for the Plague or Pestilence."

John Jones, a licensed *and* living London physician, included the plague in his 1566 compendium of fevers, *A dial for all agues*.[10] Even though he himself had contracted the plague in 1563, a victim of corrupt air but somehow also contagion, Jones relied only on classical and biblical authorities to explain his affliction. The traditional connection between putrefying fruit and pestilence was given a new twist in Jones' discourse, as he observed that one of the most plague-vulnerable neighborhoods of London was St. Sepulchre's parish, the center of the "fruiterers'" trade, and also home to many "poor people and stinking lanes." An author who was more exclusively focused on the plague, due to both his experience and concerns for the poor, was Thomas Brasbridge, whose *Poore mans iewell* was advertised as "cheap, easy to be gotten, and practiced of the poorest."[11] He followed what was a standard plague tract format of causes, preservatives, tokens and cures, and reasserted the generally accepted four causes of the contagion: divine (the sinfulness of man), astronomical (an evil constellation) and medical (corruption of the air caused by either the evil constellation or the man-made environment and "the aptness of man's body through evil humors" to receive the venomous, corrupted air). Preservatives were generally the longest section of a plague tract, but Brasbridge was determined to make his succinct, so he referred his readers to the regimens of "learned physicians" in order to craft their own compensatory, preservative diets but did recommend constant cleaning and fires for the home, as "fire takes away the force of the evil air." Outside in the pestilential air, Brasbridge advised his readers to keep an orange peel and an Angelica root in their mouths as often as possible and avail themselves of the knowledge and use of that particular herb, along with "Carduus Benedictus" or Blessed Thistle, both of which were presented as cure-alls according to the "new" herbals of Leonhart Fuchs and William Turner. Brasbridge anticipated Nicholas Culpepper in bringing these wonder herbs to the masses, and he also connected religion and medicine in ways that are representative of his time and these texts: as excess, of food and drink in particular, was seen as a cause of both sin and infection, he urged those who indulged to reduce their consumption and give their leftovers to their honest neighbors who could not work, as "this is more healthful for themselves, better for a commonweal, and more acceptable to God."

There was an expanding group of physicians, translators and apothecaries for whom traditional responses to the persistent plague—as well as a range of other ailments and conditions—were no longer enough: fire must be fought with fire through the amplification of *materia medica* by new alchemical processes and substances; for them, simply sticking a cutting of Angelica or Blessed Thistle in one's mouth was not tapping into these plants' full potential as curative agents. The quest to develop stronger, more effective (and processed) medicines to fight both old and new diseases dates to a least a century before and intensified over the sixteenth century. While early modern alchemy had its mystical and cosmographical influences, in terms of the practice of English medicine it was primarily practical and chemical: focused on the process of distillation as the means to reveal the virtues of nature, in alliance with the essential mineral substances sulfur, mercury, and salt, the composition of both macrocosmic earth and microcosmic man. Two other books, which were published within a few years of Brasbridge's *Poore mans iewell*, employed their "treasuries" to present an array of plague pills, potions, powders, perfumes, and plasters distilled through complicated distillation processes, which "drew out" the hidden powers of plants, animals, and minerals: *The newe iewell of health, wherein is contayned the most excellent secretes of phisicke and philosophie, deuided into fower books* (1576), an amplified collection of secrets presented by Swiss naturalist Conrad Gessner in the earlier *The treasure of Euonymus* published by surgeon George Baker, and *A ioyfull iewell. Contayning aswell such excellent orders, preseruatiues and precious practises for the plague, as also such meruelous medcins for diuers maladies, as hitherto haue not beene published in the English tung*, a translation of the Italian physician Leonardo Fioravanti's "secrets" published by apothecary John Hester (1579).[12]

In retrospect, alchemical medicine looks "new" but its practitioners often claimed that it was "ancient," derived from Hippocratic tradition continued by Roger Bacon in the medieval period and the radical reformer Theophrastus von Hohenheim, better known as Paracelsus, in their own time: in his 1585 apology for the "ancient chemical physick," Richard Bostocke traced its origins to "Abraham or at least from Hermes Trismegistus" and defended Paracelsus as "the restorer thereof to his purity: and that he has given more light thereunto, than any other before him," which has resulted in "great cures."[13] These "great cures" were revealed to the English people by John Hester, who was at the forefront of Elizabethan alchemical medicine both as a practitioner and a translator. The two activities were related in very practical ways: the remedies that he translated became the basis of his business, located on Paul's Wharf at the sign of the "stillatory." In his prefaces for works such as *A hundred and fourtene experiments and cures of the famous phisition Philippus Aureolus Theophrastus Paracelsus* (1583), Hester directed his readers there, where they could find ready-made remedies and the apothecary himself, creating medicines "simply and plainly without sophistication." As was the case with mathematical authors and practitioners, a demystifying message was implicit (and sometimes explicit) in the texts of alchemical advocates, along with a focus on praxis and process. A printed bill of Hester's ready-made oils, salts, extractions, essences, and compositions, both of his own invention and other authors, indicates that he would avail himself, for a reasonable stipend, "to instruct any that are desirous to learn the secrets of the same in few days," and following his death some of these remedies (combined with a pretty traditional herbal) were published under the title *The pearle of practise, or Practisers pearle*, which includes myriad treatments for wounds of all kinds, for plague, and for venereal disease.[14]

Hester's concern with teaching "spagyric" processes, with *practice* as well as products, was typical of English alchemists who presented their art as an active, even mechanical pursuit. George Baker's Gessner compilation *The newe iewell of health* includes scores of recipes for "marvelous" distilled oils, waters, balms, electuaries, and powders, as well as the "manner to make the vessels, furnaces, and other instruments thereunto belonging" to the Art of distillation, but also its fundamental process: "herein you shall learn the manner to separate by Art the pure and true substance as well manifest as hidden, which in Physick is a great help to the taking away of diseases, hard or rebellious, to be cured."[15] With respect to that most "hard or rebellious" disease, Baker accepted the traditional secondary cause of terrestrial corruption and prescribed remedies that were progressively more complex in terms of both their processes and ingredients, from waters "simply distilled of herbs" to compound elixirs distinguished by their secret, golden, strong, royal and life-giving natures like oil of antimony, a "holy liquor" made of the "flower of all metals," an aqua vitae for the pestilence, and mercury precipitate, "a remedy against all sicknesses and diseases, caused of the rottenness of humours."[16] In keeping with the comparable-component philosophy of alchemical medicine, the *Newe iewell* also features a recipe for a "caustick" made of arsenic and mercury, an appropriate remedy for the plague as it is among the "arsenical diseases" and not the only affliction in which the cure was potentially worse than the disease.[17]

Traditional medicine in the Elizabethan era was challenged not only by alchemy but also by new diseases and plants for which no classical precedents could be found. From the fourteenth century onwards, physicians had been able to establish precedents for the plague, most especially in the second-century "Plague of Galen" or Antonine Plague, which is generally, but not conclusively, thought to have been either smallpox or measles. Another great pox appeared in the late fifteenth century, and though it was described as both evil and "pestilential" it was quickly identified as something "new": syphilis. Galen could not advise a course of treatment for this scourge, alternatively referred to as the Spanish, Neapolitan, and French Pox, due to its first appearance among French soldiers based in Naples during the Italian Wars. Herbal decoctions and gum-based ointments were ineffective, and as the primary focus of treatment were the ulcers and abscesses on the skin, syphilis came under the jurisdiction of surgeons. While Galen considered quicksilver, or mercury, to be too poisonous to ever be considered as *materia medica*, there was a medieval tradition, clearly accepted in the Salernitan school, that it could be effective if properly administered, just as the correct preparation of poisonous herbs could be effective in remedies. The mercury cure was long, painful, characterized by dreadful side effects, and even its advocates acknowledged its risks, so it was "joyful news" when a "cure" was found in guaiac, the brown resin obtained from the South American guaiacum tree according to native practices observed by the Spaniards. This humble tree acquired a succession of embellished names as it was heralded across Europe: holy wood, *lignum vitae*, pockwood, *sanctum*. Ulrich von Hutten, a victim of syphilis (and the mercury cure) himself, praised the discovery, "found of late days among the new lands, which were unknown by the old time," as did the Spanish physician Nicolás Monardes, who published a three-part *Historia medicinal de las cosas que se traen de nuestras Indias occidentales* from 1565–1574, opining that European physicians could not cure the evil pox because "they were ignorant that it was a new disease, and they would reduce it to something already known." Both von Hutten's and Monardes's texts were translated and published in successive sixteenth-century editions in England, provoking curiosity about what other wonders of the New World could possibly cure the plagues of the Old. Yet despite William Bullein's claim that "there is no better remedy than sweating and drinking of guaiacum, using it in due time and order" and its conspicuous inclusion in the popular *Nova Reperta* (*New Inventions of Modern Times*) print series of Philips Galle after Johannes Stradanus, most English medical writers expressed Paracelsian doubt about its efficacy against such a strong disease and supported the proper use of mercury and other minerals, whose "venomous qualities" could be tamed through distillation and other chemical processes.[18]

A particular strong case for new techniques and approaches, as opposed to just simply employing new materials, was made by the Elizabethan surgeon William Clowes in *A short and profitable treatise touching the cure of the disease called (Morbus Gallicus) by unctions* (1579), which was corrected and expanded into a "brief and necessary" treatise a decade later (Figure 6). The efforts of Clowes were lauded by his like-minded colleagues George Baker, John Banister and John Gerard, among others in epistles and epilogues: Banister and Clowes had both served as battlefield surgeons battling another new "disease" of the sixteenth century—gunshot wounds—so they were brothers-in-arms. Clowes clearly had several goals for this text: to enhance his own reputation as well as those of other educated and experienced surgeons, to instruct young surgeons, to condemn the malpractice of "fugitive" surgeons and shady practitioners such as the notorious Valentine Russwurin, to defend the artful use of mercury, and finally, to prescribe treatment and remedies for the French pox. He claimed to have cured more than a thousand syphilis patients during his residency at St. Bartholomew's Hospital in London, and proceeded in casebook form, recommending evacuation procedures, diet, mundifying medicines, compound caustics, and both desiccative and incarnative unctions and unguents to which mercury could be added safely. Clowes allowed that many learned men were "sworn enemies" against quicksilver because of its dangerous side effects, but asserted that if it was

> compounded with the fore named unguents, oils, gums, etc. then undoubtedly it will resolve and mollify: and it opens the body, and provokes it to sweat, and empties the cause this disease, sometimes sensible and sometimes insensible, and the blood thereby is purged from infection, and all the parts of the body is cleansed from superfluous humors so that good humors are bred, and they do return to their natural course and disposition.[19]

Extreme diseases (and nothing could be more extreme than syphilis) required extreme remedies, but the "malice" of quicksilver could be "killed"

FIGURE 6 *William Clowes (1543/4–1604), A briefe and necessarie treatise, touching the cure of the disease called Morbus Gallicus, or Lues Venerea, by unctions and other approved waies of curing / newlie corrected and augmented . . . (London, 1589). Wellcome Collection (Attribution 4.0 International CC BY 4.0).*

(separated) by the complex compounds of an experienced and learned practitioner. Clowes's colleagues concurred: in John Banister's opinion, "quicksilver yields health to the body in a marvelous manner, if it is administered according to art."[20] This was an authoritative opinion: Banister gave the visceral lectures at the Barber-Surgeons' Hall, was licensed by both the Barber-Surgeons Company and the College of Physicians, had served as both a battlefield and naval surgeon, and was a prolific author. These men were practitioners first, but also open to theory, representative of the "chymists," identified by Lawrence Principe, working as "an endeavor of head and hand, a meeting of theory and practice."[21]

Among the myriad medical practitioners of early modern London, apothecaries like Hester and surgeons such as Banister, Clowes and Baker were the most attracted to alchemical medicine, with the "learned" physicians of the Royal College remaining devoted to Galenic theory and practice. Yet Elizabethan surgeons were not casually receptive to either new processes or new materials: such novelties had to be vetted, battle-tested, and put on trial through professional practice. John Banister expressed an emerging scientific method very succinctly: "there are two ways to find out the truth of any matter, that is to say, Demonstration & Induction, the first bringing knowledge of those things which are obscure, and dark to our understanding, and the other of those things contained within the compass of our capacity."[22] The virtues of all the wonderful things brought back from the New World had to be demonstrated and "approved", not merely claimed and asserted, but there was general agreement that metals had proved their medicinal worth by the beginning of the seventeenth century, when the cumulative observations of the Spanish Jesuit missionary and naturalist José de Acosta were finally translated into English as *The naturall and morall historie of the East and West Indies*, several decades after their first appearance. True to its title, de Acosta's text was a mixture of theology and empiricism: in the second chapter of its fourth book, he focused on the metallurgical "abundance" in the New World and asserted that "the wisdom of God hath made metals for phisick, and for defense, for ornament and for instruments for the work of man," embracing a wealth of practical pursuits. The novelty and the abundance of the Americas challenged and stimulated arts and crafts simultaneously, perhaps the latter more than the former. No doubt de Acosta's claims that in the West Indies "there are great store of mines of all sorts of metals, as copper, iron, lead, tin, quick-silver, silver and gold: and amongst all the regions and parts of the Indies, the realms of Peru abound most in these metals, especially with gold, silver, quick-silver, or mercury, whereof they have found great store, and daily discover new mines," were motivational in myriad ways.[23]

Of the long list of American plants and stones referenced by de Acosta's fellow Spaniard Nicolas Monardes in his *Historia medicinal*, the English translation of which was issued under the title *Ioyfull newes out of the newfound world* by merchant John Frampton in 1577, only a few made it into use and discussion in our period, and none into the demonstration phase of approved knowledge: tobacco, of course, cocoa and chocolate, mechoacan, a root from New Spain that was briefly recommended as a purgative, and sarsaparilla and sassafras. Monardes presented guaiac, "China-root" and sarsaparilla as near-wonder drugs, along with tobacco, which he claimed could cure countless (actually 65 and counting) diseases, including all diseases of "cold causes," headaches, sores, swellings, the suffering of women, kidney stones, and ailments of the stomach and joints. While Monardes's view seems to have held for much of the sixteenth century, tobacco had to go "on trial" in order to establish its virtues, and like alchemical medicine and the guaiacum cure, this trial was conducted as a public discourse via print: the erstwhile poet Anthony Chute published the first English treatise on tobacco posthumously in 1595, providing a convenient summary of continental views on the "divine" plant and a few of his own experiential observations, and then the tobacco wars ensued, gaining steam even before the publication of King James's *Counterblaste to tobacco* in 1604.[24]

As he was not a medical practitioner, Chute does not have much to say about the "outward applications" of tobacco, chiefly as a salve for wounds, aches and pains in its green-leaf form. He was much more interested in the benefits of "receiving it in pipes" or drinking tobacco, the common contemporary term for smoking. He observed that tobacco was used as a preservative against the "late dangerous infection," presumably the plague of 1593, and opined that "there is nothing that harms a man inwardly from his girdle upward but may be taken away with a moderate use of Tobacco." It was early days though, and the jury was still out, as "time and experience ... correct old and bring forth new things." In the last year of Elizabeth's reign, debate over the "new thing" broke out, with one "Philaretes" publishing the first condemnation of tobacco in *VVork for chimny-sweepers: or A warning for tabacconists. Describing the pernicious vse of tabacco, no lesse pleasant then profitable for all sorts to reade*, and provoking a rejoinder from the acclaimed College physician Roger Marbeck and a more whimsical panegyric from the then-teenaged poet John Beaumont.[25] Philaretes argued from the perspective of a Galenic practitioner, criticizing the indiscriminate use of tobacco and identifying its essential hot and dry characteristics as excessively harmful for daily use, violently purgative, and the potential cause of such random conditions as infertility, indigestion, and colds. He also claimed that it was a discovery of the Devil, revealed first to heathens and embraced by infidels, and therefore not to be used by good Christians. Marbeck countered point by point, arguing Galenic theory primarily, but also defending tobacco on grounds that could be employed for all worldly discoveries: "in condemning Tobacco, and the Tobacconists so eagerly in this point, as you do: in my opinion you do in a manner condemn all Christendom for some one thing or other used by them: which was either invented at the first: or else is now daily used by the Infidels."[26] The debate continued in the Jacobean era, even as apothecary John Clarke observed that "we see that Indian weed Tobacco has now found out both learned & honorable patrons" in his pamphlet *The trumpet of Apollo sounding out the sweete blast of recouerie, in diuers dangerous and desperate diseases*, also published in 1602.[27] Like John Hester's earlier broadside advertisement for his distilled remedies, Clarke's text foreshadowed the more commercialized medicine of the seventeenth century: it was not an advocative or instructive manual of prescriptions for the era's most threatening diseases, but an advertisement for the alchemical oils, waters, and ointments that could be purchased at his shop and the names of those whom he has cured with his art, including a "notable defensative cake against the plague" for which no ingredients—just many testimonies—are listed. He labeled himself "bold" to begin with this product (not recipe), as "diverse Physicians of great reading and judgment (whose grave censures I do greatly reverence) do expect a fearful and general infection of the plague this summer, by reason of the unnatural and intemperate season of the spring, which has already showed both his deadly and dangerous effects in the bodies and lives of many thousands of her Majesty's subjects." And in the following year, the plague came back, killing at least 30,000 people in London alone, despite the availability of Clarke's plague cakes.

Profitable Plants

Whether one was a Galenic physician, a Paracelsian surgeon, or an entrepreneurial apothecary, knowledge of plants and their virtues was essential in the Elizabethan era, and the knowledge base expanded considerably with the publication of William Turner's *A new herball* from 1551 to 1568. This was the first English herbal, even though it was printed partially abroad and illustrated with plates from the octavo edition of Leonhart Fuch's *De Historia Stirpium* (1542). Not only did Turner provide vernacular names for the 238 plants included in his herbal, thus enabling medical practitioners who were not literate in the classical languages to identify and reference their "tools," but he included their English habitats whenever possible. Exiled to the Continent twice for his devout Protestant faith, Turner was inspired by the German herbalists of his day, and equally conversant with the ancient authors: what emerges from his straightforward descriptions of plants and their properties is a dialogue of sorts with all of these authorities, with Turner himself having the final say. He is the approver, but when Turner cannot confirm, he says so: "but because I have not seen.... I cannot judge."[28] He relayed to his readers what he has seen, in straightforward and detailed descriptions of each plant and its utility, stripped of the folklore so present in medieval herbals, and where they can see each plant as well: the *New herball* is thus a dynamic document, and a baseline for further discoveries and confirmations. Comparing it to another contemporary vernacular work of natural history, John Maplet's *A greene forest* (1567), is instructive: while the latter's purview was much broader, including not only plants but also minerals and animals, its perspective is narrower, confined only to classical and humanist knowledge. For Turner, it is "I have seen," for Maplet, "it is said."[29]

Like the authors of husbandry and navigation texts of his time, Turner was also an advocate: during his time on the Continent he developed a comparative perspective that steered him towards constructive commentary. When discussing a plant that was not cultivated properly (or at all) in England, he tells us so. Flax, for example:

> which is called of the Northern men lynt / in Dutch Flachs / in French Du lyne / in Greek Linon / and in Latin Linum / grows very plenteously in the North part of England / and should grow as plenteously also in the South part / if men regarded not more their private lucre then the King's Laws and the common profit of the whole realm. I haue seen flax or lynt growing wild in Somersetshire within a mile of Wells / but it has fewer bowls in the top then the sown flax has / and a great deal longer stalk. Which things are a sure token that flax would grow there if men would take the pain to sow it.[30]

Likewise, when England deserves praise for its flora, Turner extended it: in reference to another textile herb, madder, he observed that "The wild kind grows plenteously both in Germany in woods / and also in England / and in the most that ever I saw / is in the Isle of Wight. But the fairest and greatest that ever I saw / grows in the lane beside Winchester / in the way to Southampton."[31]

Turner's detailed, personal descriptions of England's flora were inspirational but also reflective of an increasing interest in both the English land and its ability to propagate "profitable" plants, interests that were both agricultural and horticultural. The word "horticulture" will not appear for another century or so, but there is enough evidence of an enhanced focus on the culture of individual plants in the sixteenth century to brand it an Elizabethan discovery. Many factors contributed to this singular scrutiny: reports of the marvelous plants in the New World, the alchemical mission to extract the very essence of each and every plant, the commercialization of agriculture, and the emergence of gardening manuals as a distinct sub-genre of husbandry texts. The inventor of the English gardening manual was Thomas Hyll (Hill), who dominated the field in the latter half of the sixteenth century with successive editions of his two texts, *The profitable Arte of Gardening* and *The gardeners labyrinth*, in continuous print.[32] The popularity of his works can be explained by the emergence of specialized gardens over the sixteenth century: market gardens near the city, kitchen gardens in the country, nursery gardens, physic gardens, and pleasure gardens. In the 1587 edition of his *Description of England*, William Harrison included a chapter on gardens and orchards, which begins with the admission that in the recent past "we have neglected our own good gifts of God, growing here at home" but goes on to observe how "art also helps nature in the daily colouring, doubling, and enlarging the proportion of our flowers, it is incredible to report: for so curious and cunning are our gardeners now in these days that they presume to do in manner what they list with nature, and moderate her course in things as if they were her superiors." Harrison believed that these curious and cunning English gardeners would be more in sync with nature if they cultivated native plants like the humble germander or thistle rather than the "strange herbs, plants, and annual fruits [which] are daily brought unto us from the Indies, Americas, Tapobrane, Canary Isles, and all parts of the world," but he was still impressed with the number of gardens and gardeners all around him.[33]

Whether he fostered or tapped into this market, Thomas Hyll's books were popular, and not for their innovation: he was certainly a gardener, but also a "gatherer" of information, and above all a translator, having made the initial translations of the two alchemical "Jewels" issued by George Baker and John Hester. In his preface to *The newe iewell of health*, Baker informed his readers that Hyll "took great pains in this work, but before it could be brought to perfection, God took him to his mercy," and Hester observed that Hyll "deserves great praise" for the translation of Leonardo Fioravanti's recipes in *A ioyfull iewell*.[34] Hyll's gardening books were not so weighty and much more accessible, especially the first book of *The profitable Arte*, which instructed one in perfect "how-to" prose how to situate, lay out, enclose, fertilize, and protect (from weather and pests) a garden. Book Two was focused on individual plants and their "phisick helps" or virtues, as Hyll presented gardening as both an art and the "handmaiden" to medicine and surgery. While gardening was seen as in service to these "noble" pursuits, it could (and should) be pursued for profit *and* pleasure as well, points that Hyll reinforced with references to markets and illustrations of maze and knot gardens. Later editions of *The profitable Arte* included appendices on beekeeping, the seasonal tasks of the gardener, and tree-grafting: the latter was "gathered" from Richard Arnold's 1502 *Chronicle* or *Customs of London*, which was reissued in 1525.[35]

Thomas Hyll's second gardening book, *The gardeners labyrinth*, was published posthumously by his friend Henry Dethicke in 1577 with attribution to "Didymus Mountain": it expanded on the aesthetic focus of *The profitable Arte* considerably in terms of text and illustrations and acknowledged the new interest in distillation by including the virtues of the distilled waters of each herb, plant and flower. It is an amplified version of the earlier text with its characteristic mix of classical knowledge and "plainer instructions," for the daily tasks of garden maintenance. The *Labyrinth* blended utility and aesthetics by emphasizing the ideal structure of the garden, characterized by "seemly walks and alleys," which aided irrigation and fertilization, and enhanced "the delight of the owner, by which he may walk more freely hither and thither in them, and consider thoroughly all the matters wrought and done in the Garden, if the disquietness of mind hinder not the benefit of the same."[36] Hyll was very focused on approaches to the fundamental task of watering, specifically when, how, and with what vessels and tools it should be pursued: with watering pots made of copper to which "pumps" could be attached for the "handsomer delivering forth of the water," and several versions of "great Squirts" made of tin, which could achieve the effect of "drops of rain on the plants," along with a wooden "skiff" to divert water into the garden beds from a nearby pond or stream. Similar "squirts" would be specified for firefighting a bit later in the sixteenth century, and throughout the seventeenth. An enclosed, path-lined garden of distinct beds facilitated the "best watering" practices for any plant, whether for consumption or delight, as the roots must be penetrated "for water rots and kills above ground." Like William Turner, Hyll was at his most persuasive, and reflective, when he referenced his English environment in between dropping the names of classical authorities and giving his readers plain instructions: he was bound by the English calendar and climate for sowing and harvesting recommendations, of course, and his London perspective surfaced consistently, as when he admonished the "negligent" apothecaries of the city, "which hang up the Physick herbs in their open shops and ware-houses, through which the virtue of these not only breathe away, but the herbs are charged and clogged with dust, cobwebs, dung of flies, and much other filth."[37] Leather bags and wooden boxes were better alternatives for display and storage. In describing the culture and virtues of individual plants, he stepped out of his recitations of classical views frequently to offer personal perspectives and instructions: beets were "more often eaten at poor men's tables," asparagus or "sperage" requires only "small boiling" or else it will "become corrupt or without delight in eating," parsley sweetened the breath and was thus recommended to "maidens and widows to deceive their wooers," artichokes were plagued by mice and moles, so the Gardener should "learn a young cat or tame a weasel" to hunt them, "certain skillful men" have cultivated a white strawberry, "delectable to the eye," and radishes can be used to draw out all of the "evil savour and loathsomeness" of spoiled wine.[38]

The roles of gatherer, translator, and interpreter of essential horticultural information were also assumed by Hyll's contemporary Leonard Mascall, who published a diverse succession of informational manuals in the 1570s and 1580s, beginning with *A booke of the arte and manner how to plant and graffe all sortes of trees* in 1572.[39] Grafting was not a new art, but its techniques were due for revival and dissemination in the later sixteenth century particularly in regard to fruit trees, as orchards were seen as integral a part of an ideal estate as adjacent gardens. William Harrison was just as impressed with the efforts of England's grafters to fashion "artificial mixtures" as Thomas Hyll was with white strawberries: these workmen "dallied" with nature, "as if her whole trade was perfectly known to them" and brought forth tree fruit of diverse colors and tastes, more tender, sweeter, and more delicate than the natural versions. They know how to "convert the kernels of peaches into almonds, of small fruit to make far greater, and to remove or add superfluous or necessary moisture to the trees, with other things belonging to their preservation, and with no less diligence than our physicians doo commonly show upon our own diseased bodies, which to me does seem right strange."[40] The medical comparison seems very apt: while most of Mascall's manual contains basic instructions regarding grafting, "setting stones" (planting the pits of fruit), sowing seeds, and the care of trees, he also included a "little treatise" of "how one may Graft & Plant artificially, and Dexterously, and to make many things very strange in Gardens" in an expression of botanical alchemy that focused on both the alteration and preservation of tree fruits: to make an apple-pear, to make spicy cherries and peaches, to have pit-less peaches, and "keep cherries good a year."

The grafters of Elizabethan England, Mascall included, were focused exclusively on fruit, despite the contemporary perception that the country's timber trees were "spoiled" or "decayed."[41] Concerns about timber shortages were addressed in reference to several trades in Elizabethan statutes, most prominently ironworks (1558, 1581, 1585), but also tanning (1564) and the wine trade (1593): restrictions on timber use were enacted but there was no corresponding policy to expand England's woodlands.[42] Orchard trees were fruit trees, and the orchard was the sylvan counterpart of the garden; forests were royal hunting preserves in their own separate realm and woodland management fell under the larger jurisdiction of husbandry. The two most comprehensive husbandry texts of the Elizabethan era, Barnabe Googe's translation of Conrad Heresbach's *Foure bookes of husbandry* and Richard Surflet's translation of *Maison rustique, or The covntrey farme* do survey woodlands and "mast trees," grown for their timber rather than their fruit, and include instructions for the planting and maintenance of individual trees, groves and "coppice woods", which were felled or harvested continually.[43] Even before the mighty English Oak, "King of the Forest," achieved royal status with the later Stuarts, it was perceived as essential to the English economy *and* identity due to its integral role in English industry and trade (charcoal for iron and glass production; tanbark for leather, the preferred wood for wine, ale and beer casks), and residential and naval construction, but Tudor gardening and husbandry texts tended to focus on the improving aims of the individual private landowner rather than the national interest. Attitudes towards the kingdom's natural resources shifted a bit in the next century: after conducting several surveys, James I issued his *Proclamation for the Preservation of Woods* in 1609, in which he expressed his dissatisfaction with the "great spoils and devastations" committed in the royal forests, even by "our own inferior Officers, such as ought to have had the chief care of the preservation thereof" and a desire to not only preserve but also *increase* and multiply woodlands "for all future ages."[44] No concrete plan was put in place, but this was an acknowledgement of a national concern, especially as the King referenced the Navy and its "especial wants" in terms of timber. Two years later, James began licensing a succession of texts published by a local landowner named Arthur Standish entitled *The commons complaint* and *Nevv directions of experience by the authour for the planting of timber and firevvood*, which called for an ambitious planting program of trees for both timber and for fruit to address "the general destruction and waste of wood" and "the extreme dearth of victuals" so that "there may be as much timber raised as will maintain the kingdom for all uses forever." James was just as dependent on the revenues raised from leases of crown lands as his predecessor had been, however, and so Standish's vision did not turn into a reality.[45]

Like Thomas Hyll, Leonard Mascall experienced a considerable afterlife in terms of publication, with five editions of the *A Booke of the arte and maner, howe to plant and graffe* published during his lifetime, and eight after his death, up to 1656. He moved from husbandry into animal husbandry in the 1580s, with the publication of *The husbandlye ordring and gouernmente of poultrie* in 1581 and *The first booke of cattell wherein is shewed the gouernment of oxen, kine, calues* in 1587: this was expanded to *The gouernment of cattell* to encompass horses, sheep, goats, hogs and dogs after his death, and issued in twelve editions over the next century. This very practical Renaissance man also offered up texts on stain removal (and dyeing, gilding, and a range of material "secrets"), fishing, the engineering of traps for varied vermin, and distillation during his lifetime—and after. Mascall acquired the authority of a title-page portrait in his seventeenth-century publications and associations with the Archbishop of Canterbury (as Clerk of the Kitchen) and King James (as Royal Farrier, even though he died fourteen years before the Stuart succession). Such a range of topics was exemplary of an Elizabethan "gatherer," but also of a more original author of the era, Reynolde Scot, who not only wrote a trailblazing skeptical treatise on *The discouerie of witchcraft* (1584) but also a practical manual on hops published a decade earlier. *A perfite platforme of a hoppe garden* was the first English book devoted exclusively to the cultivation of a crop that had been increasing in popularity in England over the sixteenth century. Henry Buttes, author of the commentary/dietary *Dyets dry dinner* (1599) observed that "heresy and beer came hopping into England both in a year," among his "stories for table talk": presumably this year was around 1520, when Lutheran texts were first disseminated in England.[46]

In language that signals an original treatise rather than one which is compiled, Scot wrote "plainly to plain men of the Country" about how, when, and where "to plant hops with effect" by constructing "hop hills" with trellises made of alder wood onto which the hops vines were tied with rushes. This was a practice based on his own "small skill and experience," which he was compelled to set down according to his friends' urging and his own desire to limit the abilities of "strangers beyond the seas" (chiefly Flemings) to "deprive us of our commodities." He perceived the existence of a ready market and envisioned an expanding one and believed that profitable hops cultivation was in the interests of both individual landowners and the collective Commonwealth. When the private and public interests converged, a plant or crop became "profitable": Scot made the case for hops convincingly, and his manual was reprinted over the next four years and again in the mid-seventeenth century.[47] The public interest was conflicted, however: there was clearly a desire to reduce England's reliance on foreign imports of expensive commodities, but a coincidental concern about the food supply placed potentially profitable industrial crops like rapeseed, madder and woad (like hops, not a new crop but one which experienced a pronounced revival in the sixteenth century) in competition with corn.[48] The struggle to find an equitable and profitable balance between tillage and timber, and crops for consumption and industry, seems to have been constant over much of the Elizabethan era, but in its last decade, characterized by war, plague and dearth, choices would be clearer, and necessity would breed invention.

The Crisis of the 1590s

During the last decade of Elizabeth's reign, English men and women experienced an ongoing war with Spain and in Ireland, harvest failures and consequential periods of dearth, two plague pandemics, escalating inflation, and heavy taxation. There was also considerable anxiety over the aging Queen's successor, more difficult to gauge. It was as if the Death-personified character in William Bullein's early Elizabethan *Dialogue against the feuer pestilence* was prescient when he threatened to unleash his three "fearful darts" upon England and the world: a pale dart that would "destroy infinite numbers with hunger," a black dart of pestilence, and a third dart with which he would "in battle slay in number more than the stars of heaven." This Grim Reaper would "cut them down with my scythe like grass."[49] Following the onset of the first darts of war and plague, the four successive harvest failures from 1594 to 1597 provoked a flurry of governmental reactive acts: against dearth of grain and corn, abuse in diet, and "forestallers, regraters, and engrossers," but also several texts that offered practical suggestions with a remedial intent. Hugh Plat, a proto-scientist in the midst of London, published his master miscellany, *The jewell house of art and nature* in 1594, but responded specifically to the crisis at hand with several shorter texts: *A discouerie of certaine English wants* (1595), *Sundrie nevv and artificiall remedies against famine* (1596), and *The nevv and admirable arte of setting of corne* (1600), timely titles for tracts whose contents were drawn largely from the earlier book. Richard Gardiner of Shrewsbury, a market gardener and textile merchant, published several editions of *Profitable instructions for the manuring, sowing, and planting of kitchin gardens*, which he deemed "very profitable for the common wealth and greatly for the help and comfort of poor people" in 1599 and in the following year, John Taverner presented his *Certaine experiments concerning fish and fruite*. Gardiner and Taverner were both advocates for a more varied English diet in these times of scarcity: different foods rather than different ways of cultivating the staple cereal crops of wheat, rye and barley, generally and collectively referred to as "corn." Gardiner was all about root crops, and Taverner gave detailed instructions in how to create and stock estate ponds, while also encouraging his readers to take advantage of the natural fruitfulness of England: apples, pears, cider and perry could compensate for shortages of corn and malt.[50] In response to "these threatening days of sword and famine," Plat offered a range of skillful (the contemporary meaning of "artificial," which could have positive or negative connotations) substitutions for wheat: breads made of vegetable roots, pumpkins, rice, millet, lentils and beans, rape, the ground leaves of apple, pear, beech and oak trees, eggs and milk. In regard to beverages, the approach was the same: substitute readily available or cheaper ingredients for those which were dear and extract the essence of these ingredients to untap their virtues: wormwood beer, the distilled water of oats, the "licour" of the birch tree, decocted anise, fennel, caraway and licorice could compensate for shortages of other commodities. Plat encouraged his readers to "practice" their substitutions, especially of overlooked "wholesome" native plants like pepperwort, galingale, thyme, orris-root, hyssop, winter savory and pennyroyal: profitable English herbs that could replace expensive foreign spices.[51]

Very much in the method of William Turner decades before, Hugh Plat was an active and discerning observer who prioritized his own experience and experiments over the judgements of the traditional authorities, but he was still fluent in the latter. He included some "frugal notes" taken from a Latin writer in his *Sundrie nevv and artificiall remedies* but also his own annotations: *here I think that our climate will proue too cold*. Also like Turner, he learned from the community of natural philosophers and practitioners whom he lived alongside in late Elizabethan London, and most particularly the latter: his energetic and egalitarian pursuit of natural knowledge in general and processes evocative of the "managed alteration of natural substances" in particular took him into every artisanal quarter of London, where brewers, glassmakers, and apothecaries could relay and demonstrate such alterations as well as the most learned chemist or physician. Plat was both egalitarian and entrepreneurial: the artisanal secrets he gleaned from others not only inspired his own experimentation but found their way into print under his name, establishing his authority as a "public man of science" and one of England's most prolific "knowledge-mongers." His slim dearth pamphlets referenced and advertised his more comprehensive (and expensive) storehouse of useful information, *The jewell house of art and nature*, and while he was content to extend a few free aids to England's seafaring men for the good of the Commonwealth, if these should "receive entertainment according to the worth thereof and my just expectation, I may happily be encouraged to pry a little further into Nature's cabinet, and so to disperse some of her most secret Jewels, which she has long time so carefully kept, only for the use of her dearest children."[52] He believed that his gleaned knowledge had value, and sought recognition and compensation.

With his general interest in the access and alteration of nature for the benefit of society (as well as himself), Plat was not a specialist: his portfolio of inventions encompassed the fields of agriculture, horticulture, chemistry, engineering, manufacturing and medicine. It is helpful to consider and differentiate them in terms of intent: as we have seen, he was responsive to the crisis condition of the 1590s, but he also wanted to improve the daily lot of England's poor in terms of corporeal comforts and amuse his fellow gentlemen with new techniques and tricks. There was considerable overlap among these categories, as illustrated by Plat himself when he republished material for different audiences. For the navy, so much a national focus after the Armada, Plat offered protection and provisioning in the forms of water-resistant garments and a rust-proofing "defensative" for armor and artillery, along with "a certain victual in the form of hollow pipes" which could be kept for years without spoilage: in one publication he refers to this miracle food as "macaroni."[53] The preservation of beverages and foodstuffs for long periods of time was a special preoccupation of Plat's: an objective that would benefit sailors at sea as well as civilians at home. According to Plat, who was a liberal name-dropper, Francis Drake sought his provisioning inventions for the "better relief of his Mariners" and one imagines that he would have appreciated Plat's instructions for better pitch, better bullets, and a portable pump for the removal of superfluous water in ships (and fields) as well. Plat was mindful that if he extended the longevity of certain commodities he would increase their value and price and thus defeat another purpose: relief for the "poorer sort" whose numbers were clearly increasing. Considering shellfish, whose days he prolonged a bit by wrapping them in saltwater-soaked cloths and burying them in a cool and moist place, he expressed a concern that he would "raise the price of them by this discovery amongst the Fishmongers, who only in respect of their speedy decay do now and then afford a pennyworth in them."[54] Plat was just as much an advocate for root crops as his contemporary Richard Gardiner: one of his most-reprinted recipes was for "sweet and delicate cakes made without either spice or sugar" but rather with powdered parsnip roots (and no flour, unfortunately). He also offered up alternative sources of light and fuel: cheaper candles and lanterns, and "coal-balls" made of sea coal, "according to the manner of snowballs."[55] This latter invention would not only provide heat, but also occupation, for England's poor in Plat's estimation.

The sense of shortage was acute at the very end of the sixteenth century: whether it was mere perception, as in the case of England's diminished forests, or reality, as in the case of dearth. In the midst of ever-growing London, a "monstrous" metropolis that seemed to have the capacity to devour the rest of England, Plat must have known that substitution and preservation, even combined with his recommendations for conservation, could not solve the problem of food scarcity: England needed to produce more food, either through technique or enhancement of the soil. While he presented prescriptions for an alternative way of planting corn seed in his 1600 treatise, *The nevv and admirable arte of setting of corne*, and fashioned a greenhouse of sorts to accommodate the cultivation of "Indian" plants, he was much more focused on ways to unleash the productive capacity of soil, in the manner of "alchemical agriculture." Plat advertised, but did not disclose, "a new and extraordinary means for the enriching of arable grounds" in his *Sundrie nevv and artificiall remedies against famine* but included a longer treatise entitled "Diverse new Sorts of Soil not yet brought into any public use" in the *The jewell house*. Plat's discourse on husbandry in the midst of famine was both responsive and reflective, theoretical and practical. Much of it considered the theories of the ingenious French potter and scientist Bernard Palissey regarding the unleashing of the generative powers of salt and marl in the soil, but Plat was determined to proceed from French theory into English practice. He was enraptured with the potential of transforming common salt into "vegetative salt" and observed that "the salt of Clapham, those Western lands, that brine of the Cheshire Saltpits, the residence of those brackish Waters at Erith, do offer to lively demonstrate unto us of the undoubted fertility, which is ready to overflow our banks if we will but only give passage to it."[56] Plat was so focused on new ways to increase the fertility of England's soil he gave short shrift to the traditional ways, passing over all the usual dungs (cow, horse, sheep, hog, pigeon) pretty quickly with only the recommendation that muckheaps and dunghills be covered, lest their "strength" be carried away by the winter rains. In like manner, the "soil of the streets", channels, ditches, pools, ponds and riverbeds, should be mined for fertilizer, as well as the waste from London's trades: hides and hair from its tanners, ashes from its soapmakers, malt dust from its brewers, random remains from its butchers. What emerges is a strategy of digging deeper, literally and figuratively, so to discover generative spirits "concealed, and kept in the bosom of Nature" while simultaneously utilizing anything and everything that was manifest.

In an era of emerging scientific patronage, Hugh Plat was both an aspiring scientist and an aspiring courtier.[57] The son of a prosperous brewer, he was educated at Cambridge, lived the life of a London landowning gentleman, and was knighted by James I in 1605. He was consistently attentive to gearing his inventions and instructions towards the public good, addressing the needs of both seamen and privy councilors, but he also aimed to please more privileged interests. *The jewell house of art and nature* contains more inventions aimed at the gentry than the "poorer sort," including a "perspective ring" that would allow the wearer to cheat at card games, a two-foot-long pistol, various forms of ink, a process to dissolve gold and carry it around in a secret manner, "sweet and tender dentifrices, or rubbers for the teeth," and "a Wagon to be drawn with men" among other innovations. The distillation recipes included in *The jewell house* tend more to the delightful than the beneficial, including "sweet" fragrant waters, herbal butters, salad oil, and well-spiced wines. In offering up these culinary creations, Plat was appealing not only to a refined audience but also a new one: women, whom he would address more directly in his most popular text, *Delights for ladies, to adorne their persons, tables, closets, and distillatories with beauties, banquets, perfumes, and waters.*[58]

Busy Housewives

By the time that Hugh Plat published *Delights for ladies* in 1600 the feminine audience for household help and "stillroom secrets" seems established, or at least identified. The English "huswife" had been acknowledged from the thirteenth century but Thomas Tusser identified the *work* of "huswifery" and separated this sphere of activities from general husbandry only in the second edition of his *A hundreth good pointes of husbandrie* in 1562 while also maintaining that it was equally integral to the success of the estate: *Though husbandry seemeth, to bring in the gains/ Yet huswifry labours, seeme equal in pains/ Some respite to husbands, the wether many send, But huswifes affaires, have never an end.*[59] According to the prescriptions of all the men who wrote books addressed to England's "huswives" from this point on—an increasing number—their affairs were indeed never-ending:

Tusser's whimsical rhymes present a daunting list of daily tasks and general expectations for the "wife of the house", from morning until night and throughout the seasonal year and the tasks get more numerous and detailed as this genre expanded over the sixteenth and seventeenth centuries.

The expansion of books addressed to women in early modern England was largely due to these practical publications. With the exception of Juan Luis Vives's *A very fruteful and pleasant booke called the instruction of a christen woman*, Renaissance conduct and courtesy books were not aimed at English women: this was a genre more commonplace in the later seventeenth and eighteenth centuries.[60] Before the emergence of the housewife, however, there was the mother, addressed generally in the full range of medical literature in the sixteenth century but more specifically in a succession of midwifery texts beginning with "The Rosengarten" of Eucharius Rosslin, first published in 1513 as *der Schwangern Frauen und Hebamen*, reissued by Rosslin's son as *De partu hominis, et quae circa ipsum accidunt* in 1532, and translated into English as *The byrth of mankynde, otherwyse named the womans booke* by Richard Jonas (1540) and Thomas Raynalde (1545) successively. Both the *Rosengarten* and *The byrth of mankynde* benefitted immensely from their illustrations: Raynalde's 1545 edition is one of the first English books to feature copperplate engravings. The pictures of infants in utero, in every possible position, and a very practical birthing chair, must have provoked interesting reactions.[61] While Eucharias Rosslin utilized his original *Rosengarten* for commentary, specifically criticizing the negligent practices of midwives he observed in his capacity as the city physician of Frankfort and Worms, his English translators were focused primarily on edification, and consequently *The byrth of mankynde* aimed for a more general audience: Raynolde's prologue is addressed to women and allows that some "wise women and good midwives" may be ignorant of some of the knowledge and practices contained in his book.

A practicing physician himself, Raynalde apparently wanted nothing to remain "obscure and dark" as he proceeded through four books covering women's reproductive anatomy, conception, pregnancy, childbirth, and infant care, offering both clear description, advice, and helpful remedies along the way—along with the annotated illustrations. His anatomical survey focused, quite logically, on the womb, or matrix, and its function in great detail, from its "privy passage" to its "mother port," dispensing many age-old beliefs about conception as "lies, dreams, and.... fantasies." Few ancient authors appear: indeed, Raynalde interrupted his long descriptive discourse on menstruation only to abhor the "shameful lies and slanders that Pliny, Albertus Magnus, *De secretes mulierum*, and diverse others have written of the venous and dangerous infective nature of the woman's flowers or terms: which all be but dreams and plain dotage: to rehearse their words here were but loss of ink and paper: wherefore let them pass with their authors." As childbirth and its aftermath "lying in" period constituted the most dangerous moments and days of a woman's life, Raynalde gave considerable time and space to the hours and days after birth, as well as to "unnatural," untimely, and dead births. Detailed advice for the care and nourishment of infants was directed at mothers, who are urged by Raynalde to breastfeed their children but also given the preferred attributes of a worthy wet-nurse if they could not. Every infant ailment, from "windiness" to "fearful and terrible dreams" to "google eyes," was addressed with remedies and directions. The last book of *The byrth of mankynde* addressed infertility for the most part (somehow ending with random recipes for dandruff, hair removal, toothpaste and deodorant): while Raynalde focused primarily on deficiencies of the womb, he also offered his readers several ways to discern "whether lack of conception be of the woman or the man," though instructs them not to trust these experiments entirely.

The byrth of mankynde was but the first of a succession of books focused on women's reproductive health in England, followed by translations of the Swiss physician Jacob Rüff's *The expert midwife* and the French surgeon Jacques Guillemeau's *Child-birth, or the happy deliuery of vvomen*; after 1640 the titles increased with popular texts like Thomas Chamberlayne's *Compleat midwifes practice* issued in multiple successive editions.[62] While Rüff's text was essentially derivative of the *Rosengarten*, Guillemeau's work is much more comprehensive, particularly in the realm of pediatrics. He was more apt to indulge his readers than Raynalde was on questions and concerns such as how gender could be determined in pregnancy and the unnatural behavior of pregnant women and new mothers (noting that some women developed *malacia* or *pica* in the former state—and desired to eat very strange things like plaster, ashes, coal, old shoes, and even man's flesh) and also offered detailed instructions on how to help women through their "travails," both natural and unnatural. The uterus was the central focus of medical authors who addressed women's health: either its ability to reproduce or its "suffocation," a contemporary phrase for hysteria brought on by the "rising" of the womb, which was often referred to as the "mother." In more comprehensive textbooks like Philip Barrough's *The method of physick* and Christopher Wirsung's *General practice of physick*, women experienced many of the same conditions as men but also had their unique concerns; Barrough discusses the occurrence and treatment of myriad diseases for both genders, and each alone. Women were diagnosed as "less troubled with dropsy than men," but equally susceptible to sciatica, tonsillitis, and venereal disease. Menstruation and menopause (discussed at some length) were their exclusive domain, of course.[63] As we have seen, the regimens occasionally offered specific prescriptions for women, but almost exclusively pregnant women. Women's health *was* reproductive health, for the most part, but the sensational witchcraft trial of Elizabeth Jackson in 1602 cast quite a different light on the womb. Jackson was accused of bewitching, through demonic possession, her fourteen-year-old neighbor, Mary Glover, who clutched at her throat, unable to speak or eat, in a series of intermittent fits. During the trial, several members of the College of Physicians (always ready to exert their authority in this contested time) testified to their diagnoses of Glover's condition. In support of Jackson, Edward Jorden asserted that Mary was suffering with hysteria or "suffocation of the mother," an unprecedented diagnosis in an age when such symptoms, if deemed "natural," were generally ascribed to melancholy. Jackson was nonetheless convicted, but perhaps the "medical" evidence presented resulted in her relatively light sentence: a year in prison and four appearances at the pillory. Dr. Jorden would go on to expand upon his views of hysteria in the next year, in a work entitled *A briefe discourse of a disease called the suffocation of the mother* (1603) and serve as an "expert witness" of sorts in other witchcraft trials. His dual assertions of ascribing natural causation for behavioral disorders and connecting such disorders to the "wandering womb" would be tested repeatedly throughout the seventeenth century.[64]

The emphasis shifted from women as medical *subjects* to women as medical *provisioners* in the most popular books addressed to women in the sixteenth and seventeenth centuries: recipe books and domestic manuals. These didactic books, encompassing medicinal, culinary, and housekeeping receipts, accounted for the majority of books published for women over the 1475–1640 period, and began to increase in editions notably in the later Elizabethan era.[65] Doubtless "artisanal literacy," or experiential learning, was a more important factor and process than textual literacy in the transmission of much of this information, but again, the drive to compile, "set down" and publish instructive texts on domestic practice is indicative of its increasing value. The preponderance of male authors (or compilers) instructing women practitioners mandated the prescriptive nature of most of these publications, but the printed domestic manual or recipe book developed in tandem with a thriving manuscript culture in England that showcased women as producers as well as consumers. The dynamic nature of this textual culture is particularly apparent in the culinary realm: England rather surprisingly emerged as a leader in European "cookery" publications from the 1570s through the mid-seventeenth century, as the genre transformed from rather random miscellanies to more formal cookbooks.[66]

Two texts credited to recipe "collector" John Partridge illustrate the range of women's activities within the home from a publishing perspective: *The treasurie of commodious conceits, & hidden secrets, and may be called, The huswiues closet, of healthfull prouision* and *The widowes treasure plentifully furnished with sundry precious and approoued secretes in phisicke and chirurgery for the health and pleasure of mankind*.[67] There was little new or experimental in either volume, and Partridge adopted the humanistic stance of a mediator or disseminator, setting forth valuable information for the public good and posterity. Something was new, however, in his allowance of whom he was mediating *for*: in the prefatory comments of *The treasurie*, he admitted that he was urged to publish his gathered secrets "at the instance of a certain Gentlewoman (being my dear and special friend)." This anonymous gentlewoman was further characterized by her "importance," lending an air of authority to Partridge's text beyond that of his classical sources. Partridge's audience of women, addressed both in the *The treasurie* and the *The widowes treasure*, were not Tusser's rural housewives: they had no responsibilities over the kitchen garden, but plenty of provisioning to do inside the house: of food, medicine, and cleaning agents. The *Treasurie* offered women an assortment of recipes in these three basic categories, with instructions for both food preparation and preservation, remedies for canker sores and pomanders, and a range of fumigations and perfumes for the house. It seems as if anything and everything could be turned into a preserve or a conserve, and marmalades and syrups were also essential forms of preservation provisioning. Likewise, one could never have enough rose-water or powder, preferably made from damask roses, said to be introduced to England by Henry VIII's Royal Physician and the founder of the College of Physicians, Thomas Linacre. This rose variety, "whereof is no mention in any olde writer" in the words of William Turner, was perceived as particularly efficacious in its distilled form, or rose absolute, and Partridge included it in cooking, cleaning and aromatic recipes. The near-coincidental arrival of distillation and damask roses earlier in the sixteenth century was an essential requisite of the late Tudor domestic manual.[68] In keeping with the contemporary inclination to identify universal cure-alls, Partridge included a recipe for "Dr. Stevens Water," a staple in both print and manuscript recipe collections through the mid-eighteenth century. According to Partridge, this "sovereign" water or cordial was used by the "cunning" yet secretive Dr. Stevens in his practice for many years, effecting very many cures: only at the end of his life was he persuaded by a "special" friend to write it down. The receipt contains ample herbs and spices, both imported and domestic, steeped in "Gascon" wine and then distilled: this was not a simple concoction intended for the poorer sort. Its purported cures were also extensive: melancholy, aging, palsy and dropsy, infertility, gout, toothaches and stomach aches, gallstones, and even bad breath.

Partridge also included a "brief treatise of urines" at the end of his *Treasurie*, the first uroscopy text to be directed towards women, albeit quite brief indeed and without the usual partially filled flasks (*matulas*) characteristic of the genre. The *widowes treasure* is more of a medical text, with the majority of its recipes for a full range of illnesses, from the plague to pimples. Again, Partridge credited women in his preface, or at least one woman: the source of his recipes was lent to him by "a special friend," and he was once again urged to publish them "at the earnest request and suit of a Gentlewoman in the Country for her private use, which by these singular practices has obtained such fame, that her name shall be remembered forever to posterity."[69] Based on the nature of the recipes included in *The widowes treasure*, this famous country gentlewoman had slightly different responsibilities than the *Treasurie*'s housewife: not only was her medical arsenal much larger, more diverse (including, oddly enough for a "widow," a recipe for "the swelling of the Yard or Cods") and inclusive of treatments for both humans and animals, she had fewer culinary interests and obligations and more responsibility for the household provisioning of the standard cordials, dyes, and inks. Apart from the cure-all cordials, many of the recipes in *The widowes treasure* are easily assembled compounds of domestic ingredients: sugar was an indispensable agent of preserves, and pepper and other Asian spices do make their appearance, but the more exotic guaiacum is reserved for only one treatment for strangury, and American "brasill" wood for a red dye recipe. Quicksilver was recommended only as a topical treatment for lice, utilizing a "girdle": domestic alchemy was clearly a much simpler practice than that practiced by the London Paracelsians.

As Wendy Wall and others have shown, Partridge's popular pamphlets opened the door for a succession of printed domestic manuals prior to the English Revolution, which made England "the most active site of cookery publication in Europe and the only country marketing recipe books for women."[70] This is notable as England was situated squarely in the "periphery" of European publishing in the sixteenth century, and consequently English culinary texts represent a unique leadership category.[71] Between the first appearance of *The treasurie of commodious receipts* and that of John Murrell's *New booke of cookerie* in 1617, more than thirty editions of English recipe books were published, encompassing multiple editions of anonymous *bokes* of cookery, Thomas Dawson's "Jewel," "Treasury," and "Handmaid" for *The good husvvifes ievvell*, and Hugh Plat's *Delights for ladies*.[72] There is an obvious courtesy dimension to these culinary texts, as they all featured the essential preliminaries laid out in the foundational *A proper newe booke of cokerye* (1545): *seasons, service, and sauces*. One must know what foods were in season, what order to serve dishes on both "flesh and fish days," and the sauces that should accompany the meats laid on the table. The more fanciful recipes of the *Propre new booke* were featured in the later cookbooks as well, including "A dishful of snow," made of cream, eight egg whites, sugar, and the ever-present rosewater cast upon a rosemary bush. Simple recipes appeared in the later Elizabethan cookbooks, but there was a clear interest in expensive ingredients and the appearance of what were obviously banquet dishes. The anonymously gathered *New book of cookery* (no Proper) built on its predecessor with more recipes for both savory and sweet dishes dense with flavor from imported citrus fruits, spices and sugar and made the case for baking pudding in *anything*: carrots, "cowcumbers," and the belly of a cony (rabbit) which was then boiled. There are many recipes for tarts, of the standard fruit variety and more unusual "vaunts" (fruit pies), Florentines, and "Farts of Portingale," little meat-stuffed pastries in the Portuguese style. Apparently, the rules of health had been well-established by the succession of regimens published over the century, as later Elizabethan cookery books do not assume the responsibility of stating the virtues or degrees of their dishes, but preservation of foodstuffs, if not health, was a major part of culinary creation.

Thomas Dawson's *The good husvvifes ievvell* (1596) offered "most excellent and rare devices for conceits in cookery" as well as medical receipts and a few key points of animal husbandry, "very necessary for all husbandmen to know": a mixed message in terms of readership and also the sources of his offerings, culled from his own practice as well as other "approved" authorities.[73] Dawson clearly intended that his *Jewel* should serve as a more comprehensive manual, following the example of John Partridge and anticipating Gervase Markham in the next century. While most of his conceits are derivative, there were some innovations, including the first reference to "humble pie" as Dawson provided an alternative spelling of *umbles* (the inwards of a deer or other beast) in his recipe for "a pie of Humbles": *Take your humbles being parboiled and chop them very small with a good quantity of mutton sweet, and half a handful of herbs, following thyme, marjoram, borage, parsley, and a little rosemary, and season the same being chopped with pepper, cloves and mace, and so close your pie and bake him.* He also included an early recipe for baked (American) turkey, trussed, de-boned, and in a pastry "coffin," as well as another American import, the sweet potato or "Potaton," which was a key ingredient in his "tart that is a courage to man or woman."[74] To expand his readership in imitation of Partridge, *The good husvvifes ievvell* was followed by a "second part" in 1597, promising, but not delivering, distillation instructions for "many wholesome and sweet waters" as well as a book of carving: preservation and soapmaking recipes were the only supplements to his culinary conceits. In the same year, Dawson issued the second edition of his *A booke of cookerie, otherwise called the good huswiues handmaid*, which liberated several gentlewomen from the preface, enhancing their authority as well as that of his book. The recipes for Mistress Duffeld's boiled capon with oranges, Mistress Horsman's clouted cream, Mistress Drake's soft, "Rowen-like" cheese and Lady Gray's manchets, were revealed for *every* lady's use along with two manners of "keeping lard" attributed to Lady Weston Browne and the esteemed Marchioness of Dorset (Figure 7).[75]

The genteel patrons and "contributors," the exclusive ingredients, and the focus on service take these texts out of their time: a time of war, famines, plague and anxiety over the succession in the waning years of Elizabeth's reign. In his most popular text, *Delightes for ladies to adorne their persons, tables, closets, and distillatories with beauties, banquets, perfumes and waters* (1600), Hugh Plat announced that that dark time was over: he had served his country with his past writings irrespective of "labor, time or charge," but now that the "Spanish fear" had been "hushed," he finds that his "pen and paper are perfum'd," and he will use his "painfully-practiced" skills at artifice for more pleasant pursuits and products. Plat's prefatory plea *let piercing bullets turn to sugar balls* was not just metaphorical: the vast majority of the recipes in his *Delightes for ladies* contain sugar: *lots* of sugar, sugar for candying and sandying, for plate, paste, and molds, for preservation of anything, a process that involved at least "as much sugar as

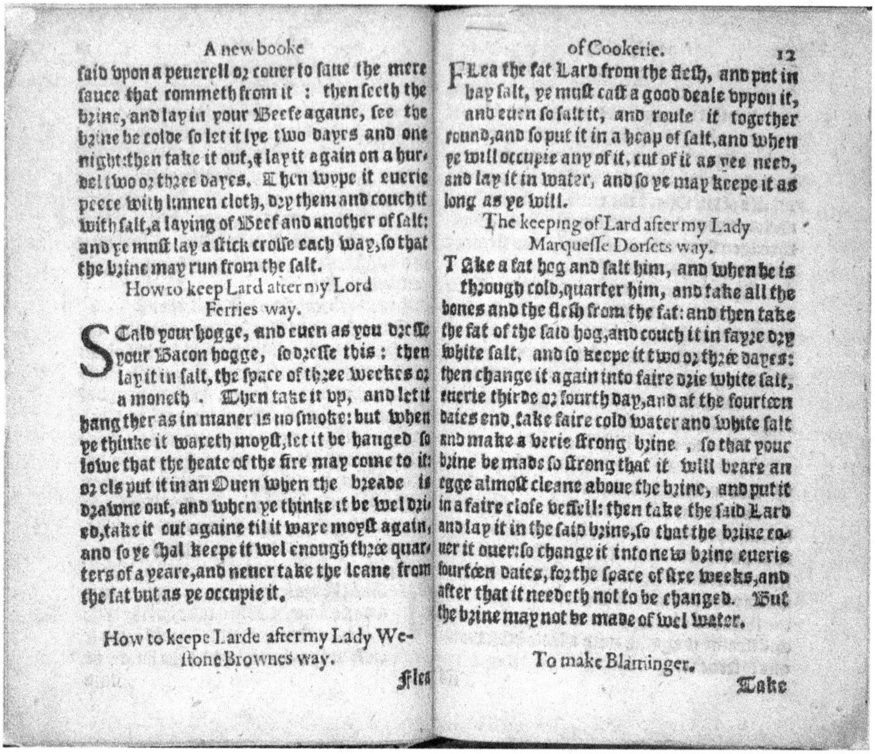

A new booke

said vpon a peuerell or couer to saue the mere sauce that commeth from it : then seeth the brine, and lay in your Beefe againe, see the brine be colde so let it lye two dayes and one night: then take it out, & lay it again on a hurdel two or three dayes. Then wype it euerie peece with linnen cloth, dry them and couch it with salt, a laying of Beef and another of salt: and ye must lay a stick crosse each way, so that the brine may run from the salt.

How to keep Lard after my Lord Ferries way.

SCald your hogge, and euen as you dresse your Bacon hogge, so dresse this : then lay it in salt, the space of three weekes or a moneth. Then take it vp, and let it hang ther as in maner is no smoke: but when ye thinke it wareth moyst, let it be hanged so lowe that the heate of the fire may come to it: or els put it in an Ouen when the breade is drawne out, and when ye thinke it be wel dried, take it out againe til it ware moyst again, and so ye shal keepe it wel enough three quarters of a yeare, and neuer take the leane from the fat but as ye occupie it.

How to keepe Larde after my Lady Westone Brownes way.

Flea

of Cookerie. 12

FLea the fat Lard from the flesh, and put in bay salt, ye must cast a good deale vppon it, and euen so salt it, and roule it together round, and so put it in a heap of salt, and when ye will occupie any of it, cut of it as yee need, and lay it in water, and so ye may keepe it as long as ye will.

The keeping of Lard after my Lady Marquesse Dorsets way.

TAke a fat hog and salt him, and when he is through cold, quarter him, and take all the bones and the flesh from the fat: and then take the fat of the said hog, and couch it in fayre dry white salt, and so keepe it two or three dayes: then change it again into faire drie white salt, euerie thirde or fourth day, and at the fourteen daies end, take faire cold water and white salt and make a verie strong brine, so that your brine be made so strong that it will beare an egge almost cleane aboue the brine, and put it in a faire close vessell: then take the said Lard and lay it in the said brine, so that the brine couer it ouer: so change it into new brine euerie fourteen daies, for the space of sixe weeks, and after that it needeth not to be changed. But the brine may not be made of wel water.

To make Blaminger.

Take

FIGURE 7 *Thomas Dawson (active 1568–1620),* A booke of cookerie, otherwise called the good huswifes handmaid *(London, 1597). © British Library / Bridgeman Images.*

the pulp does weigh." Plat's sweet tooth was impressive, but he had his limits, and improved upon a marchpane recipe given to him by yet another anonymous benefactress, a "country Gentlewoman whom I could name, which venteth great store of sugar cakes made of this composition. But the only fault which I find in this paste is, that it tastes too much of the sugar, and too little of the almonds, and therefore you may prove the making thereof with such almonds."[76] *Delightes* is a perfect expression of the characteristic Renaissance themes of intensely sugared foodstuffs and strong distilled spirits with its emphasis on "confit-making" and recipes for the classic cordials of rosa solis, aqua rubea, and usquebaugh, or "Irish aqua vitae." Plat repeated only a few of his recipes from the dearth time, including his sugar-free parsnip cakes, instructions for "how beef might be carried at sea," and "sweet and delicate dentifrices or rubbers for the teeth" made of gum dragacanth and alabaster powder, and focused more on the little things that might improve daily life on an individual basis rather than grand artificial alterations for the public good: "dainty" butters and cheeses, salad oil, candles, stain-removers, damask powders, toothpaste, hair dyes (for both ladies' hair and men's beards), sachets and pomanders.

The range of innovations, inventions, and alterations evident in Plat's body of work is representative of both the demands and instincts of his age: new approaches to persistent problems like plague and dearth, a focus on both public improvements and personal comforts, provisioning for those at sea and those at home. He discerned different audiences: privy councilors, gentlemen, ladies. There were challenges, but also opportunities: for a general and individual improvement, for commercial gain. This was an age that generated both needs and wants. Gathering and compiling from "approved" authorities, whether they were classical or continental, was no longer sufficient: approval came from experience and applicability and was more of a reciprocal process than a century before: Plat admonished his readers to *Reade, Practise and Censure* on his title page, engaging them in an evolving dialogue of knowledge production.

4

Maritime Matters

Most authors of instructive literature contended that their efforts were oriented towards a collective audience and the public good, but Elizabethan texts about navigation were more explicit in their assertions of national interest and national expediency: several even adopted the guise of a competitive call to arms. In his first book, the great imperial advocate Richard Hakluyt began with a preface to Sir Philip Sidney that expressed this concern/call well:

> I Marvel not a little (right worshipful) that since the first discovery of America (which is now full fourscore and ten years) after so great conquests and plantings of the Spaniards and Portingales there, that we of England could never have the grace to set fast footing in such fertile and temperate places, as are left as yet unpossessed of them. But again when I consider that there is a time for all men, and see the Portingales time to be out of date, & that the nakedness of the Spaniards, and their long hidden secrets are now at length espied, whereby they went about to delude the world, I conceive great hope, that the time approaches and now is, that we of England may share and part stakes (if we will ourselves) both with the Spaniard and the Portingale in part of America, and other regions as yet undiscovered.[1]

This was 1582: Hakluyt perceived that the Iberians were losing their global dominance, but several developments were necessary if England was going to claim her rightful share of the New World, principally an "increase of knowledge in the art of navigation & breeding of skillfulness in the seamen" following the example of Spain's *Casa de Contratación*. The Spanish imperial infrastructure did not provide a template for England's westward expansion in the Elizabethan era or later, but Spanish navigational texts did aid navigational knowledge, both in terms of inspiration and adaptation, beginning with Richard Eden's translation of Martin Cortés's *Breve compendio de la sphera y de la art de navegar con nuevos instrumentos y reglas exemplificado con muy subtiles demonstraciones* in 1561. Eden's *Arte of nauigation* was reprinted in ten editions up to 1630, commencing a succession of increasingly comprehensive navigation publications over the Elizabethan and Jacobean eras.[2]

The value of experience and the ability to verify characterized both agricultural and navigational practice in the early modern era, but the latter experienced a structural transformation over the later sixteenth century through the expansion and application of geographical, mathematical and instrumental knowledge. Prior to Elizabeth's reign, navigational knowledge was essentially empirical and local: the only written (and consequently printed) texts were guides to coastal navigation called *rutters*, an English variation on the French *routier*. These were pilot manuals, containing the essential information necessary for maritime travel in a particular region: England's first printed rutters were translations of French pilot Pierre Garcie's fifteenth-century *Grand routier* and *Le Routier de la mer*, focused on the English Channel and Bay of Biscay, first printed in 1528 and expanded to include the North Sea in 1557.[3] These rutters focused necessarily on precise tidal information, depths, distances, directions, physical features of both land and sea, and customs of maritime commerce, but included more universal "rough and ready rules" for estimating the phases of the moon, telling time by the "star clock" and traversing. The well-equipped pre-Elizabethan mariner, armed with a magnetic compass, a sand-glass, a traverse table, and a rutter, could navigate his region with confidence, but the vast ocean sea was not only beyond his experience, but also his abilities and resources. If England was going to widen its horizons and assert sovereignty over some share of the expansive new world, a navigational revolution would have to occur.

Two books published near the end of Elizabeth's reign represent this revolution well, even though they were very different texts aimed at very different audiences: John Davis's *The seamans secrets* (1595) and Thomas Blundeville's *Exercises* (1594).[4] One of the most experienced and prominent shipmasters of his era, Davis was very precise in his list of what was "needfully required in a sufficient seaman": "a Sea Compass, a Cross staff, a Quadrant, an Astrolabe, a Chart, an instrument magnetical for the finding of the variation of the Compass, an Horizontal plain Sphere, a Globe, and a paradoxal Compass" as well as the knowledge to use these instruments (Figure 8). That knowledge was practical but also essentially and fundamentally mathematical, as illustrated by Davis in straightforward text *and* ready tables, an acknowledgement that his target audience of seaman might not be "acquainted with such calculations." Even more so than vernacular medical manuals, navigational texts were tasked with the charge of providing *regiments* for their readers given the complexity and urgency of their missions. Davis provided his seamen with ephemerides applicable from 1593 to 1612 based on Johannes Stadius's Copernican tables, a sea chart annotated with text in dialogue to demonstrate its use, and a sample log book, and while he omitted the more challenging calculations he also asserted the absolute precision of "navigation arithmetical."

FIGURE 8 *John Davis (d. 1621), The Seamens Secrets (London, 1626), sig. C4v. Used by permission of the Folger Shakespeare Library under a Creative Commons Attribution-ShareAlike 4.0 International License.*

Unlike Davis, Thomas Blundeville was not an experienced and famous navigator, but rather an educator and "explainer," and author of popular texts on horsemanship, history, and logic. The first edition of his *Exercises* was a compilation of six different treatises, on arithmetic, cosmography, terrestrial and celestial globes, the "universal map" of Petrus Pancius, the "mathematical jewel" (an astrolabe) of John Blagrave, and navigation, which he has compiled for "all the young gentlemen" who have not been "exercised in such kind of studies." Blundeville's book is big, meant for a library rather than a ship's deck or cabin, and much more derivative than original, but it confirmed the mathematical basis of the new navigation for a more general audience, including not only all the basic arithmetical processes but also a trigonometry table. As the title of his individual treatises implies, Blundeville's book was intended to be both a comprehensive and *current* reference to all of the disciplines associated with navigation, and he instructed his young gentlemen to read its contents in order. Though more descriptive than analytical, he also encouraged his readers to engage in exercises, and like any good instructor he was prepared to offer supplemental help: one assignment, or proposition, "that you might exercise yourself in finding out by the Globe, the place, Longitude, Latitude, and declination of any star that is described in the Globe," was aided by his inclusion of

> the Table of Garceus, showing not only the Longitude, Latitude and declination of the most notable stars that are both Northward and Southward, but also the right ascension, magnitude or bigness, the quality or nature of every such star, and also the Arch of the Ecliptic line, which accompanies the right ascension of every star, which Table though by the said Garceus was calculated out of the Astronomical Tables for the year of our Lord 1564.[5]

as well as "such Longitude, Latitude, declination, magnitude, and right ascension, and all other things contained in the said Table, according as they are to be found out by the Celestial Globe of Mercator, and not calculated by any of the Astronomical Tables."[6] In keeping with the rule and practice of the evolving navigational manual, Blundeville included so many aids, in the form of illustrations and tables, that his cumulative treatise anticipated the "ready" references of the seventeenth century, which reduced the necessity of their readers to engage in "busy and tedious" calculations even further. But he was not quite there yet: he was a teacher, with an awareness that there was a generation of young men out there, inspired by the glorious exploits of Davis and Frobisher and Drake, eager to learn.

The last treatise of Blundeville's *Excercises*, on the art of navigation, is the culmination of all that came before. Navigation was defined simply as the art of directing a ship from one port to another in the "shortest and most commodious way possible" through a combination of method and practice. Blundeville distinguished between pilotage, "small", local, or "common" navigation, and that of the "grander" variety: the former was governed by experience and so not in his purview. With their emphasis on currency and expertise, early modern navigational texts characteristically referenced myriad contemporaries, giving the impression that there was a circle of theorists, educators, and practitioners working together to expand knowledge of the world as well as the ways to get to its most "profitable" places. Blundeville acknowledged that coastal topography has been covered by William Bourne and Leonard Digges, so he need "not speak any further thereof" but that left quite a lot of ground—or sea—to traverse, especially as he incorporated instruction from his earlier treatises, primarily arithmetic but also cosmography and geography, to illustrate computations of the calendar and instrumental and celestial navigation in a grand synthetic conclusion. The end result, in the words of Eric Ash, was the essential (and first) linkage between practical arithmetic and navigation "through a logical, even inexorable progression."[7] The wandering miscellany, still popular in late Elizabethan England, had no currency in the realm of navigation.

The mathematization of navigation over the Elizabethan era was the result of a succession of forces: first and foremost was the general maritime trend of the sixteenth century, when the average length of voyages among European ocean-going kingdoms tripled, radically altering and expanding the requisite skills for seamen in the process.[8] As Hakluyt's preface asserted, this trend was somewhat delayed in England by Continental standards, but it started to emerge coincidentally with the decline of the woolen trade at mid-century. This trade with the Low Countries and northern France was exemplified by the rutters of the era, but they would not be sufficient to steer English seamen out into the open sea. The establishment of the Merchant Adventurers to New Lands in 1551, later chartered as the Muscovy Company and England's first joint-stock company, was a focused attempt to find new lands and new markets in the East, but there was interest, and envy, about Spanish possessions in the West as well. Eric Ash credits two "expert mediators" associated with the Muscovy Company—and very familiar with the operations of the Spanish Casa de Contratación—Sebastian Cabot and Stephen Borough, with inspiring the expansion and reform of the English naval and maritime initiatives in the early Elizabethan era, in collaboration with Robert Recorde and John Dee.[9]

It was Borough who commissioned Richard Eden, a notable alchemist/translator who seems to have been able to navigate the turbulent religious waters of the 1550s with some success, to translate Martín Cortés de Albacar's *Arte de navigar* as *The arte of nauigation* in 1561, based on his earlier translations of Sebastian Muenster's *Cosmographia* as *A treatyse of the newe India* (1553) and Peter Martyr d'Anghiera's *De Orba Nova* as *The decades of the newe worlde or west India* (1555). The preface of *Decades* reveals a strong sense of English envy, several decades before Hakluyt, as Eden remarked upon Spain's "great plenty of fine wools little inferior unto ours (indeed, the preference for Spanish merino wool was one of the causes of the English woolen trade's decline)," and an abundance of sugar, vines, pomegranates, lemons and oranges, "whereas the apples and crabs of England are scarcely able to serve itself." Eden declared further that "England is in few years decayed and impoverished," while Spain has been "enriched" by both its own "flourishing" as well as the great riches that were "yearly brought thither from the Indies," including copious cargoes of silver and gold. At the beginning of Elizabeth's reign, the motives for expanding England's overseas voyages seem clear; the means less so, but an experienced *and* educated like seaman like Stephen Borough was in the best possession to chart the way forward: he had done so for the Muscovy Company, quite literally, he had first-hand knowledge of the Casa de Contratación, and he became the most prominent—and *public*—pilot in England in the 1560s through his masterships of the Muscovy Company, the royal navy, and Trinity House, incorporated by Henry VIII in 1514 to oversee pilotage on the River Thames and Port of London. Yet navigation was a collaborative enterprise, endeavor, and cause: an expanding circle of courtiers, merchants, and experts were advocating for maritime ventures in the early Elizabethan era and John Dee was certainly at its center in terms of mathematical consultation and instruction from about 1566 to 1583. While Dee's imperial visions (and angelic conversations) are manifest, his mathematical mentorship is a bit more under the radar; nevertheless, his consultancy with the Muscovy Company and membership in the Mercer's Company placed him in a position of mathematical mentorship to aspiring overseas adventurers, both through print and personal audiences at his house in Mortlake, with its well-stocked library and laboratory.

John Dee's conception of navigation and all of its constituent disciplines, expressed succinctly in his masterful "Mathematical Praeface" to Henry Billinglsey's 1570 translation of Euclid's *Elements of geometrie*, was definitive in and for its time, and repeated in a succession of navigational manuals: Davis's and Blundeville's definitions are clearly dependent upon it:

> The Art of Nauigation, demonstrates how, by the shortest good way, by the aptest Direction & in the shortest time, a sufficient Ship, between any two places (in passage Navigable) assigned: may be conducted: and in all storms, & natural disturbances chancing, how, to use the best possible meane, whereby to recover the place first assigned. What need, the Master Pilot, has of other Arts, here before recited, it is easy to know: as, of Hydrography, Astronomy, Astrology, and Horometry. Presupposing continually, the common Base, and foundation of all: namely Arithmetic and Geometry. So that, he is able to understand, and judge his own necessary Instruments, and furniture Necessary: Whether they be perfectly made or not: and also can, (if need be) make them, himself. As Quadrants, The Astronomers Ring, The Astronomers staff, The Astrolabe universal. An Hydrographical Globe. Charts Hydrographical, true, (not with parallel Meridians). The Common Sea Compass: The Compass of

variation: The Proportional, and Paradoxal Compasses (invented by me for our two Moscovy Master Pilots [in 1559], at the request of the Company) Clocks with spring: hour, half hour, and three hour Sandglasses: & sundry other Instruments: And also, be able, on Globe, or Plane to describe the Paradoxal Compass: and duly to use the same, to all manner of purposes, whereto it was invented. And also, be able to Calculate the Planets places for all times.[10]

All the key aspects of the Elizabethan navigational revolution or "awakening" are here: the foundational mathematics, the new instruments *and* the knowledge to use them, and even make them. At this time, Dee's authority was based on both his expertise and his experience, both of which were shaped by his time abroad, just like that of Sebastian Cabot and Stephen Borough. For him, the University of Leuven was the equivalent of their Casa de Contratación: there he studied with the leading mathematical cosmographers and instrument makers of the day, Gemma Frisius, Gerard Mercator and Gaspar à Mirica, and he widened his circle to include cartographers Abraham Ortelius, Oronce Finé and Pedro Nunes, among others, over the next decades. Dee's continental education also enabled him to acquire instruments and texts unavailable in England, which he brought back to the river-front Mortlake house he inherited from his mother, thus establishing his role as both a conduit and a resource for the expansion of mathematical knowledge and navigational practice during Stephen Borough's contemporaneous reign as England's preeminent pilot. Dee's authority and ambitions were confirmed in the *General and rare memorials pertayning to the perfect arte of nauigation* (1577), in which he advocated for an expanded English presence on the seas to protect the interests of the "British Empire," a new and conspicuous use of that phrase. The kingdom needed a "Pety Navy Royal" of "three score Tall ships, (or more:) but in no case, fewer, and they to be very well appointed, thoroughly manned, and sufficiently victualled" in order to protect its national security in general and mercantile and fishing interests in particular. Dee presented several economic arguments for the new navy, which would not only defend England's current interests but also support future claims for treasure and trade routes and provide employment and maintenance for the "hundreds of lusty and handsome Men" who "are either Idle, or, want sustenance: or, both: In too many places, of this renown Monarchy." There is the sense of urgency characteristic in all texts advocating for an expanded maritime commitment and presence, as this was not an age of free trade but rather one in which sovereignty and jurisdiction must be proclaimed and defended: England must assert its "sea-rights" in order to attain "sea-security," and a force of "sea-soldiers" will emerge in the process. The *Memorials* was the first chapter of a larger and more technical navigational text that Dee had planned, so he never gets to the "paradoxal compass" of its title: the audience for this brief comprised the Elizabethan courtiers and councilors, not merchants and mariners.[11]

The more centralized visions of Dee and Borough did not become reality, but private ventures projected maritime progress in the later 1570s, beginning with the chronicle of Martin Frobisher's three Northwest Passage expeditions in 1578. George Best, who accompanied Frobisher on the second and third voyages, made the argument the English mariners were superior to their Iberian counterparts as they were sailing in colder waters, and dealing with intemperate challenges, principally ice. In his dedication to Sir Christopher Hatton, Best asserted that England had been "reformed" in matters maritime:

> there have been two special causes in the former age, that have greatly hindered the English nation in their attempts. The one has been, lack of liberality in the Nobility, & the other want of skill in Cosmography, and the Art of Navigation. Which kind of knowledge, is very necessary for all our noble men, for that we are Islanders, our chief strength consists by Sea. But these two causes are now in this present age (God be thanked) very well reformed: for not only her majesty now, but all the nobility also, having perfect knowledge in Cosmography, do not only with good words, countenance the forward minds of men, but also with their purses do liberally and bountifully contribute unto the same, whereby it comes to pass, that Navigation, which in the time of King Henry the 7th was very raw & "toke" (as it were) but beginning (and ever since has had by little and little continual increase) is now in her Majesty's reign, grown to his highest perfection.[12]

The association of the English geographical identity as "islanders" with their natural proclivity for navigation became almost commonplace in texts such as Best's, as did the assertion of "the great industry of our age," but the claims that both the Queen herself, and the English nobility, have "perfect" knowledge in cosmography and that navigation has achieved its "highest perfection" in 1578 were contradicted by contemporary maritime manuals, which asserted that Englishmen still had a lot to learn about the sea around them.

William Bourne's popular *Regiment for the sea*, first published in 1574, aimed to be a more basic text, "base and simple" in his words, and "needful and necessary for all sorts of seamen," not just ambitious explorers from the ranks of the nobility. Utilizing an incongruous metaphor, Bourne allowed that while "a great number of excellent learned men in the Mathematical Science have written diverse books of Cosmography and Navigation," notwithstanding he has written "this Regiment for the Sea with a few rules of Navigation, as it were a nosegay whose flowers are of mine own gathering."[13] Bourne had other goals too: principally to integrate the old empirical tradition of seafaring with the new navigation, and supplement Cortés's authoritative *Art de navegar* with "other necessary things meet to be known in navigation." Integration is a theme running throughout the text: the familiar calendar time of saints' days, terms and seasons serves as a natural introduction to celestial navigation, and Bourne's shipmaster was expected to be able to read (and *correct*) sea charts, maps, and instruments as well as the seascape and landscape as a "good coaster." If he did not possess the ability to calculate the Sun's declination or some other important indicator, he should have at his disposal a "true regiment" or table, such as Bourne was providing. Again, *regiment*, an important concept and word in all instructional literature of the era, has a double meaning in navigational texts, which provided not only the rules of conduct but reference tools for their readers. Bourne equipped his seamen with a series of illustrations and tables, including the compass and its 32 points, a table of the Prime and Epact for 19 years, a "regiment of the sun," indicating its declination for four years, the cross staff or "Bella Stella," various spherical measurements, the North Star, distances of league and degree, a table for the declination of fixed stars, and an equinoctial dial. Following the Frobisher voyages, a "hydrographical discourse" about the various passages to Cathay was added by Bourne in the second edition of the *Regiment*, and after his death, England's famed and first mathematical lecturer Thomas Hood contributed to a corrected edition, supplemented with the "Mariner's Guide" to the use of the sea chart.[14]

In both their tendency to present compartmentalized reference materials and their mandate to present updated and corrected information on a continual basis, navigational texts previewed and encouraged the development of more portable *vade mecums* of the next century, the ultimate epitomes. The focus on identifying errors—a general Renaissance preoccupation first centered on updating classical knowledge and then extended to contemporary debate—ultimately led to English discoveries which equaled or surpassed those of Iberian and Dutch navigators. The most groundbreaking example of this trend was Edward Wright's *Certaine errors in nauigation, arising either of the ordinarie erroneous making or vsing of the sea chart, compasse, crosse staffe, and tables of declination of the sunne, and fixed starres detected and corrected* (1599), which facilitated the nautical application of the Mercator map projection and presented revised tables of compass variations and declinations of the sun and fixed stars, all derived from the combination of Wright's personal and practical experiences (principally as part of the Earl of Cumberland's 1589 royal-sanctioned expedition to the Azores, which were not quite where they were supposed to be according to the sea charts then in use) and mathematical skill.[15] In the preface to *Certaine errors*, Wright asserted that seamen such as himself were equipped with charts that contained a veritable and "inextricable labyrinth of error" in places, utilizing language reserved for the religious discourse of the Reformation earlier in the century. The increasing secular use of "errors" over the Elizabethan era is particularly apparent in instructional texts in all disciplines: in William Turner's *A new herball* and *A new boke of the natures and properties of all wines*, André Thevet's *New found vvorlde, or Antarctike*, "now newly translated into English, wherein is reformed the errors of the ancient Cosmographers," various medical treatises by surgeons identifying the errors of physicians and the latter exposing the "manifold errors" of apothecaries, Edward Worsop's indictment of unschooled surveyors in the *A discouerie of sundrie errours and faults daily committed by lande-meaters, ignorant of arithmetike and geometrie*, and Richard More's *The carpenters rule*, all expressing errors of perception and practice rather than errors of opinion.

Instruments and Invention

Elizabethan navigational culture was characterized necessarily by processes of verification and correction, as well as continuous innovation. There would be no grand navigation without instruments, and every prescriptive text asserted that mastery of the sea involved not only their use but the ability to produce, or reproduce, them. Richard Polter, master mariner as well as the Master of Trinity House, asserted that masters had to have "artificial" capabilities, and if such "courses be too deep for his understanding.... he is not worthy to take charge at all" in *The pathway to perfect sayling*.[16] The foundational *Art de navegar* included instructions on how to make a mariner's astrolabe, and both John Davis and Thomas Hood devised their own instruments, the latter marketing them quite aggressively following his appointment as "Mathematical Lecturer" to the City of London. Perhaps the most inventive men were enclosed within the widening circle of Elizabethan nautical experts, but not seamen themselves: William Bourne and John Blagrave. Bourne followed up his *Regiment* with three books in 1578: *A booke called the treasure for traueilers*; *The Arte of shooting in great Ordnaunce*; and *Inuentions or deuises Very necessary for all generalles and captaines, or leaders of men, as wel be sea as by land*.[17] He fulfilled several roles over his varied career, including innkeeper, mathematician, and gunner, and the skills of the latter occupations are most evident in these works, which are characterized by considerable overlap and cross-referencing. As was the case with his equally-inventive contemporary, Hugh Plat, Bourne offered his readers more tactics and techniques than innovative *entities*, but *Inuentions or deuises* does feature some notable examples of the latter, including a "sunken ship" or submarine (Device 22), a diving suit made of leather with eyeglasses (Device 23), a night signal system (Device 75), and an early telescope likely based on Bourne's familiarity with that of Leonard Digges (Device 110). Bourne's purpose was to instruct and demonstrate that the arts were "good and lawful," emphasizing that "the making of any strange works that the world has marveled at, as the brazen head that did seem to speak: and the Serpent of brass for to hiss: or a Dove of wood for to fly: or an Eagle made by art of wood and other metals to fly: and birds made of brass, tin or other metal to sing sweetly" were not "done by enchantment, which is no such thing" but rather by the skillful fashioning and alignment of wheels and springs.[18]

It is clear that sea charts were perceived to be as much of a nautical instrument as astrolabes or quadrants in sixteenth-century England, and if paper could be instrumental then a book could be just as essential and inventive as a map. This was certainly the intended function of John Blagrave's *The mathematical ievvel*, the title of an instructive book about an invention of the same name, an astrolabe of the author's own design. Blagrave made the ambitious claim on his title page that one reinforced the other: while the instrument "performs with wonderful dexterity, whatsoever is to be done, either by quadrant, ship, circle, cylinder, ring, dial, horoscope, astrolabe, sphere, globe, or any such like heretofore devised: yea or by most tables commonly extant: and that generally to all places from Pole to Pole," its use (which is laid out in the book) will "lead any man practicing thereon, the direct pathway (from the first step to the last) through the whole arts of astronomy, cosmography, geography, topography, navigation, longitudes of regions, dialing, spherical triangles, setting figures, and briefly of whatsoever concerns the globe or sphere."[19] Blagrave was a university-educated mathematician and professional instrument-maker, much more of a specialist and an expert than Bourne, who assumed the role of a translator of technical information and seldom ceased reminding his readers of the simplicity and "rudeness" of his understanding. *The mathematical ievvel* was the first, and the most ambitious, of a series of texts on Blagrave's inventions, all representative of the emerging genre of *usus et fabra*, "how to use" devices. Such texts were craft examples of a more universal inclination to expose secretive knowledge, for the greater good, also very much apparent in medical and distillation texts. In his preface addressed to William Cecil, he presented his work as

> a Jewel, not wrought of Minerals, or set with stately stones, or brought home from beyond the seas by sundry our countrymen, in their venturous and worthy voyages lately performed. But a Mathematical Jewel, of no small virtue and efficacy, to furnish the willing wits of this our age for the like enterprises. Containing in sum, A reduction of the Arts Mathematic tending thereunto, and to diverse other good uses, from that deep difficulty, wherewith hitherto they have been sequestered and closed up as it were in several, only to the most learned: into an easy, methodical, plain, and practical discipline, lying wide open unto every ingenious practicer, whence I presume, many singular inventions, and notable commodities in time shall ensue and spring, yea a number yet unthought of, even from the common sort of handicrafts men and travaillers.[20]

His "reduction" takes the form of six books, encompassing the rudiments of geometry, astronomy, and cosmography, a treatise on the Jewel's construction and operation, a more comprehensive treatise on the Jewel's capacity, in reference to the works of other mathematicians, and books on astronomical propositions and the "knowledge of the sphere." Like Blundeville's *Exercises*, the *Mathematical jewel* (the text) was a progression, a pathway to use Blagrave's term, towards knowledge of both the instrument and the disciplines that it served.

Blagrave's aim to "furnish the willing wits of this our age" with the knowledge and the tools to devise "singular inventions" was facilitated by his active learning approach: he instructed his readers to abridge his text themselves, engage with his copious diagrams with their pencils and dividers, construct their own Mathematical Jewels with the templates he provided, and *perform* observations and calculations on *their* Jewels. He utilizes the verbs stamp, strike, pierce (but don't "chisel"). At least a couple of readers, including the famed annotator Gabriel Harvey, well-known for his engagement with texts, followed Blagrave's instructions and produced their own paper Jewels, but apparently the instrument, if not the book, proved to be a bit too complicated for nautical use and the average seaman.[21] Undeterred, Blagrave followed up with manuals on another universal instrument, the "familiar staff," which he advertised as "so general that it readily performs all the several uses of the Cross staff, the Quadrate, the Circle, the Quadrant, the Gunners Quadrant, the Trigon, every one in his own kind, and with no less method and facility, both for Sea and Land," another astrolabe, which could provide "necessary and pleasant solace and recreation for navigators in their long journeying," and a two-part guide to the construction and use of various types of sundials.[22] His approach remained very visual and interactive: with an abundance of workable diagrams to engage his readers in both the creation and utility of his instruments. Blagrave's focus on the mechanical could not ignore the structural changes occurring in cosmographical circles altogether: his *Jewel* described a geocentric elemental world, "after the opinion of old writers" but noted that "Copernicus hath ascribed another order" while his uranical astrolabe of a decade later was built to reveal the dimensions of a Copernican system, with a moving earth or fixed horizon.

The relationship between instrument crafting and invention is illustrated particularly well by Robert Norman's groundbreaking work on magnetic inclination, *The newe attractiue Containyng a short discourse of the magnes or lodestone*, first published in 1581.[23] *The newe attractiue* contains succinct expressions of an emerging scientific method and also reflects the importance of collaboration between craftsmen and seamen in this era. Norman was generally self-styled as an "hydrographer" and instrument-maker, but he served at sea for decades and then began making compasses, which he advertised for sale at his house in Ratcliff, the "sailor town" along the Thames. He clearly had a respectful working relationship with one of his clients, William Borough, younger brother of Steven, and an experienced mariner, mathematician, and Comptroller of the Royal Navy, as Norman dedicated his text to him and the influential Borough endorsed the work by annexing his own *A Discovrs of the Variation of the Cumpas* to create one volume, representing a wealth of empirical and mathematical knowledge. As a teen, William had accompanied Stephen on his 1556 northern voyage for the Muscovy Company, during which the first observation of the magnetic variation of the compass was logged.[24] And now, many years later, the two men were taking on one of the trickiest challenges in northern navigation, in print. Though Borough expressed his desire to appeal to both average seamen and the "learned sort," his mathematical discourse definitely trended towards the latter, but the treatise of the "expert Artificer" (Borough's description of Norman) and "unlearned Mechanician" (Norman's description of himself) is grounded in a much more accessible narrative of the discovery, by observation, trial, and experiment, of magnetic dip, "this strange and new property of Declining of the Needle," the downward incline of a magnetized compass needle below the horizontal plane. In his introduction, Norman informed his readers that his arguments would be based only on experience, reason and demonstration, which are the "grounds of arts," a phrase generally reserved for mathematics. While he exhibited a certain respect for both the ancient authors and the mathematicians of his own time, Norman maintained that the authority of both does not prohibit "mechanicians and mariners" from taking part in an ongoing discourse on all matters maritime.

Robert Norman's expertise relative to magnetic variation was derived from his experience and *practice* as a compass-maker. His observations and explanations of both magnetic "declining" and variation referenced instruments and their creation and operation, his own path through experimentation and towards understanding. A working craftsman rather than a gentleman of leisure, he admits to making *many* compasses during which he noticed that the northward-pointing needle would always dip down after it was magnetized, provoking him to add a "counterposing" piece of "ware" on the southern tip, and not giving the phenomenon a second thought. Then one day, in the midst of another compass commission that required a compensatory action, he snapped and spoiled the needle, fell into a rage (a choler), and decided to try to figure out what was going on: after consulting some "learned" friends, he began to engage in experiments to determine the cause of the dip, and isolated its source to the magnetized needle itself rather than some external force. It would take William Gilbert, the Queen's physician, to expand upon terrestrial magnetism considerably in *De magnete, magneticisque corporibus, et de magno magnete tellure* twenty years later, building on the pioneering work of Norman, whom he referred to as a "skilled navigator and ingenious artificer," albeit in Latin. When Gilbert trod into the realm of practical navigation in *De magnete*, he followed Norman very closely, as for example his discussion of the diversity of common mariner's compasses according to region and the corresponding variety of sea charts: "from those differences most serious errors have arisen in navigation, and in marine science ... For one who should use the British compass and should follow the directions of the marine charts of the Mediterranean Sea would necessarily wander very much out of the straight course."[25] Such assertive statements from one who had no experience in navigation must have been based on an esteemed source, and that source was Robert Norman, compass-maker.

Despite its antiquity, the compass remained a central focus of navigational texts in the later Elizabethan era, exceeding more novel instruments in terms of technical and utilitarian analysis. This was largely due to the ongoing discussion over its variation, but William Barlow, a friend of Gilbert's and author of *The nauigators supply*, asserted that even the "ordinary sailing compass" could and should be improved, along with the compass of variation. He did both, and also offered up directions and textual demonstrations for more examples of "sail-ware," including a compact equinoctial sundial called the "traveller's jewel," a "pantometer" for measuring angles, a portable globe called the "hemisphere," and a plotting board with protractor called the "traveller's board."[26] Barlow's instrumental improvements were in keeping with the computational discourse of his era, but he was more innovative in his marketing approach, with eight plates illustrating each of the instruments by the London engraver and instrument-maker Charles Whitwell, giving his text a catalogue appeal. On the title page, adjacent to his improved sailing compass, is an advertisement: *If any man desire more ample instructions concerning the use of these instruments, hee may repayre unto John Goodwin dwellinge in Bucklebury teacher of the grounds of these artes. The instruments are made by Charles Whitwell, over agaynste Essex howse, maker of all sortes of mathematicall instruments, and the graver of these portraytures.* Barlow gave Goodwin another plug in his concluding "Friendly Advertisement to the Navigators of England" as one who, though "unskillful in the Latin tongue" was nevertheless knowledgeable in arithmetic, surveying, and the use of "sundry other instruments" having obtained "partly by his own industry, and by reading of English Writers (whereof there are many very good) and partly with conference with learned men (of which he is passing desirous), such ready knowledge and dexterity of teaching and practicing the grounds of those Arts, as (giving him but his due) I haue not beene acquainted with his like." England needed more of such men in general; *London*, "standing upon merchandise and marine trades," needed more of such men in particular.

After the Armada

It is traditional to divide Elizabeth's reign by the English victory over the "invincible" Spanish Armada in 1588, but as this triumph was a testament to superior English ship design, gunnery, naval tactics, and general seamanship it seems like an appropriate juncture from the perspective of navigation, even more so than political, diplomatic, or social history. Yet it was only one event in an ongoing Anglo-Spanish War that would continue, and characterize, the remainder of the Elizabethan era, shaping the course of English maritime history in some ways, but not in others: the roles of individuals would continue to trump those of officials, but integrated goals of maritime defense and expansion would serve as inspiration for both. After its mid-century "awakening," English navigation was transitioning even before the Armada, with John Dee's departure for the Continent (and spiritual drift) in 1583 and Stephen Borough's death in the following year. Though the Armada looms very large in 1588, two other developments in that year arguably had a greater impact on the development and dissemination of English navigation practice: the appointment of Thomas Hood as "Mathematics Lecturer" to the City of London and the publication of England's first comprehensive sea atlas, *The mariners mirrour*, an English translation of Lucas Janszoon Waghenaer's *Spieghel der Zeevaerdt* by Sir Anthony Ashley. For quite some time thereafter, "waggoners" would be an essential shipboard "instrument."

Thomas Hood was yet another mathematically-inclined physician, with connections at court and among London's mercantile community, both of which were increasingly convinced that England's naval commanders, merchants and shipmasters needed a stronger foundation in mathematics and its applications. Hood petitioned the Privy Council for a subsidized lectureship in 1588 and received approval for a two-year appointment in "the reading of the Mathematical Science and other necessary matters for warlike service both by sea and land" provided that the City of London paid for it.[27] Consequently, Hood became England's first *official* mathematical lecturer, a decade before the establishment of Gresham College would expand mathematical instruction to a wider audience on a more permanent basis. It is impossible to glean how much practical information was discussed by Hood in the course of his lectures as the transcript of only the inaugural event exists: in it, he relays only fevered enthusiasm for the subject and excitement about his appointment, using the actual phrase *leapt for joy*. This was just the first lecture, however, so he was setting the scene and establishing the importance of his topic:

> ...if Geometry reaches so high that it can justly measure the Cope of heaven: no doubt on earth it performs most excellent things. Let Geography witness in universal Maps, let Topography witness in several Cards, let Hydrography witness in the Mariners plat, you yourselves may witness in Martial affairs, let the Gunner witness in planting his shot, witness the Surveyor in measuring land, witness all those, that labor in mines, and those that practice conveying of water, whose skill being told us, we would scarcely believe it, were it not lying at our door.[28]

Hood's texts, published before and after the conclusion of his lectureship in 1592, were primarily focused on the utility of instruments, including the celestial globe, the terrestrial globe, the cross-staff, the Jacob's staff, and the sector.[29] His use of dialogues between master and scholar was perhaps not the best way to convey practical information to seamen, but his corrections and additions (including several tables and a "mariner's guide" to the use of sea charts) to Bourne's *Regiment for the sea* continued that text's currency into the seventeenth century. In the preface to his guide, Hood informs "industrious sailors" that he has taken these pains for their sake: "I have had to do a long time with diverse of your profession both for the making of Sea Cards, and also for instructing them in mathematical matters belonging to navigation. Amongst whom I have found many willing to learn and by that means had an insight into their wants."[30]

The same approach to establishing authority—mathematical knowledge in consultation with experienced practitioners—was utilized by Anthony Ashley, the translator of Waghenaer's *Spieghel der zeevaerdt*, Europe's first sea atlas. The translation was another official commission, completed over twenty-five years after Richard Eden's pioneering *Arte of nauigation*: English navigators once looked to Spain for guidance, but now their "pilots" were Dutch. Ashley, the clerk to the Privy Council, was commissioned by Sir Christopher Hatton to undertake the project: he followed Waghenaer's text closely but consulted men with "knowledge or experience" on the details, and familiarized the text by using English place names, Old Style calendar dating, and referencing the "exploits" of Sir Francis Drake on the title page. The end result was a comprehensive navigation manual, which equipped its referencers with forty-five sea charts covering the entire western European coast, precise sailing directions for these regions, essential declination tables, instructions in the use and construction of the cross staff and astrolabe and the estimation of latitude based on stellar observations: descriptive *and* analytical tools, information *and* instructions. *The mariners mirrour* could be viewed as an amplified rutter with its focus on the physical details of the coastline, evident not only in the sea charts but also in its explicit "Exhortation to the Apprentices of the Art of Navigation" with its emphasis on learning to "mark" all landmarks with pen and on the compass upon setting forth and arrival: "Any Mariner that will diligently, and with understanding practice these precepts, shall attain the true skill and science of Navigation." The practice of careful pilotage, however, was just the beginning of the apprentice seaman's course:

> let him not neglect, nor shame to enquire of the Master of the ship, and other men exercised in this study, the situation of countries, the courses upon several points, the depths or soundings, and the elevations of the Pole: and practice with the Cross staff, and Astrolabe. The which two, are the principal instruments (next the Compass) that belong to safe and skillful seafaring.[31]

In a now-established industry, recognized as central to the country's prosperity, the requisite skills for practitioners included traditional tasks, mathematical calculation, and instrumental adeptness, and they were also expected to engage with the ongoing process through which navigational and geographical knowledge was being advanced. This first English "waggoner," a term that first applied specifically to Waghenaer's text and then more generally to any book of sea charts, became instrumental for its "workbook" nature as well: it was a book to work *with*, as Ashley explained in his preface:

> in most of the Plots, the Sea is purposely left in blank, because the Traveler, finding perchance some point of the Compass, risings of Lands, Depths, Soundings, or ought else mistaken; or some Rock, Sand, or other danger left out, or not rightly expressed (for nothing so perfect but has his fault) may as he travels set down and correct the same with his own hand, as it shall best like himself: which doubtless will be no small furtherance and contentment even to the best Doctors in this science.[32]

The collaborative nature of navigation is apparent here, not just among the "doctors" or acknowledged experts in this emerging art or science: any "traveler" (one who is traveling but also *travailing*) can be a doctor as all are contributing to both an expanding physical world as well as one of knowledge discovered and charted rather than compiled.

An Anglicized model of this expanding world was another product of the post-Armada period: even though London merchant William Sanderson commissioned the first English globes from instrument maker Emery Molyneux in 1587. The Armada portraits of 1588, with their conspicuous placement of the Queen's right hand on the globe, might have accelerated the demand for the creation of an English sphere. Richard Hakluyt announced "the coming out of a very large and most exact terrestrially Globe, collected and reformed according to the newest, secretest, and latest discoveries" in the preface to *The Principall nauigations* in the following year, and in July of 1591 Molyneux delivered a cosmographical pair of terrestrial and celestial globes to the Queen, almost a century after the appearance of the first European globe fabricated by Martin Behaim. While the celestial globe was a standard Mercator reproduction, the terrestrial globe was as "new" as Hakluyt promised, with lines and notes marking the voyages and discoveries of the prominent English navigators of the era, including Martin Frobisher, Francis Drake, Thomas Cavendish, Walter Ralegh and John Davis, and the placement of the English coat of arms on the North American continent. It was not only an instrument, but also a cartographic record, and referenced as such by contemporaries, and according to at least one source, also visual inspiration to expand and possess. The Tuscan courtier Petruccio Ubaldini, who witnessed the globes as a work in progress and revealed at Greenwich, noted that Molyneux gave Queen Elizabeth the terrestrial globe "to let her see at a glance how much of the seas she could control by means of her naval forces."[33]

Hakluyt was also correct in his characterization of the coming Molyneux globes as "very large": they were indeed the largest in Europe when completed and presented, two feet, two inches in diameter by several accounts. Presentation globes were different than "instruments" however, and Sanderson commissioned "other smaller Globes, also, which as they are of a lesser bulk and magnitude, so are they of a cheaper price, that so the meaner Students might herein also be provided for."[34] The ever-observant Ubaldini also noted that Molyneux "makes his globes not of wood or cardboard, as these are altered by the passage of time, but of a mixture which dries very hard and (he says) will not be affected by wet or dry weather."[35] While a smaller, weatherproof globe might have served as a useful shipboard instrument, we have only prescriptive advice. The arrival of the Molyneux globes necessitated the publication of manuals to illustrate (and encourage) their use, and the most successful of these was written by the mathematician-navigator Robert Hues, recently returned from the disastrous last voyage of Thomas Cavendish. Hues was a bit contradictory regarding his mission to elevate the skills of geometry and astronomy in service of navigation, as he wrote in Latin and declared that the globes might be an "easy" way to simply see, rather than calculate, longitude and latitude, declination and ascension, positions and distances, and "an infinite number of other like things" simply through informed inspection. While "all these things may be performed far more accurately by the help of numbers, and the doctrine of Triangles, Plains, and Spherical bodies is a thing very well known to those that are acquainted with the Mathematics" he advertised that "the same things may be found out readily and easily by the help of the Globe with little or no knowledge of the Mathematics at all."[36] The educators Thomas Hood and Thomas Blundeville expounded upon the navigational uses of the globe as well, and John Davis (friend of Molyneux, and whose exploits were noted on his globe) included it among his essential instruments for navigation in the 1595 edition of his *Seamans secrets*. For Davis, the globe was the most "rare and excellent" instrument, producing "infallible" conclusions relative to "the true line, angle, and circular motion of any Course or traverse that may in Navigation happen, whereby the longitude and latitude is most precisely known, and the certainty of distance very plainly manifested, according to the true nature thereof." The miraculous globe

> gives the variation of the Compass, and the hour or time of the day at all seasons, and in all places. And by the Globe the Poles height may at all instants and upon euery point or azimuth, of the Horizon, by the Suns altitude taken, be most precisely known, by the certainty of whose excellent use, the skillful Pilot shall receive great content in his pleasing practice.[37]

Whether or not ship pilots had globes on board in the 1590s and after, they were probably not English-made, as Emery Molyneux did not establish a native industry: in 1596 he departed for the Low Countries, where his collaborator Jodocus Hondius, the engraver of the Sanderson globes' gores, was contributing to the establishment of Amsterdam as the center of the European cartographic community. In the later seventeenth century, Joseph Moxon, printer, instrument-maker, author, and expert in all things mechanical, as well as the official hydrographer to King Charles II, resurrected the English globe-making craft with the production of pocket globes as well as the decorative "English Globe," neither of which were particularly useful for navigation.

Planning Ahead

The literature of navigation in the Elizabethan era was characterized by several common claims, chief among them the intensifying declarations of the "ignorance" of the ancients in geographical matters, and assertions of the collaborative nature of its knowledge, evident in both cause and effect. John Davis, for example, pointed to the shoulders of doctors of the "Arts Mathematic" on which he stood on, including Thomas Digges, Thomas Harriot, and John Dee, as well as the application of their teaching in the "Mechanical Practices" by globe-maker Emery Molyneux, artist Nicholas Hillier, and shipwright Matthew Baker. It is a bit surprising to find Hillier in this august company, but obviously Baker, a second-generation master shipwright, and Digges, a second-generation "public" mathematician who served as the chief overseer of the restoration and fortification of Dover Harbor in 1582, played key roles in the emerging English maritime presence. Their roles in the construction of ships, docks, fortifications, and the infrastructure of empire in Elizabethan England were both inherently practical and literally foundational, but they continued initiatives from earlier in the sixteenth century, including coastal surveying, fortification and dockyard construction, and the dramatic expansion of the royal navy (both in terms of ships and administration) during the reign of Henry VIII. Elizabeth continued these initiatives and investments, although she was more limited in her funds and inclinations, and the joint-stock companies chartered during her reign, including the Muscovy, Spanish, Levant, and East India Companies provided additional incentive for shipbuilding and storehouses. We can trace the evolution of ship design over this era, but the cumulative effect that shipbuilding had on all the subsidiary crafts and crops, from forestry to the production of iron, hemp, flax, pitch and tar, is a bit more difficult to ascertain, though the connection between the expanding royal and merchant fleets and the Wealden iron industry is well-established.[38] Matthew Baker's accounts of his work as a master shipwright, however, can illustrate the process of building a ship going forward, if not the supply chain of materials.[39] Because Baker was the first English shipwright to proceed with plans on paper (a process that is memorialized by an illustration of the shipwright/Baker standing over a plat with a very large pair of dividers in hand), it is tempting to envision a process by which the work of actually building a ship was conducted by carpenters, joiners and sawyers bound by his design rather than their craft traditions, and a consequential separation of design and construction (and of designers from makers) but there is insufficient evidence to support that conclusion.[40] Nevertheless a ship, or any large structure, was simply too expensive a construction to go forward without some sort of planning process, incorporating multiple perspectives and calculations. Baker's planning inspired William Borough, then Comptroller of the Navy, to place him in the company of the most esteemed classical architect and Renaissance artist: the "studious practice and exercise" of arithmetic and geometry has resulted in the "rare and singular knowledge" of Vitruvius in architecture, "that famous Germaine Albertus Durerus" in painting, "And in building of Ships, Mathew Baker our countryman."[41]

Based on the notes and calculations in the "Fragments of Ancient English Shipwrightry," Baker agreed with Borough: he refers to arithmetic and geometry as the "two supporting pillars of every art" but acknowledges their rarity in his trade by including "mechanical demonstrations" for workmen unskilled in these arts. There is instructive text among the "Fragments", and also critical verse about those "filching filchers" who have published his knowledge as their own (William Bourne), but in large part the documents constitute a "working notebook" for Baker, who was searching for new rules of proportion for different-sized ships with calculations and diagrams.[42] The two big changes in northern shipbuilding had already occurred earlier in the century: the introduction of cannon onboard and the transition from "clinker-built" (overlapping planks) to carvel (edge-to-edge planks adhered to a skeleton) construction, which was more suited both to the integration of gunports and open-ocean sailing. Baker's challenges were to build purpose-built warships that incorporated the "race-built" design preferred by John Hawkins, who became Treasurer of the Navy Board in 1577, and to establish proportional rules, through "art" (mathematics) rather than just rule of thumb, which could serve as a shipbuilding standard in an era of increasing specialization. He seems to have worked out a flexible formula in the "Fragments": "The breadth is arbitrary, the depth must never be more than ½ the breadth, nor less than ¼. The length never less than double the breadth nor more than treble. The floor never more than ½ nor less than ¼ of the breadth. . . ."[43] Baker's focus on the proportions of ship design were just one aspect of the reform of the naval administration during Elizabeth's reign, which resulted in a series of "proportions" relating to a ship's crew, guns, ordnance, stores and capacity. Naval Comptroller William Borough laid out the "orders" for both merchant and warships in 1592, based on size and structure of the midship: the mean and best proportion for the former, "for the most profit," was a keel length two or 2 ¼ times that of the breadth, while warships should be built with a keel three times that of the breadth, with the depth of holds conforming to

Baker's general standards as well.[44] In another continuation of an early Tudor policy designed to encourage the construction of larger ships for both trade and requisition purposes, the Crown offered a bounty of five shillings per ton to builders of ships over a certain tonnage, which required a more specific and standardized measurement of capacity: Baker supplied another formula/rule in use until 1628.[45]

The work at the royal shipyards—Woolwich and Deptford on the Thames, Elizabeth's newer Chatham on the Medway—did not encompass the totality of shipbuilding in England, of course, and one should not overemphasize the role or distinction of royal ships. Of the 226 ships that faced the Spanish Armada only 34 belonged to the Queen, and a decade earlier William Harrison seems to utilize the word "navy" for all of England's ships, private and public, in the service of war, trade, and even fishing, yet distinguishing between the "Navy Royal and the common fleet." He was well aware the former has been built up:

> Certes there is no prince in Europe that has a more beautiful or gallant sort of ships than the Queen's Majesty of England at this present, and those generally are of such exceeding force that two of them, being very well appointed and furnished as they ought, will not let to encounter with three or four of those of other countries, and either bouge them [stave them in] or put them to flight if they may not bring them home.[46]

Harrison knew the names of Her Majesty's ships and the speeds at which merchantmen could sail to the West Indies and back, and clearly considered ships and navigation to be essential to the kingdom's security and prosperity; his contemporary William Lambarde likewise listed the names of the Crown's "moving castles."[47] Of the two chief enterprises of matters maritime, shipbuilding and navigation, the former seems something to marvel at rather than engage in, and was still cast in a web of some secrecy in terms of the public discourse. We have insights into Baker's design discretion because of the "Fragments," but not his more mundane tasks of organization and oversight: he was responsible for repairs and routine maintenance as well as new construction, and he took on private projects as well as public commissions. The incorporation of an integrated Company of Shipwrights in the seventeenth century, combined with the publication of the first treatises on shipbuilding, made the profession and its practice a bit less mysterious but also less majestic. Sir John Smith built a ship in a few chapters in *A sea grammar* (1626), but stopped short of providing

> a true Arithmetical and Geometrical proportion for the building of all sorts of Ships, were they all built after one mould, as also of their Masts, Yards, Cables, Cordage, and Sails..... a methodical rule as you see might be projected as their lengths, breadths, depths, rakes and burthens are so variable and different, that nothing but experience can possibly teach it.[48]

When addressing aspiring young seamen, Smith always stressed that "practice is best" but he also recommended a few texts, including the requisite "waggoner," John Davis's *The Seamans secrets*, Edward Wright's *Certaine errors*, and the *Pantometria* of Leonard and Thomas Digges. As a protégé of John Dee, the latter Digges distinguished himself as an early apologist of Copernicus and an infinite universe, but his focus was earthly and utilitarian in both *Pantometria* and *Stratioticos* (1579), on mathematical applications in the military realm. His chief contribution to the maritime infrastructure of England was his plotting, planning and oversight of the work on Dover Harbor and its fortifications in the 1580s, a massive public-works project implemented to transform the strategic-yet-silted port into a safeguard and staple. A semi-circle of coastal fortifications from Milford Haven in the west to Hull in the east had been built, and mapped, during the last part of Henry VIII's reign with funds provided by the Dissolution of the Monasteries, but many of these "Device Forts" required rehabilitation by the beginning of Elizabeth's reign. The attempt to restore Dover Harbor at this time resulted in complete failure under local supervision, so when entreaties from the town resumed in the 1570s the Privy Council considered the potential project a national matter and enlisted the aid of prominent experts, including William Borough and Thomas Digges, who eventually became the project overseer. Digges's qualifications were scholarly, social, and experiential: he was a published author of mathematical and astronomical analysis, trained by his prestigious father and John Dee, he had been a member of Parliament from 1572, with committee work on the ports, the draining of salt marshes, and the maintenance of the navy, and his patron was Robert Dudley, the Earl of Leicester, for whom he had carried out a reconnaissance mission in the Low Countries in 1579, in anticipation of English intervention in the Dutch Revolt. While on the Continent, he had been able to inspect Dutch and Flemish water works and fortifications, "havens artificial" made by the cutting-edge engineers of the era.[49] The Privy Council had solicited the ideas of Flemish experts for the Dover project, and in his "Brief discourse declaring how honorable and profitable to your most excellent majesty, and how necessary and commodious for your realm, the making of Dover Haven shall be," Digges presented a comparison of his own plan with that of the "strangers," based on his own surveys, calculated costs, and consultations with local officials.[50] In order to convince the Queen of the necessity of what would be a considerable investment, Digges asserted that "there is not one thing of greater necessities . . . then by all convenient means to increase Navigation, Shipping, and Mariners" with the creation and improvement of "safe receptacles" or harbors. Because of its situation, Dover was a "jewel" well worth polishing: its rehabilitation would provide a place of refuge and safeguard for English merchants and travelers, facilitate "alluring intercourse by sea," create opportunities of employment for regional laborers both during the project and after, increase customs revenue, protect English fishing, increase security by "annoying" England's enemies and enabling Her Majesty's ships to "scour the sea of pirates." Digges emphasized his own assessment of the situation and potential plans based on his experience and ability to set down the physical terrain "exactly in plat"; no doubt he did not need to assert his patronage and parliamentary connections.

The Dover project went forward with Digges in his supervisory position, and by all contemporary and historical accounts was an unqualified success. His public service was compounded in 1585 when he was appointed Muster-Master General to the Earl of Leicester's army in the Netherlands, an experience that gave him the authority to "review, correct, and augment" his *Arithmetical militare treatise, named Stratioticos*, first published in 1579 and issued again in 1590.[51] The original *Stratioticos* was comprised of three books, the first of which, on arithmetical applications for military formations, was the work of Thomas's father Leonard Digges. Thomas added sections on algebra and military laws, offices and duties, after having witnessed "extreme disorders' among English soldiers on his first visit to the Low Countries. An appendix on "the art of managing great artillery" represents the first English treatise on ballistics, which was expanded in the 1590 edition. Throughout the text, and most particularly in his prefaces, Digges adopted the guise of a scholar in service, which was also evident in his discourse regarding Dover Harbor. He expressed his eagerness to bridge the gap between mathematical theory and practice and transcend from the "demonstrative contemplative" to "experimental actions for the service of my prince and country." In 1579, not only was Digges seeking patronage from Robert Dudley, to whom he dedicated the *Stratioticos*, but also validation of his expertise. Echoing the constant refrain of the central importance of navigation in his time, he complained that he had tried to correct the "great imperfection" and "gross Errors" of that art but was rebuffed by mariners who relegated his demonstrations as "pretty devices" and inventions as "toys": he simply did not have enough "sea service" in that realm. He hoped to have a better reception as a purveyor of military science, as English soldiers must receive more, and better training: "For if a mason, a Painter, or other Mechanical Artificer be scarcely able in seven years to learn the perfection of his Science, shall we think the Art of a Soldier so base and abject, that it is to be attained in a few Weeks or Months?"[52] To establish his authority, Digges listed his prior publications at the beginning of the text, as well as works in progress, including treatises on navigation and "architecture nautical," which never made it into print.[53]

While it is not immediately apparent how the mathematical problem-solving of the first two books of the *Stratioticos* might enhance the effectiveness of the common soldier, Digges was able to illustrate the utility of calculation with applications specific to officers' duties and challenges. For example, concerning the Sergeant Major, to whom has been delivered "60 Ensigns, in every Ensign 160 Pikes and short weapon. The Generals pleasure is, that he shall put them into one main Squadron, and to arm it round with seven ranks of Pikes, I demand how many Pikes, how many Halberds, he shall use to make the greatest Squadron, and how many Ranks shall be in that Battle." Digges answered his question, provided the additional aid of a diagram of the scientific formation for his readers, and proceeded to illustrate how marching, encampment, ammunition, trench-digging, victualling, and other military endeavors could all be aided by the "plain, easy, and requisite Rules" of mathematics in general, and algebra in particular. In recognition of the reality that order could not be achieved entirely through calculation, the last book of the *Stratioticos* presents standards for military behavior and discipline, based primarily on classical precedents, except for officers and soldiers of the artillery: the *terra nova* of the military for which new rules had to be made. Digges included "Certain Questions in the Art of Artillery, by Mathematical Science joined with Experience, to be debated and discussed" in 1579, and expanded his treatment of "great Ordinance" the 1590 edition, when he was on firmer ground to "reduce Imaginative contemplations to sensible Practical Conclusions" based on his experiences in the field. The second edition of the *Stratioticos* is indeed an illustration in the benefits of experience as Digges had a lot *more* to say about military affairs: there are more "masters" (and he includes his own duties as Muster-Master), more contemporary continental examples as compared to classical precedents, more diagrams of formations and encampments, more errors in the developmental practice of ballistics to expose, and more concern for the defense of England in this post-Armada period.

The work and life of Thomas Digges is representative of two "revolutionary" trends of the sixteenth century: military and cartographic. These were European-wide trends initiated with the introduction of gunpowder and the geographical discoveries of the fifteenth century, and their impact in England was a bit delayed but on full display in the Elizabethan era. The diffusion of surveying knowledge and instruments, combined with the extensive coastal mapping of Henry VIII's reign, created a standard of practice best represented by the national surveys of Christopher Saxton and John Norden but also encompassing estate plans and Digges's detailed survey of Dover. As the ongoing effort to fortify England in response to the challenge of gunpowder continued over the Elizabethan era and beyond, a new focus on trained bands within the traditional militia emerged, exemplified by the emphasis on military discipline and training in Digges's *Stratioticos*. Yet, as all of England's authors on matters maritime asserted, the security and prosperity of the island kingdom was based on both its mastery and "sovereignty" over the seas, and so master shipwright Mathew Baker's contribution to England's military transformation was both more consequential and more revolutionary. Baker's *Dreadnought* was completed in 1573, the first in a long line of powerful warships, purposefully designed and planned, fully-rigged and "race-built" for maneuverability and accommodating an unprecedented concentration of cannon on board: these were the means towards mastery, and eventually empire.[54]

5

Public Discourses; Practical Concerns

The context in which practical knowledge about health, household, husbandry, and all the constituent arts and crafts associated with the evolving enterprise of England was diffused in the seventeenth century was characterized by a marked appeal to collective utility as compared to a century before, as the cumulative experience of crisis and discovery in the latter half of Elizabeth's reign forged a general awareness of the powers of utilitarian information to improve lives, lots, and the kingdom-at-large. Thomas Elyot's *The castle of helth* seems almost intimate in its attention to individual regimens compared to the wider perspectives of the three most popular seventeenth-century regimens, which took on old age, tobacco, and colonization, and the manorial perspectives of John Fitzgerald and Richard Benese seem parochial compared to John Norden's *The surueyors dialogue* (1607), which asserted that *The King consisteth by the field that is tilled*. Norden *was* the royal surveyor, but he was also the author, or creator, of *An intended guyde for English travailers*, a guide in its most literal or practical sense in that it consists of nothing more than tables of distances between the chief towns of England and Wales. Gervase Markham's texts on horsemanship and husbandry had a broad appeal that was also nativist, with his aptly-named *The English husbandman* (1613) written to "set down the true manner and nature of our right English Husbandry, our soil being as delicate, apt, and fit for increase as any foreign soil whatsoever, and as far outgoing other kingdoms in some commodity, as they us in other some."[1] The expanded purview of seventeenth-century texts stems from the success of the genre itself, and its impact in creating an audience for its "products," but there were also external and political factors, including the ambitious public works projects of the Crown—from the coastal fortifications of Henry VIII through the reconstruction of Dover Harbor under Elizabeth and Thomas Digges to the draining of the Fens over several decades. National crises, such as the dearth and plague of the last years of Elizabeth's reign, also focused attention on agricultural and medical discourses. The agrarian and trade crises of the early Stuart regime would have the same effect, along with the plagues of 1603, 1625, and 1636.

Navigation also bore the promise of enrichment and advancement, if not improvement. This was certainly the opinion of Francis Bacon, who "made a small Globe of the Intellectual World, as truly and faithfully as I could discover; with a note and description of those parts which seem to me not constantly occupied, or not well converted by the labour of man."[2] His classification of knowledge and its acquisition came at the beginning of a new era, and looked both backward and forward with an assessment of "helps and lights" as well as deficiencies. In the former category was navigation, which had opened the world and "disclosed multitudes of experiments, and a mass of natural history" as well as printing, "which communicates books to men of all fortunes." Bacon was less impressed by other practices of "history mechanical," but he still believed that it had potential to be

> operative to the endowment and benefit of man's life: for it will not only minister and suggest for the present many ingenious practices in all trades, by a connection and transferring of the observations of one art to the use of another, when the experiences of several mysteries shall fall under the consideration of one man's mind; but farther, it will give a more true and real illumination concerning causes and axioms than is hitherto attained.

Medicine was not, of course, within the jurisdiction of history mechanical but rather the philosophy of the body, and Bacon deemed the state of the "art of the cure" not so artful in 1605, for physicians were constrained by the general theories that prevented them from addressing the particular concerns of their patients as well as the particular symptoms of disease, and these failings were exceedingly apparent during epidemics such as the recent plague of 1603. While the most learned of physicians held fast to their "general intentions of purging, opening, comforting, altering," the unlearned "empirics and old women are more happy many times in their cures ... because they are more religious in holding their medicines." And when physicians did prescribe, their medicines were too "compendious," inexact, "inconstancies and every day's devices, without any settled providence or project." So many sovereign waters were sold as panaceas for every disease: "more exact knowledge in prescribing and more precise obedience in observing" would result in a more artful practice of medicine.[3]

Bacon would develop and expand upon his critique of the medical profession in later works, re-emphasizing its role as a public concern. As we have seen, disorder in the ranks and debate among the varied medical practitioners of early modern England had been ongoing for some time, a result of the clash between university-educated physicians incorporated in the College of Physicians and an array of irregular practitioners as well as the dissemination of Paracelsian medical theories in Elizabethan England, prompting barber-surgeons and apothecaries like William Clowes, George

Baker, John Banister and John Hester to challenge the established Galenist order, along with a few learned physicians like Thomas Muffet. By the turn of the seventeenth century, distilled "mineral medicines" (to use Bacon's term) were not quite as outlandish as viewed previously, and in its second decade a very prominent Paracelsian, Dr. Theodore de Mayerne, was appointed Royal Physician to King James and Queen Anne. There were still differences of opinion, but the variety and vendibility of both medicines and medical practitioners in early Stuart London were the greater source of division and the deterioration of the reputation of all those associated with healing: Dr. Mayerne reported that the King wanted only relief from pain and finding none, "laughs at medicine and holds it so cheap that he declares physicians to be of very little use and hardly necessary. He asserts the art of medicine to be supported by mere conjectures and useless because uncertain," echoing the critique of Bacon.[4]

The Plague and Public Health

The "uselessness" of physicians and "uncertainly" of medicine were never more apparent than during plague "seasons," including the epidemics of 1603, 1625, and 1636 and endemic outbursts in between. The public discourse during these crises was dominated not by considerations of potential preservatives or cures, but rather by the incidence and morality of "flight," the departure of the wealthy from plague-infested London, along with their learned physicians, leaving the city to the poor and the irregular practitioners and "inferior foot-physicians" in the words of the anonymous author of *Lachrymæ Londinenses: or, Londons lamentations and teares for Gods heauie visitation of the plague of pestilence* (1626). In language that was not quite as angry as that of his contemporary Thomas Dekker, this lamenter for London saw "no reason why the Physician, who hath the care of men's bodies, should flee and leave us destitute of his help, for which he was ordained" and asked:

> Can he gather so much out of the time of a common Mortality, by his Fees of us, that the ground will not hold him, but he is mounted on his Foot-cloth? and must he needs flee from us, when we have most use and need of his company and his Counsel, when thousands are daily sick, and many die for want of means?[5]

It seemed blatantly hypocritical for doctors incorporated in the College of Physicians, endowed with a monopoly on medical practice within the City and the censorial powers of enforcement along with inherent public responsibilities, to vacate London and blame those healers who remained, and indeed, Margaret Pelling's detailed study of the College physicians and their conflicts during this period asserts that this very "moral issue had a greater effect on their credibility than doubts over the effectiveness of treatment."[6]

The central policy regarding plague was first expressed in 1578 with the *Orders, thought meete by her Maiestie, and her priuie Councell*, which attempted to regulate the movement of those stricken by plague, to give care to those who became ill, and to provide for the orderly burial of the dead, which was issued with an "Advice set down upon her Majesties express commandment, by the best learned in physick within this realm," and reprinted relatively unchanged up to 1660.[7] *Orders thought meete* contained seventeen regulations instructing local magistrates on their duties in controlling and preventing the spread of the pestilence, essentially through the system of "keepers and searchers" through which the infected were "shut in" by the former until their death could be confirmed by the latter: the "watchman" of these orders prevented the plague from getting out, into the streets. The Advice of the College of Physicians included "sundry good rules and easy medicines" both to preserve and treat the "meaner sort of people," including sweet-smelling herbal preservatives to "correct the air" both inside the house and out—if you must go outside—and "inward" and "outward" medicines for preservation, purgation, and treatment of plague sores. The plague was perceived as both cardiological and poisonous, so cordials, antidotes, and sweat- and vomit-inducing medicines were prescribed, including a very cheap and "easy" version of the panacea Mithridatium, a cousin antidote to the 64-ingredient Theriac or Treacle, well beyond the reach of the meaner sort of people to whom the *Orders* and *Advice* were addressed. Presenting advice to the people through the proclamation and prerogative powers of the Crown was the extent of the College's response to an ongoing health crisis that was squarely centered in their jurisdiction.

The royal plague orders were essentially unfunded mandates: proclaimed and printed from on high with instructions to local magistrates to enforce them, ensuring that the primary responsibilities were municipal and parochial. In the case of London, there was clearly a dialogue about plague regulations between Crown officials and the City's Court of Common Council over what public places to close and when, and the latter also issued a succession of increasingly-long orders which reveal all the details of "plague management" in the later sixteenth and seventeenth centuries. The 1625 *Orders heertofore conceiued and agreed to bee published, by the Lord Mayor and Aldermen of the citie of London, and the iustices of peace of the counties of Middlesex and Surrey by direction from the Lords of his Maiesties most honourable priuie councell* called for the appointment of two or three examiners of health for each parish (and there was no power of refusal for the tapped, which might also account for "flight"), in addition to watchmen for the infected houses, up to six surgeons (three for the parish and three for the pest-house, if there was one), women searchers, and buriers, all of whom must not pass through the city streets without holding a three-foot red rod or wand, clearly visible to all passers-by, and also "abstain from company."[8] Householders were obligated to report illness in their houses within two hours of its appearance to the examiner, a surgeon or a searcher: from that time the house was "shut up" and watchmen put in place, one for the daytime and one for the night. Some parishes pursued a dual policy of quarantine and transportation of some victims to pest-houses, but for others it was all about shutting up. A shut-up house was marked with a red cross beneath or above the printed words "Lord, have mercy upon us" and would remain quarantined from anywhere from 20 days to four weeks. Burials took place at night with no friends or neighbors in attendance. Householders were obligated to sweep the streets in front of their houses daily, but the parishes also employed rakers and scavengers and nightmen who took it from there, carrying away "the sweeping and filth of houses" as far as possible, and giving notice of their arrival with the blowing of a horn. It is quite clear that the parish and its employees, surgeons, searchers, watchmen and rakers, constituted the front lines of the plague in early modern London. The weekly Bills of Mortality were another tool of public health initiated and overseen by the city government: dating from the mid-sixteenth century, they were first printed in in 1596 and issued regularly from 1603 "in quantities that were far in excess of a normal print run for a broadside or pamphlet," indicating the public interest in the enumerated threat.[9]

With London's incorporated physicians confined to a general advisory role and *fleeing* while surgeons were in the streets and the trenches, criticism and conflicts with other medical provisioners intensified. The College of Physicians was determined to prevent Barber-Surgeons, organized in a larger and more London-integrated livery company, from practicing "inward" medicine at all costs, but both the seemingly-subordinate surgeons and the other partners in medicinal practice, the apothecaries, had benefitted from their association with the new anatomical and chemical learning as well as the perceived absence (and limited number) of physicians. Still, the three arts were supposed to work together to preserve individual and collective health and the manual operations of surgery and pharmacy were deemed subsidiary to the more theoretical medicine in the seventeenth century, just as they had been a century before; and despite King James's personal feelings about physicians, he was eager to expand his authority in partnership with the College and in pursuit of public health.[10] Several important developments of his reign testify to the collaboration of Crown and College: the formal incorporation of the Worshipful Company of Apothecaries in 1617, the publication of the London *Pharmacopeia* in 1618, and the granting of a new royal charter to the College in the same year, prompting petitionary protests in Parliament. All aimed to establish a more orderly prescription of medicine and bolstered the position of the College. Tudor Acts of Parliament had placed pharmaceutical preparations under the supervision of physicians, who were authorized "to survey and examine the stocks of apothecaries, druggists, distillers and sellers of waters and oils, and preparers of chemical medicines" in 1553, but as the Apothecaries were part of the influential Grocers Company of London, they possessed a certain amount of leverage against the physicians and were among the highest percentage of illegal practitioners censored by the College in the later sixteenth and seventeenth centuries.[11] The royal charter granted to the new Worshipful Company of Apothecaries in 1617 (despite the protests of the City of London) was quite clear in its intent that the new company would serve the interests of Royal Physician Theodore de Mayerne, the apothecaries themselves, and "our Royal Respect and Regard to promote the State of our Commonwealth and to procure the Public Good, that the ignorance and rashness of presumptuous Empiricks and ignorant inexpert men . . . may be restraint." While the new company received all the usual powers of self-regulation, the charter also gave the "Faculty of Physicians of London" oversight authority with respect to the examination and approval of all those apothecaries who desired to open a shop or "otherwise by any other ways or means exercise the Art of an Apothecary" within the city of London or its seven-mile perimeter.[12]

A standardized pharmacopeia, another regulatory mechanism for these newly incorporated Apothecaries, had been under discussion since the 1580s but now became a reality over the next year: the definitive second edition of the *Pharmacopoeia Londinensis* included the King's proclamation "commanding all Apothecaries of this Realm to follow the dispensatory lately compiled by the College of Physicians of London," rendering it the first *national* pharmacopeia. Nicholas Culpepper's English translation of the Latin *Pharmacopoeia* asserted that it had been "*imposed* upon all the apothecaries of England to make up their medicines by" and the author of the *Pharmacopoeia*'s Epistle Dedicatory, the very influential Theodore de Mayerne, would agree with that word; in fact, he used it:

> we impose and enforce one and only one law and one method of compounding, from which we would allow no deviation whatsoever, not even that of a finger's breadth, so to speak. We do this in order that physicians as well as pharmacists being, as it were, strung on the same thread, may work in harmony and proceed on a cooperative basis, the former in a more secure mode of prescription, and the latter in a more accurate compounding of preparations.[13]

Writing with the authority of the Crown and two Companies, the Royal Physician described a vast "forest" and "sea" of varietal remedies, and a "plague" of deceit and "filthy concoctions": the new *Pharmacoepia*, "neither obviously lacking in medicaments nor crammed with them," would clear a path through this confusing terrain. As its language mandated, it was not, however, a remedy book, but only "for the learned, for the disciples of Apollo, and for the welfare, not for the information, of the common people."[14] Several decades later, during the less-regulated revolutionary environment, Nicholas Culpeper issued his unauthorized English translation, complete with dosages and attributes, under the title *A physicall directory, or, A translation of the London dispensatory made by the Colledge of Physicians in London* in which he admonished the Physicians for their privileged positioning: "you profess yourselves to be a College of Doctors; Doctor comes of *doceo* to Teach: Be Teachers."[15]

Culpeper also asserted that the Physicians had transformed both the Apothecaries and the Barber-Surgeons into "crutches," but corporate conflicts continued for the rest of the century. London's Barber-Surgeons constituted a large and influential company, with established procedures for training based on both theory and practice, its own regulatory powers, and notable members like anatomical and surgical lecturer Alexander Read and naval surgeon John Woodall. As both a fellow of the College of Physicians and a brother of the Worshipful Company of Barber-Surgeons and one who labored "to instruct thy mind, and to direct thy hand in the knowledge and curation" of diseases, Read was in the influential position of bridging the disciplinary gap between physicians and surgeons, whom he viewed as partners and "nature's friends," bound by the same goal. In the published versions of his lectures at the Barber-Surgeons' Hall in the 1630s, Read grounded surgery in both antiquity and utility, asserting that it "is by reason of absolute necessity more often required, than the ministration of medicaments."[16] The tumors of plague and pox were perfect illustrations, and by delineating both the external and internal causes of these very public diseases, Read was able to avoid addressing the major issue of contention between physicians and surgeons: the latter's desire to prescribe "inward" medicines as part of their practice. Read not only included instructions for the treatment of tumors and ulcers with medicines, but also for the preparation of these medicines, conjoining the work of physician, surgeon and apothecary in one practitioner. From his positions as physician, surgeon, and lecturer, Read strove to be nonpartisan in pursuit of the "impartial balance of reason," but defenses of surgery appeared in his discourse intermittently: echoing the critiques of Francis Bacon and King James, he stressed its comparative certainty when he observed that "the means which Physicians use in curing, sometimes take effect, sometimes avail not, it may be doubted whether health may be ascribed to the good constitution of the body, or to the means applied, but the effect of Chirurgerie is most evident."[17]

As the first surgeon-general of the East India Company, John Woodall was also in a position of experience and influence when he published the first compendium of naval medicine, *The svrgions mate*, in 1617. Out on the open sea, far from London and its physicians, medical specialization was impossible, and the surgeon had to fulfill the roles of physician and apothecary as well as respond to the specific challenges of seaboard life: Woodall included the key medicines and surgical procedures with which a shipboard surgeon should be equipped, as well as a treatise on scurvy and its treatment with lemon juice, "a precious medicine and well-tried, being found & good, let it have chief place for it will deserve it." After the Barber-

Surgeons Company was charged with supplying surgeons' chests for the English navy by royal commission in 1626, this responsibility became Woodall's, and his recommendations for the requisite military medicines and instructions for the treatment of gunshot wounds were outlined in *Woodalls viaticum: the path-way to the surgions chest*: this treatise along with others on the plague and gangrene were included in the revised and augmented *The surgeons mate, or, Military & domestique surgery* in 1639, with an equestrian engraving of King Charles on its frontispiece. Woodall was fulfilling a lot of roles in these publications: practitioner, educator, purveyor, poet (he favored Galenic regimens but paid tribute to the Paracelsian *tria prima* of salt, sulphur, and mercury in verse).[18] His long career illustrates some of the key advantages that the Barber-Surgeons had over London's learned physicians: public service that was characteristically active rather than advisory, field experience, whether in the hospital, on board a ship, or on the battlefield, a focus on practical problem-solving, and a corporate brotherhood that was integrated with both the city and royal governments. Expediency and necessity, whether in the midst of a plague epidemic or on a ship in the middle of the Atlantic, favored the Barber-Surgeons: in his preface to the 1639 edition of *The surgeons mate*, Woodall offered a utilitarian defense of his art and craft: acknowledging, as every medical writer in the early modern era did, that "Surgery, Diet, and Medicine (I mean outward and inward) are inseparable companions, and therefore all to be used in the art of curing man's body" he noted that in military contexts those roles had to be exercised by one man, always a surgeon as "neither his Majesty nor the Merchant allows Physicians nor Apothecaries any place." With this heavy burden laid on his brethren,

> it is an ungodly thing, and in reason most unjust, to forbid a surgeon to learn all, or anything that concerns his calling: and all those that are of the opinion to hinder a Surgeon from using outward and inward medicines, have quite misconstrued *Hippocrates* and *Galen*, showing themselves enemies to art, reason, and true experience, for that it is manifest, each of these three branches of healing, do mightily further the other, and not by any one of them simply of itself and alone, we may boldly conclude to have healed well and honestly, as we should do.[19]

He goes on, making comparisons between the collaborative work of the joiners, carpenters and shipwrights, to call for a collaborative medical "industry" as unified as harmonious on land as that which existed at sea in the guise of one learned and skillful surgeon. This was a constant cause for the venerable surgeon, who was one of the authors of the 1624 petition to the House of Commons protesting the College of Physician's attempt, through royal patent and confirmation by an Act of Parliament to impose "a superintendency over the petitioners in their own profession," and "restrain them from using part of their art, which they have studied and served for, and have done and do lawfully use, and without which many times they cannot perform their Cures, nor give such ease and remedy to their patients as is fit they should do."[20] The plague of 1625 interfered with the deliberations, which continued into the 1630s without resolution, and the jurisdictional struggles within London's medical marketplace persevered over the Revolutionary regimes and beyond.

Mercantile Medicine

While it is tempting to condemn the College of Physicians for prioritizing corporate control over public health, professional physicians in the sixteenth and seventeenth centuries were not trained "responders" but rather councilors for the lifelong preservation of health, based on their knowledge of established medical theories. Several factors were pushing learned physicians to become more responsive, including the endemic plague, "new" diseases and *materia medica*, and the increasing commercialization of medicine and conflicts between medical practitioners, trends that were manifest in the deliberations of the College, but also in the medium of print. When reading the prefaces of publications by licensed physicians in the early seventeenth century, it is impossible not to notice the references to irregular practitioners who were perhaps outside the reach of the College's censors: foolish and ignorant empirics and "quacksalvers" appear to be everywhere. The Northampton physician John Cotta devoted a chapter to each offender in his *A short discouerie of the vnobserued dangers of seuerall sorts of ignorant and vnconsiderate practisers of physicke in England* prefaced with a general plea for more scrutiny among medical "consumers": tobacco was supposed to be a universal panacea but was now (in 1612) a "monster of many diseases" and beware of the "barbarous medicine-mongers." There followed chapters on empirics, "trusting unto experience alone without reason" (contrasted with "methodians" and "travailers" who rely too much on theory and foreign ideas, respectfully), "wise women," "fugitive" and "heretical" physicians, quacksalvers, unlearned surgeons and apothecaries, spellcasters and wizards, physicians' helpers posing as their masters, clergy posing as physicians, astrologers and "emphemerides-masters," and "conjectors by urine," practicing deception through uroscopy.[21] While the medical connotations of "empiric" date back to the fifteenth century, the two words used most consistently to refer to the most brazen of irregular practitioners were "quacksalver," a play on Paracelsian abusers of quicksilver, and the Italian-derived "mountebank," both of which had more recent Elizabethan origins. Francis Herring, a College Fellow and Censor, was the first physician to use the word in reference to medical "imposters" and "counterfeiters" in *The anatomyes of the true physition, and counterfeit mounte-banke wherein both of them, are graphically described, and set out in their right, and orient colours*, a translation of a German exposé, which he reissued under the title *Beware of pick-purses*.²² For Herring, mountebanks were not just itinerant, unlearned and unlicensed medical practitioners, they were deceitful, both ignorant *and* insolent, incapable of being "reduced to order" and thus "bad and dangerous Members of the State, and in no sort sufferable in any well-ordered Common-wealth." Even more disturbing to Herring and his fellow "true" physicians was the popularity of these imposters among the "ruder and simpler sort of people," providing a rationale for members of the College to offer redress and expose stratagems in print. Herring asserted that he and "all the learned Gentlemen of our College" were intent and bound to the "prosecution and persecution" of "intruding and shifting Mountebanks" by their royal charters, and certainly not (as some must have claimed) "because they take away our profit."²³ This was the subtext in several texts authored by established physicians: Thomas Lodge asserted that his 1603 plague treatise was issued not to make himself "vendible," which was "ill-beseeming" and unworthy for a physician and philosopher, but rather for his

> poor countrymen and afflicted brethren turmoiled and attainted with the grievous sickness of the Plague: and left without guide or counsel how to succor themselves in extremity: For where the infection most rages there poverty reigns among the Commons, which having no supplies to satisfy the greedy desire of those that should attend them, are for the most part left desolate & die without relief.²⁴

Lodge admitted tacitly that his colleagues were not particularly attentive to the needs of the commonwealth in crisis, and one wonders if the "promised preservatives" and cordial waters referenced in his preface were sold to the multitude who descended upon his doors, as the College had granted permission to its fellows to sell medicines a decade before. He also expressed his belief in the efficacy of one of the most "vendible" plague preservatives in London: amulets or "cakes" made of arsenic worn around the neck or under the arm which could "void the poison of the plague" as one venom draws out another. This endorsement was contrary to that of another "learned physician" in the College, none other than Francis Herring, who condemned "poisoned amulets" in a treatise published in the same year as that of Lodge. *Certaine rules, directions, or aduertisments for this time of pestilentiall contagion: with a caueat to those that weare about their neckes impoisoned amulets as a preseruatiue from the plague* was reissued with successive seventeenth-century plague epidemics, including that of 1665, decades after Herring's death.²⁵ Herring revealed himself to be a strict Galenist in his *Certain rules*, with an argument focused on the medical harm that such amulets might cause, rather than a condemnation of quackery. In his steadfast support of the Galenic principle of contrary cures, arsenic, "a perpetual enemy to our nature," can only worsen the condition of those armed with amulets, rather than preserve them from the plague, a "monster" which must be fought with antidotes rather than poisons. Following up in a longer and more comprehensive treatise in the following year, directed perhaps to his medical colleagues rather the general public, Herring called for "the learned Masters of our Profession with one voice [to] proclaim that forasmuch as the special weapon to kill that Monster is not yet found out," and not advocate for dangerous Paracelsian panaceas: "How then shall Arsenic be their Curer, when all Diseases are cured by their contraries? unless you will maintain that dotage of Paracelsus (for so I must needs call it) against Galen, That Diseases are cured *per similia*, by their like."[26]

In the second edition of his *Certain rules*, published during the 1625 plague epidemic in London, Herring added a section "for the poorer sort of people when they shall be visited," which included "cheap medicines, as may come within the compass of their short and mean ability." He recommended sweat-inducing herbal vinegars to induce sweating sessions, but "if any be in that extremity of poverty and misery that they cannot procure these parable and easy cheap medicines, let them drink twice in the day, a draught of their own urine, in the morning and five in the afternoon." After all that, if the plague botches still appeared, Herring advised his readers to go to a surgeon, but not too soon: he warns against applying "forcible and sharp" external medicines hastily, as surgeons, physicians and the patients themselves were prone to do, with harmful consequences. Inward medicines were best, and "the preservatives mentioned in this book, may be had from Mr. James the Apothecary, at his house in Aldermanbury, near to the sign of the axe; with others of like nature, well approved and experimented."[27] Printed advertisements for medicines were more common in the second half of the century than the first, but they do appear on single-sheet publications as well as at the end of treatises like Herring's *Certain rules* before the Revolution. Irregular practitioners could not issue them without fear of search, seizure and censor by the College, of course, but certain brazen fugitives were willing to take the chance, particularly during plague times when the learned physicians were perceived to be absent. An anonymous German "professor," aged and experienced with the plague by his own account, issued *A directions concerning the Plague or pestilence, for poore and rich* in broadside form during the epidemic of 1625, advertising a preservative, a "certain precious pill, to keep in your mouth, when you go abroad or perceive any danger," as well as "poultices, balsams, oils, plasters & all things else belonging to this disease," all available at his residence at "Great Woodstreet at the sign of the Mere Maid near the corner of Maiden Lane." The Professor concluded that perhaps "some Caluminating Night-owls" might speak against his intent, but "let them show better or else let this alone."[28] Stephen Bradwell, the grandson of the eminent surgeon John Banister and a university-educated but unlicensed physician who was censored by the College on at least one occasion, published plague tracts in both 1625 and 1636, citing a Hippocratic rule in his *A VVatch-man for the pest* "that good Physicians do apply themselves to the present Time, and to take hold of the Occasion. The present Time (good Reader) is Woefull, & the Occasion, Dangerous" and including his address in Mugwell Street, where readers could purchase his pedigreed medicines. Bradwell added a menu and price list at the end of *A VVatch-man*, advertising plague powders, an "excellent Electuary," lozenges and pomanders, all of his grandfather's invention: "I confess they are costly: but slight means and cheap Medicines (however they promise) prove as dear as death." He also urged caution, as

> there is a Fellow in Distaff Lane, that disperses Bills abroad, bragging of a Medicine that was my Grandfather Banisters; thinking upon the fame of his name to get both glory and gain to himself. But let me warn all men to take heed of such impudent liars. My Grand-father was very scrupulous of giving any special Receipts to others. But if any man can say he hath any Receipt of his: I am sure, (if it were of any value) I have the Copy of it.[29]

The competition for cures was fierce, causing conflict not only between licensed practitioners and unlicensed ones, but also among the latter.

Probably the most conspicuous irregular practitioner in the marketplace of medical print, both because of his product and his advertising strategy, was Francis Anthony, a promoter of the ultimate mineral medicine, *aurum potabile* or "drinkable gold." There was nothing really new about this golden cordial: references to it date back to at least the thirteenth century, and it became one of the Paracelsian universal cures in the sixteenth, when Surgeon John Caius disdained all the dubious panaceas "promising help of all diseases, yea incurable, with one or two drinks, by waters six months in continual distilling, by Aurum potabile, or quintessence, by drinks of great and high prices, as though they were made of the sun, moon, or stars" in his treatise on the English sweating sickness.[30] A half century later, it was associated with the enterprising mountebanks who descended upon London during the "wonderful" plague year of 1603 by Thomas Dekker, right after he skewered the physicians, who "hid their synodical heads":

> [the] empirical mad-caps, for they could never be worth velvet caps, turned themselves into bees, or more properly into drones, and went humming up and down, with honey-brags in their mouths, sucking the sweetness of silver, and then of *aurum potabile*, out of the poison of blains and carbuncles. And these jolly mountebanks clapped up their bills upon every post, like a fencer's challenge, threatening to canvas the Plague, and to fight with him at all his own several weapons. I know not how they sped, but some they sped, I am sure, for I have heard them banned for the heavens because they sent those thither, that were wished to tarry longer upon earth.[31]

Francis Anthony, son of a London goldsmith who was educated at Cambridge, began practicing about 1600 without a license and was reproached by the College of Physicians on numerous occasions over the next two decades. The accusations leveled at him included at least two deaths, but he was apparently so successful in his "practice" that two members of the College were commissioned to write tracts condemning it: Matthew Gwinne in Latin for the medical community, and John Cotta in English for a wider audience of potential consumers.[32] In between these attacks, Anthony mounted a spirited defense, producing no less than nineteen testimonials and many more specific references in his *The apologie, or defence of a verity heretofore published concerning a medicine called aurum potabile*.[33] Cotta refuted several of the testimonies in his *Ant-Antony*, and so a dispute within the confines of practice and profession became even more public, an inevitable progression as such "lowly-learned Practisers, prodigiously climb into a wondered and undeserved height of popular fame and common esteem."

The equally enterprising but authorized practitioner John Woodall, surgeon and provisioner of surgeon's chests to the English navy, invented and sold another golden antidote: *aurum vitae*. Whereas approval a century before came from established ancient or continental authorities, it was now the opinion of consumers, especially if they were "worthy personages." Extending the endorsement of individuals, Woodall presented a certificate of the collective testimonies of the officers of St. Margaret's Parish in Westminster in his short tract *The cure of the plague by an antidote called aurum vitae*: testifying to the fact that Woodall's pills were administered to

> threescore several persons, some of this new Fever, some of the small Pox, some Agues, and some other diseases, but most, to them that were visited with the Plague, which had risings, Sores, Carbuncles, Blains, and were certainly known to have that fearful disease, all which persons recovered, and not one of all them that have taken the said Pills, died, thanks be given to Almighty God: neither can we do less than publish the great skill, judgement, and charity of the said John Woodall, by whose industry and care this Antidote hath wrought so good effect, and did bestow them freely, without one penny recompence for the same.[34]

Woodall allowed that he had invented this universal antidote quite some time ago, but had omitted it from his previous publication *The surgeons mate* as that was a comprehensive treatise and thus much too expensive for the poor: the slightness of the present treatise would render it more "common," "open," and "easy," for those of less means. The medicine itself, which had the additional attribute, a natural advantage of metal cures over vegetable ones, of being "permanent," and efficacious for at least seven years or more, could be purchased (as proclaimed on the title page) at the shop of Nicholas Bourne, Stationer, at the South Entrance of the Royal Exchange.

The Last Herbals

Most *materia medica* remained vegetative, manifest, and native, qualities emphasized in Timothy Bright's *Sufficiencie of English medicines*, an Elizabethan treatise reissued in 1615 with the aim of encouraging "others to deal with the same argument more plentifully, and kindle in us a greater diligence to inquire after the medicines of our own Country's yield and more care to put them in practice."[35] The reprint of a treatise about the over-reliance on "strange" plants might have been provoked by the medical debate over that most "outlandish weed," tobacco, of the decade before, but expressions of the necessity of national self-sufficiency were always current. Bright's text asserted that there was no reason to accept the premises that "the East and West Indies *Arabia, Barbarie*, the red Sea, are the Mines, as it were, and the fountains of medicines; and *Spain, Portugal, and Venice*, the vents of such things, and navigation the means to obtain them" when there were perfectly good simples available in England. Foreign medicines were subject to "corruptions and counterfeiting" more easily than native ones, which were also much more efficacious in their treatment of "English bodies." A generation before, Bright noted the cultivation of strange simples in London gardens and opined that in time, they might become more "framed" to English use, but ultimately he fell back on the same argument that Woodall would use much less effectively for his plague treatise and golden cordial: medicines should be easily "come by of the common people" and "homely" matter was much more so than "foreign-fetched." Bright died in the same year as his *Sufficiencie of English medicines* was reissued, so he was likely not responsible for its amendment with catalogs of English medicines for common diseases, transforming it into a reference, and also a text representative of the era: both discourse and directory. In this same year, 1615, tobacco was the subject of another text focused on its cultivation rather than its consumption: *An aduice hovv to plant tobacco in England and how to bring it to colour and perfection*, written by the semi-anonymous "C.T." A perfect example of "national husbandry," the dual goals of this *Advice* were to promote the planting of tobacco in England and discourage the purchase of the Indian or Spanish product, so to decrease the drain of treasure to Spain and avoid all of the unhealthy additives to the "outlandish weed," including an "artificial" (here used in a very negative sense) dressing of a mixture made of "the dregs or filth of sugar, called Molasses" and *poison*. Not all tobacco was harmful, just Spanish tobacco, and if England could grow its own product, additive-free and imbued with the plant's natural tawny color, consumers, cultivators and the Commonwealth would all benefit.[36]

The first decades of the seventeenth century engendered medical debate—over whether tobacco was helpful or harmful, over the curative powers of similar substances as opposed to contrary ones, over the complete or "topical" aspects of the surgeon's professional practice—as well as the urge to codify and compile: as illustrated by the publication of the *London Pharmaecopia* and the publication of an improved and augmented second edition of John Gerard's famous herbal and the new flora and herbal of John Parkinson. This was the last era of the herbal, a genre that had defined medical knowledge and practice since time immemorial. The first edition of Gerard's *The herball, or Generall historie of plantes* seems like a text out of time following forty years after William Turner's groundbreaking herbal, despite its inclusion of the outlandish "Virginian potato": it was a work of unoriginal and unattributed text, translation and images, largely based on Flemish botanist Rembert Dodoens's *Stirpium Historiae Pemptades Sex* (1583) and its English translation by College physician Robert Priest, who died before his work was completed. John Gerard was a well-connected Barber-Surgeon and gardener, who was brought in as Priest's replacement: not only did he fail to acknowledge his predecessor's efforts, but he also rearranged the text according to the classifications of another Flemish botanist, Matthias de l'Obel, and appropriated woodcut illustrations from previously published continental works, many of which did not match their botanical descriptions. In the dedicatory epistle to his patron and employer William Cecil, as well as in the preface to the reader of "his" work, Gerard conflated the considerable labor that he had dedicated to tilling the soil with his labors over the text, and the frontispiece portrait by pioneering English engraver no doubt enhanced his editorial authority as well. The second edition of *The herball, or Generall historie of plantes* was "much enlarged and amended" and published in 1633 by Matthew Johnson, a London apothecary, and furnished with an extraordinary new preface, which explained the historiography of herbals in some detail and placed the first edition in a comprehensive context: Gerard was accounted as someone whose "chief commendation is, that he out of a propense good will to the public advancement of this knowledge, endeavored to perform therein more than he could well accomplish; which was partly through want of sufficient learning . . . he also was very little conversant in the writings of the Ancients, neither, as it may be seen by diverse passages, could he well distinguish between the ancient and modern writers," a rather serious deficiency for a Renaissance compiler. Johnson made so many alterations and editions that it was necessary to include a catalogue thereof, and in contrast to Gerard, took responsibility for any errors therein and thanked his one assistant, a Mr. John Goodyer of Maple-Durham in Hampshire, for his contributions.[37]

Despite John Gerard's academic deficiencies, he was by all accounts an enthusiastic plantsman, and that inclination and avocation surfaced in the text of the *Herball* time and time again, increasing its accessibility and popularity. His experience in his own garden in greater London, documented in a published catalog of its more than a thousand plants, as well as in William Cecil's garden at Theobalds and that of the College of Physicians, were his major qualifications for the *Herball* commission. Consequently, there is quite a bit of personal testimony in the text. For every chapter/entry, there are considerations of kinds or varieties of the plant in question, the place where it naturally grows or where it can be grown, the time of the year when it blooms, its classical and vernacular names, its nature, the climate it prefers, and its medicinal virtues. The second category was where Gerard made his contribution, or his mark: establishing a strong sense of place for English botany. He noted whether plants were native or "strange," but not with the same kind of nativism expressed by Dr. Bright: Gerard expressed the confidence that he could make that foreign plant grow in his garden, or perhaps one of his fellow London experimental gardeners might cultivate it, even if it did not grow elsewhere, "wild" in England. Sometimes he cast himself as an English Johnny Appleseed, as with a particular type of garden mustard not common in England, but he had "dispersed the seeds thereof unto sandy parts of this land, so that I think it is reasonably well-known at this day." A particular type of lily grew naturally in Constantinople and those parts, "from whence we had plants for our English gardens, where they flourish as in their own country." His naturalist friends furnished him with cuttings and seeds, including a strange epimedium sent to him by the French King's herbalist: he planted it in his London garden and it came up every year, except for the very hot summer of 1590. Not content with that name, "I have thought to call it Barren-wort in English; not because Dioscorides says it is barren both of leaves and flowers, because as some authors affirm, being drunk it is an enemy of conception." Licorice grew wild or naturally in Germany, France and Spain, but only in English gardens: Gerard noted that he has plenty in his own garden, but also that "the poor people of the north parts of England do manure it with great diligence, whereby they obtain great plenty thereof, replanting the same once in three or four years." And then there were all those "Indian" plants, not just tobacco and potatoes, but pumpkins, corn, bindweed, swallow-wort, and prickly fig, nut and sassafras trees: a veritable *world* of plants, ready to be fashioned or harvested to English tastes or demands.[38] In his corrected, supplemented and re-organized editions issued decades later, Johnson preserved Gerard's "voice" and added additional observations primarily regarding cultivation rather than medical utility. Though botany was still an integrative part of medicine it would seem that medicine was no longer *the* integrative part of botany.

Gerard's fellow London gardener and Johnson's fellow apothecary John Parkinson produced both one of England's first floras and last herbals over the period of Charles I's Personal Rule: *Paradisi in sole paradisus terrestris* (1629) and *Theatrum botanicum: the theater of plantes* (1640).[39] His presentation of each book was gendered: the *Paridisi in sole*, "feminine of flowers" (Figure 9), was dedicated to Queen Henrietta Maria and the *Theatrum*, a "manlike work of herbs and plants," to the King himself. Both texts included species new to England, both transplanted introductions and domestic discoveries, like the small, wild hellebore with blush flowers discovered near the Lancashire and Yorkshire border by a certain "courteous

Gentlewoman" named Mistress Thomasin Tunstall, who sent Parkinson roots for his Long Acre Garden, where they bore "fair flowers."[40] These compendia were testaments to Parkinson's "travail, industry and experience," but also to that of his fellow English gardeners, who seem to have reported in to him in his capacity as the chief herbalist of the realm. Clearly he relied on his "gatherers" for both roots and reports, as Parkinson was even more detailed than Gerard in his physical placement of plants. In his discussion of a small variety of Solomon's Seal, for example, he remarks that it

> is frequent in diverse places of our Land, as besides those Gerard has named, it grows in a wood two miles from Canterbury by Fishpool Hill, as also in a bushy close belonging to the Parsonage of Alderberry near Clarindon, two miles from Salisbury, the next Close thereunto is called Speltes, and in Chesson wood, on Chesson hill, between Newington and Sittingburn in Kent.[41]

All of the English herbalists from William Turner on were as "unabashedly concerned with particulars and their description" as their continental colleagues, but they seem particularly focused on *place*.[42]

Parkinson employed a division of pleasant and profitable plants in both his flora and his herbal: the former was devoted primarily to the first category but included sections on the kitchen garden and orchard, while the latter is a more comprehensive manual of utilitarian plants. To impose order on his grand compendium, Parkinson created a transitional classification system, dividing his material into several classes or "tribes" based on pharmacological, ecological, taxonomical, geographical and "leftover" criteria: sweet-smelling plants, purging plants, venomous, sleepy, and hurtful plants (plus their counter-poisons), wound herbs, cooling herbs, hot, biting herbs, umbelliferous plants, thistles and thorny plants, ferns and capillary herbs, legumes and cereals, plants found in watery and damp places, trees and shrubs, "strange and outlandish plants" from all over the world, and "the unordered tribe," a "gathering camp" created for everything from potatoes to peonies, "stragglers that have lost their ranks or were not placed in some of the foregoing orders, that so I may preserve them from loss, and apply them to some convenient service for work" in the commonwealth of gardeners.[43]

Native Soil

The herbals of John Gerard and John Parkinson were useful texts in their time, but they were not *usable*: at least not by those engaged in the commercial practice of cultivation rather than gardening or medicine. For husbandmen, the focus was first and foremost on the soil rather than what was sown. The most prolific and popular author of husbandry texts in the

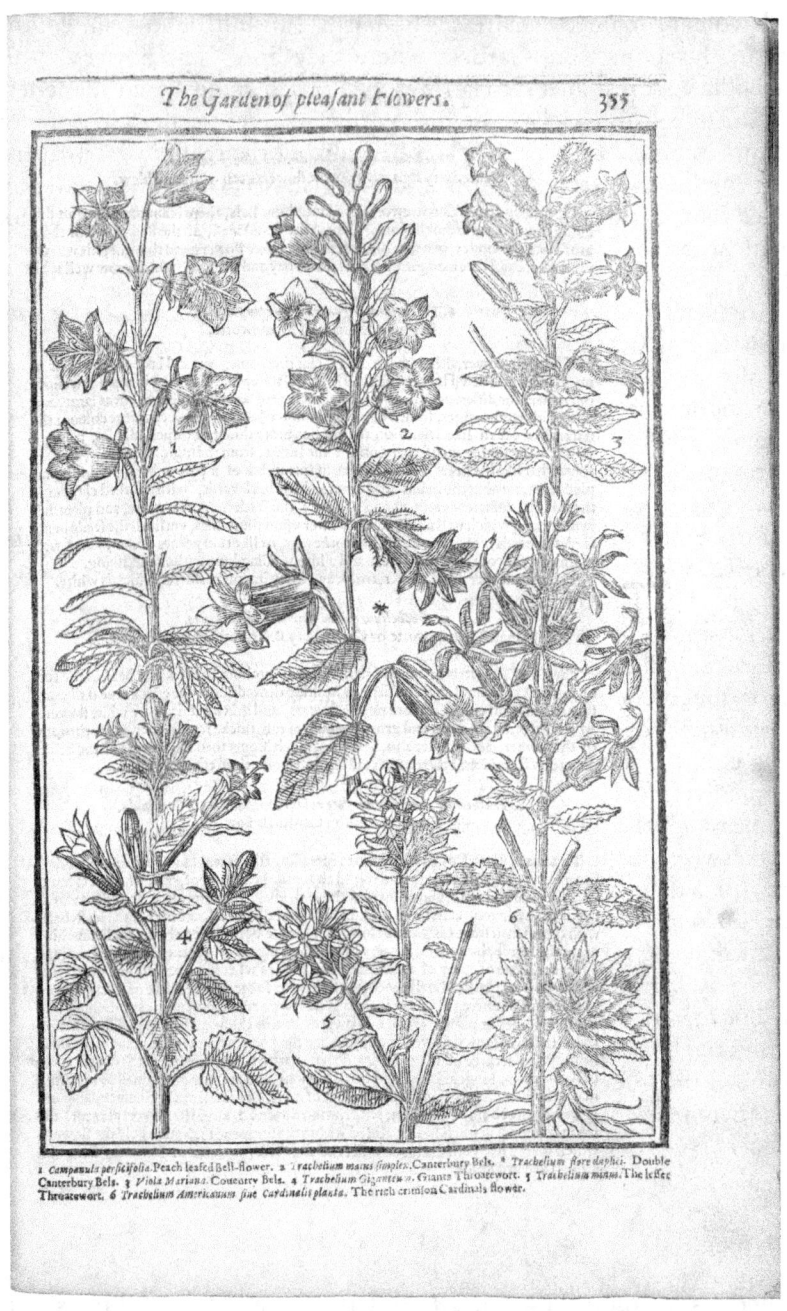

FIGURE 9 *John Parkinson (1567–1650)*, Paradisi in sole paradisus terrestris. Or, a garden of all sorts of pleasant flowers which our English ayre will permitt to be noursed vp *(London, 1629), p. 355. Used by permission of the Folger Shakespeare Library under a Creative Commons Attribution-ShareAlike 4.0 International License.*

first half of the seventeenth century, Gervase Markham, came to the topic through a common method, compilation and critique.[44] A former soldier, he began his career in advice literature with a series of books on horses and horsemanship, in the company of navigational author Thomas Blundeville. Twenty years after his first *Discourse of horsemanship* (1593), Markham published the first part of *The English husbandman*, revealing that the inspiration for his path from animal husbandry to husbandry in general was his work on an updated edition of the *Maison rustique, or The covntrey farme*, originally compiled in French by the physicians Charles Estienne and Jean Liebault, and translated into English by Richard Surflet. Markham's assignment was to review, correct, augment, and reconcile French husbandry with that of England, and in doing so he realized that the text, while "a work of infinite excellency," was "only proper and natural to the French." He noted a recent translation of Virgil's *Georgics*, "a work only belonging to the Italian climate," as well as Englished works of Xenophon, also "utterly unacquainted with our climate," and also noted the popularity of all of these agricultural works, and resolved to "set down the true manner and nature of our right English Husbandry, our soil being as delicate, apt, and fit for increase as any foreign soil whatsoever." Markham pledged that he would not cease writing about his new preoccupation until he had surveyed "all manner of English Husbandry and Huswifery whatsoever, without omission of the least scruple that can any way belong to either of their knowledges."[45] He might have stopped writing (as he became the exemplar of issuing old texts under new and/or variant titles), but he certainly did not stop publishing tracts on husbandry until his death in 1637—and Markham texts continued to be issued well after that date. Just one of his later titles, *Markhams farwell to husbandry* was issued in three editions over the last decades of his life, and two after his death.

Certainly, Markham was following in the tradition of John Fitzherbert, Thomas Tusser, Thomas Hyll, Leonard Mascall, Hugh Plat and other sixteenth-century agricultural authors: husbandry was by nature an empirical endeavor, rooted in the soil. Tusser discovered the English "huswife" and Plat offered her a whole volume of "delights." Andrew Borde discussed the preferred situation of a rural residence decades before Markham, and Plat dug into all things marl. Markham was not an original theorist, researcher, or pitcher of practical information, but like all effective instructional texts, the content and countenance of his treatises reflected the context of their time. He presented himself as a "husbandman among husbandman," unlike the men who produced *Maison rustique*, scholar-physicians who "never meddled with a plough," and a keen observer of its practice. For Markham, husbandmen were nothing less than "masters of the earth," and their endeavors "the great nerve and sinew which holds together all the joints of a monarchy," a rather awkward anatomical allegory employed in the preface to the first part of *The English husbandman*. Markham's moment, essentially the quarter-century from 1613 until his death in 1637 during which he published agricultural treatises nearly every single year, was a period of economic crisis and transition triggered by a decline in exports of England's traditional textile, white woolen broadcloth, due to the consequential Cockayne project and the beginning of the Thirty Years' War in central Europe. The general concern over the "decay of trade" intensified with the Parliament of 1621, which met after a seven-year absence from London and led to an airing of economic grievances and pamphlets. Against this background, Markham was focusing on the fundamentals of agricultural production while also advocating for a more diversified rural economy from the manorial level on up, following the recommendations raised by authors like Reginald Scot, Richard Gardiner and John Taverner during the last economic crisis: hops, "curious outlandish stone-fruit" like apricots, and grapes, in a rather futile effort to reduce English dependency on continental imported wines during the midst of the Little Ice Age.[46] Markham also followed his Elizabethan predecessors in his focus on improving, increasing, and *altering* the quality of the soil, which was the essential and most elementary endeavor of both the farm and the kingdom. His faith in the ability of the *English* husbandman, armed with his native knowledge, characteristic resourcefulness (and of course Markham's book), to increase yields was also the primary reason why he discounted "foreign" advice, whether it be classical or continental: "some of our translated Authors do utterly disavow for Gardens many Soils, as namely, all Sands, all Chalky earths, all Gravel, all Earths like dust, and any Earth which chaps or opens in the heat of summer, by that means depriving almost half of our kingdom of the benefit of Gardens."[47] There was nowhere in England that the soil could not be amended to bear fruit in Markham's estimation, except for lands which were "absolutely boggy" like the Fens, the focus of a succession of ambitious draining projects from the 1590s.

Before he began his intensive reprinting program, Markham established a systematic tree of husbandry knowledge and practice, starting from the ground up: soils, tools, sowing seeds, combating pests, "reading" the weather, pastoral and animal husbandry, including everything about his beloved horses and that most English of animals (and that most attuned to the soil), sheep, bee-keeping, poultry provisioning, kitchen and pleasure gardens, the cultivation of orchards, woodland, meadows, and fish ponds, and the realm of the housewife. Several themes run through Markham's works, reinforced with each successive publication: the manor as a microcosm of the macrocosm kingdom, a belief that all lands could be improved or better-utilized, a desire to save labor through better practice. There are few more succinct statements of the contemporary belief in man's ability to master nature through knowledge than those found in a Markham manual: addressed to those who sought to "conquer Nature by altering Nature," and make her "better than she was before."[48] As we have seen, the rationale of "the good of the kingdom" was utilized fairly consistently in a variety of didactic texts, but Markham was more specific. While he would include such language in his titles and prefaces, his works also maintained the general assertion that the collective prosperity of the kingdom was based on the individual prosperity (and labor) of the household and more specific recommendations for his husbandmen and housewives: identifying soils that could "bear abundance" of hemp or flax, both of no "small use in this our Kingdom, as witnessed by the abundance of all manner of cordage daily used for ships and other purposes; the infinite store both of coarse and fine linen cloth, and a world of other things, without which families cannot be sustained," providing instructions for "how to keep Grain, either for transportation by Sea, or for use in a town of War or Garrison, from one year, to one hundred and twenty" because the world was larger and more contentious than that of their forefathers. *Hungers preuention*, Markham's 1621 work on fowling, was addressed to "all such as travel by Sea, and come into uninhabited places: especially, all those that have anything to do with new Plantations," which he referred to as an *action*.[49] One of Markham's most popular compilations in England, *A vvay to get vvealth*, was also popular in its American colonies, appearing in collections from Virginia to Massachusetts. After foraging and fowling, apparently Markham's recommendations for planting in lands that were very different from that of England were authoritative, or at least memorials of English practices.[50]

A vvay to get vvealth is indicative of Markham's currency and marketability, as well as of contemporary publishing strategies. The title was just that, a title-page affixed to reprints of his other works advertising the six vocations or "callings" through which husbandmen and housewives might "fully employ themselves" and supposedly gain wealth. This was a relatively new secular use of that term but the callings had been covered by Markham before: the care and feeding of all animals in the service of men, country recreations for gentlemen, the "office" of a housewife, with all of the responsibilities of a "complete woman," soil enrichment, in general and in the Weald of Kent, orchard cultivation, along with bee-keeping.[51] Only *The inrichment of the vveald of Kent* was first published as part of *A vvay to get vvealth* and it was issued in successive separate editions afterwards. Much of the instructions for enrichment had been published previously in *Markhams farwell to husbandry*, but the focus on Kent was typical of Markham's comparative perspective regarding the agricultural challenges and opportunities of English counties as well as his systematic regimens for soil amendment and improvement. The Weald had always been a "barren," and "unfruitful" wilderness because of the disposition of its soil, but Markham believed that any English soil could be improved through "some manner of comfort, as Dung, Marle, Fresh earth, Fodder, Ashes, or such other refreshings." As marl was native to the region, this was Markham's recommendation, along with the implementation of a convertible or ley farming rotation, which could accommodate both tillage and livestock. Markham's ideal farmers were always very busy, juggling their animals and their crops in a constant state of rotation, but that was the way to wealth, as "Butter, cheese, and the flesh of beef and mutton, be advanced in price equally, if not beyond wheat, rye, barley, and the other grains. Howbeit a good Husbandman will make his profit of them both." And as one Kentish holding prospered so would England, as "the increase of corn and pasture through the Kingdom" would ensue with the adoption of best practices based on every county's nature and resources.[52] There is no question that Markham was repetitive, but his early works presented a consistent and comprehensive argument for a more intensive, diversified, and resilient agricultural economy, in response to the economic circumstances of his time. In his *Farwell to husbandry*, he addressed the anonymous critics who asserted that he had said it all before, and at the same time proclaimed that it just might be possible for regimented English husbandmen to eliminate their fallow fields, and "have all your ground to bear you continually either Corn or Grass in good abundance," an achievement that would not be attained for at least a century later. In the same text, Markham also presented a "computation" of estimated labor on the farm, of both men and animals, so that it "might stand for a precedent" and enable a man to better "direct the work of his family/resources," servants and animals, so that they all might be "employed for the best use and profit" in order to take advantage of England's changeable economy.[53]

Markham did not compute the labor of his English housewife, who was featured in several editions of his works and also in a succession of individual titles, but if she fulfilled all the duties of a "complete" woman her hours would represent an impressive sum.[54] Perhaps her work was outside of his jurisdiction, as it was located within the house, rather than "abroad." Following the example of Partridge's popular treasuries of receipts for women, Markham disclosed that much of his content relative to women's work came from "a Manuscript which many years ago belonged to an Honourable Countess, one of the greatest Glories of our Kingdom, and were the opinions of the greatest Physicians which then lived" in his dedication to Frances Cecil, the dowager Countess of Exeter. Markham divided the considerable duties of the housewife, encompassing the preservation (through the maintenance of their health), feeding, and clothing of her family, into categories of "inward" and "outward" knowledge. In addition to all the personal virtues necessary for the "completeness" of her character, the English Housewife should possess a "physical kind of knowledge," referring to the mastery of medical prescriptions. Markham emphasized that "the depth and secrets of this most excellent art of phisick, is far beyond the capacity of the most skillful woman, as lodging only in the breast of the learned Professors, yet that our hous-wife may from them receive some ordinary rules, and medicines," which he supplied: for a variety of fevers, including the pestilence, palsy, pleurisy, dropsy, the stone, headaches, toothaches, swellings, pains, all sorts of skin and women's problems, and sores and wounds, including those from gunpowder. The "outward and active" knowledge required of the Housewife included her cooking, distilling and outfitting responsibilities, for which Markham provided an orderly succession of recipes and instructions. There was a clear emphasis on self-sufficiency, as a good housewife was one who relied on the "provision of her own yard" rather than "strange markets," but Markham's Housewife also had lots of sugar in her pantry. The Markham cookbook began with an epitome of harvest times for all of the herbs in the housewife's kitchen garden, "so not to burden her memory," and then proceeded through the courses of service, from salads to fricassees ("dishes of many compositions"), to boiled, roasted and stewed meats and fish, savory pies, sauces and pastes: "banqueting" recipes are provided along with everyday dishes, "great feasts and ordinary contentments."[55]

Distilling had been part of the ideal housewife's duties since the Elizabethan era, and Markham recommended stills of tin or "sweet earth" for his Housewife, on which she would distil a variety of medicinal, cosmetic, and perfuming waters, among them an *aqua vita* and a multi-metallic water that contained a "world" of virtues, including the ability to make men (but not women) look young even when old. There is also a very complicated recipe with precious ingredients, perhaps the *aurum potabile* of household physic:

> take Limmell of Gold, Silver, Lattin, Copper, Iron, Steel, and Lead; and take Lethargy of Gold and Silver, take Calamint, and Columbine, and steep all together, the first day in the Urine of a man-child, that is between a day and a night, the second day in white wine, the third day in the juice of Fennel, the fourth day in the whites of Eggs, the fifth day in woman's milk that nourished a man-child, the sixth in red wine, the seventh day in the whites of eggs, and upon the eighth day bind all of these together, and distil the waters of them, and keep this water in a vessel of Gold or Silver.[56]

Markham reminded his housewives that just as they needed to know (or possess a reference which would tell them) when herbs for cookery were in harvest, they must also learn (or consult their reference) those times of the year when medicinal herbs were at their strongest. An entire chapter was devoted to the essential task of "ordering, preserving, and helping all sorts of wines" as this was an imported commodity of great value and necessity for which "self-sufficiency" could only be obtained through proper storage and clever embellishment. The characteristics of continental wines were relayed in an almost-modern manner, but the additives that "made" them suitable for contemporary English tastes are representative of the early modern palate: spices, honey, eggs, milk, fruit. The *English house-vvife* also assigned dairy responsibilities to its "complete" women, in a chapter which seems to tread on the husbandman's territory in reference to the choice and breeding of cows. After the milk has "come home," into the house, the work of "fleeting" (skimming off the cream), churning, and cheesemaking proceeded, according to a timely schedule adjusted to the fasting days, the general rhythm of the household, and markets, where of course this self-sufficient housewife would sell rather than buy. The dairy waste-products, buttermilk and whey, had their uses, including nourishment for the poor, "whose wants do daily cry out for sustenance."[57]

Markham assigned additional malting and brewing duties to his very busy housewife, extensions of her knowledge and experience in distilling and dairy. While he acknowledged the existence of "Men-malsters," malting was still "housework" and thus "properly the work and care of the woman." It was also a commodity and "merchandise" that was essential to the maintenance not only of her household but also towns, counties, "the whole kingdom and diverse others of our neighboring Nations." This is another provisioning task that seems to belong more in the realm of husbandry according to Markham's criteria, especially as he spends considerable time on the selection of grain and the construction of the malt-house and the "framing and fashioning" of its kiln and cistern. He has less to say about the furnishings of the brew- and bake-houses and more about their products: beer, ale, perry, cider, mead, metheglin, manchet, cheat bread and brown bread. Nearly a century after Andrew Borde proclaimed that ale was the natural drink for Englishmen, Markham asserted the popularity of beer, particularly the "ordinary beer" with which "Nobleman, Gentleman, Yeoman, or Husbandman shall maintain his family the whole year." Ordinary beer was more long-lasting than either "March beer" or ale, for which Markham was an early adopter of the addition of hops over the traditional herbs and spices, following the practice of the "best brewers."[58] Markham's instructions for the bake-house were limited to the production of the basic hierarchy of breads: manchet, cheat, and brown, distinguished by their grains and the processing and lightness of their flour. Manchet and cheat were breads made from wheat for the most part, with the former more "dressed and boulted" (sifted) and brown bread, made of a mixture of barley and other grains, was the "coarsest bread for man's use" and thus suitable for the servants.[59]

As brief and idealistic as they are, Markham's descriptions of the tasks of the domestic maltster, brewster, and baker and all the other "offices" of his housewife do provide narratives of the nature of domestic provisioning that go far beyond other texts referencing women's household work in the pre-Hannah Woolley era. Markham's *The English house-vvife* bridged the more random recipe books published from the later sixteenth century on with the comprehensive "domestic management" manuals published later in the seventeenth century. Even though it was a prescribed one, his somewhat self-sufficient household does seem representative of the culmination of a century-long trend from 1550 to 1650 during which a "particular kind of middling domestic environment" developed, "fostering highly skilled behaviors whose productive outputs are focused both inwards, and outwards towards the market beyond its own doors."[60] This was a development largely discerned through the analysis of probate inventories, which have determined that the vast majority of seventeenth-century households were engaging in some combination of agricultural, brewing, baking, milling, and dairying activities, with the latter and spinning even more widespread.[61] It seems that Markham was trying to cover all the bases with his housewife's dairy duties and sugar cakes in her pantry, and he laid out her clothing responsibilities as well in a relatively rare foray into the realm of material culture. Using his inward/outward framework in a very literal way, Markham asserted that in addition to acquiring knowledge of preserving and feeding her family, the housewife "must learn also how out of her own endeavors, she ought to clothe them outwardly and inwardly for defense from the cold and comeliness to the person; and inwardly, for cleanliness and neatness of the skin, whereby it may be kept from the filth of sweat, or vermin; the first consisting of woolen cloth, the latter of linen."[62] The husbandman came in from "abroad" with the newly-shorn wool, and our housewife takes it from there: carding, sorting, dyeing, oiling (or greasing, as the "plain housewife terms it"), tumming, spinning, and warping (the domain of the weaver, but the housewife still needs to have such knowledge, in much the same way that patients must be forearmed for visits to their physicians), before she turns it over to the weaver for weaving, walking, and dressing. Many different external craftsmen now entered the production line, not only weavers, but the walker or fuller, as well as the clothworker and "sheerman," before it is delivered into the hands of the tailor and then back to the housewife. Markham had to dwell on soils in his discussion of hemp and flax: these were more novel crops for England, which required a bit more introduction. Both required considerable processing (including "swingling") before they could be turned over to the housewife and her heckle, "which instrument needs no demonstration, because it is hardly unknown to any woman whatsoever," followed by spinning, scouring, whiting, and weaving.[63] A range of options was presented for the housewife, depending on her resources, necessity, and location: spinning could occur in-house or at the spinner's shop; she could make mere linen or fine Holland cloth.

Prescriptive literature does not open too many windows into material culture, so this detailed discourse of household cloth production is unique, but because it is so detailed one wonders about its source. Markham's authority and popularity as an author were based on his own experience as a practitioner; as a soldier, a horseman or a husbandman, but not as a craftsman. The anonymous Countess acknowledged in his preface could hardly be the source of all this clothmaking knowledge, much less malting, brewing and baking. In his discourse on wines, Markham discloses that he had "polished" a "rudely-written" treatise and perhaps a similar manuscript about spinning or malting fell into his hands at the stationer's. This polishing of practical information, whether derived from his own experience or others, was Markham's characteristic method. Though much of his content was empirical, he was also a compiler, and his compilations were valued as much for their currency and craftmanship as their contents. As his first editions were issued in "best-of" anthologies, Markham emphasized his constant editing in his addresses to his readers, assuring them that what they were about to read was "neither epitome, relation, extraction, nor repetition," but rather a "plain form of doing things by a nearer and more easy and safer way than ever had hitherto been discovered." Making the path towards knowledge ever more manifest was the goal of both Markham and the genre in which he was working, illustrating the shifting epistemological focus from memory to book. There are many references in Markham's works to aiding memory, or the burden on the memory: all of his polishing and epitomizing was for that purpose, but he also included the occasional Tusser-like rhyme. Occasionally he asserted that his books *were* memories, portable, physical objects that a man could keep in his pocket and access at any time: "for in sober truth, this Book is fit for every Gentleman, Husbandman, and good man's pocket, being a memory which a man carrying about him will when it is called to account, give a man full satisfaction, whether it be in the field, in the town, or any other place where a man is most unprovided."[64] In a utilitarian twist on commonplace books, fashioned of excerpts of great works to fortify memory, the pocket memory/pocket book metaphor was referenced increasingly over the seventeenth century, illustrating the effective containment and consequential commercialization of knowledge.

6

The Knowledge-Mongers

In the introduction to his *Catalogue of the most vendible books in England*, the bookseller William London asserted that "there's nothing comparable to the purchase of Knowledge, and whenever men begin to taste it, they will say I speak truth with a witness."[1] If knowledge could indeed be purchased, as a commodity and in the form of a book, then it could also be sold, by a "knowledge-monger" in the phrase of Gabriel Plattes, the author of several tracts on mining and soil amendment published just before the English Revolution. Plattes was not a compiler, and he was not interested in producing compendia for the sake of reference or his reputation: his works were pure discourses of information gathered from his own experience in the mines or the fields published for individual and collective enrichment. He was not enriched by their publication himself and died impoverished (and by some accounts *shirtless*) on the streets of London, just a few years after a much more prolific, but apparently equally poor, Gervase Markham. Plattes's association with Samuel Harlib led to the publication of his utopian *Description of the famous Kingdome of Macaria* under the latter's name, but also to the republication of his works posthumously.

In both his work on mining and metallurgy, *A discovery of subterraneall treasure*, and his text on husbandry, *A discovery of infinite treasure, hidden since the vvorlds beginning*, Plattes pursued the theme of underutilized resources lying underneath the soil and in plain sight. Knowledge—his knowledge—was the key to finding these treasures: techniques of mineral detection and refining, soil amendment and the "sowing and setting of profitable seeds" developed through his years of observation and experimentation would uncover them. There is no evidence that Plattes was university-educated, but his references point to reading contemporary cosmographical and geographical texts, and he loved to use medical allegories: in *A discovery of infinite treasure*, he expressed his desire "to turn plow-men into philosophers, and to make them excel their predecessors, even as a Learned Physician excels Empericks." He offered alchemical analyses of the earth's composition and Galenic remedies for restoring the "fatness" of the earth's soil through a combination of contrary fertilizers. He was as detailed about different regions of England as different kinds of manure. Plattes was part-environmentalist, part-pacifist, all idealist and very attuned to contemporary social conditions: not only did he want to turn plowmen into philosophers, but also swords into ploughshares, as a focus on increasing the fertility and productivity of the soil would transform the "over-peopled" commonwealth of England into a self-sufficient kingdom no longer intent on making "violent incursions upon others' territories." He envisioned a better world, in which everyone would "break our swords, and instruments of War, into Ploughshares, and other instruments of Husbandry and would spend the charges of Gunpowder, Shot, &c. in the building, repairing, and beautifying of Churches; and turn the noise of Drums and Cannon, into Hallelujahs."[2]

Gabriel Plattes had big dreams, but he was also practical in his recommendations: put all the people suffering from want of food and employment to work in intensive mining and agricultural operations, which would produce treasuries of metals, minerals and crops and keep it going: *generate* wealth for all. The argument for wealth by creation rather than by extraction was obviously stronger in his agricultural treatise, *A discovery of infinite treasure*, where he made the case that even the New World was an insufficient valve for overpopulation in the Old: agricultural production must be intensified through enclosure, improved landlord–tenant relations, and as always, the enrichment of the soil by both natural and mechanical means. He was also very much in the timber-shortage camp and believed that timber and fruit trees could serve as hedgerows, and as focused on the eradication of pests and prevention of mildew as any agricultural author. In his consideration of the common occurrence of powdery mildew, he believed that he had a remedy, but had not "brought the experiment to full perfection." So he asked for volunteers, expressing not only his process but also his identity in doing so:

> if anyone will try this experiment fully, that has better opportunity than I have, and then publish it for the general good, he shall be my brother; for that we are both of a Trade, or profession, which shall be called Knowledge-mongers, differing from Fishmongers, Iron-mongers, &c. in that we pay so dear for our wares, and give them away for nothing, which is the cause why we thrive no better of our Trades; but let us not be disheartened, for we will lay our heads together, to bring our Trade into request, by laying open the benefit of our Inventions, and by discovering the vanity of other devices, where one man's gain comes by another's loss; so will the Major part come to us, through their good dispositions, and love to virtue, honesty, and goodness, and so the rest must come to us by force, or else want and poverty will expel them out of the School of Husbandry; and we will comfort ourselves in the meantime, with the incomparable joy of a good conscience, and fear no disaster in our enterprise, assuring ourselves, that God is on our sides, and so conclude with the saying, *Si Deus nobiscum quis contra nos?*[3]

Because of the emphasis on experimentation, Plattes seems to be using the occupational phrase "knowledge-monger" in such a way to suggest a "lowly" or perhaps "middling" *virtuouso*, not in the continental manner or that of Henry Peacham's *Complete Gentleman* but rather of Robert Boyle, who observed that Parisian *virtuosi* "were very intent upon the examination of the interest of the air, in hindering the descent of quick-silver, in the famous experiment touching a vacuum."[4] The examinations and experiments of Plattes were by contrast thoroughly grounded.

Given that knowledge had become associated with personal expertise by the seventeenth century, Plattes's identity was connected to the trades he was representing, even if he wasn't practicing them at the time. He also might have identified himself as a "mechanic": certainly the organization of bookseller William London catalogue of vendible books supports that designation. Following the early modern preoccupation with order, London laid out a conventional classification of England's best-selling books that also represents the classification of knowledge: the two major classes are divine (accounting for more than half the books in the catalogue) and humane knowledge, and the latter is divided into History, Poetry, Law, Physic and Mathematics. By this time, algebra was recognized as one of the three key mathematical arts, along with arithmetic and geometry. Derived from physic and geometry are distillation, alchemy, and chemistry, astronomy, astrology, music, optics, dialing, geography, architecture, and mechanics—and the essential husbandry, navigation and military discipline were additional derivatives of mechanics. The physic and mathematics categories account for an eighth of the total books listed, and these are subjects that have formed the foundation of this book. London divided his wares in other ways apart from this content classification: he asserted that knowledge could be pursued for profit or for pleasure, and in particular and in general. These are useful categories to explore and assess the long history of knowledge-mongering over the entire 1500–1640 period.

Because the most popular texts about health, regimens, advocated both knowledge and practice they impacted the presentation of all practical information throughout our period. They constituted a conservative genre, structured around prescriptions for the Galenic "non-naturals," but at the same time gave their readers "rules" by which they could govern their own health. Regimens were assembled from various classical and medieval texts, and the first popular title, Thomas Elyot's *The castel of helth*, was the standard for the rest in both its format and accessible language: Elyot was a courtier whose ambitions for "service" were fulfilled both in appointments and print. He was in the first generation of England's knowledge-mongers, translating useful texts out of Latin and Italian into English for public use. Translation was a key act and ability of knowledge-mongering throughout the sixteenth century and well into the seventeenth: from ancient texts on just about every subject, from Italian mathematical texts and books of "secrets," from Dutch texts on husbandry and navigation. To be a knowledge-monger in the sixteenth century was for the most part to be a translator, engaged essentially in "Englishing" and "gathering," or compiling. Elyot was gifted at both endeavors, but he faced criticism from physicians, organized in their recently chartered College, for providing laymen with the tools of self-diagnosis. This was the first clash between an amateur and professionals over the transmission of knowledge, and professional expertise, gained by both learning and experience, would gradually emerge as a credential for authority over our period. The popularity of *The castel of helth* led to other consequential developments: the four humours of Galenic medicine were diffused into English literary culture and English physicians entered the realm of print, publishing for both their colleagues in Latin and a wider audience in English.

Medical publishing was not medical practice. The College of Physicians was granted powers of license and censor by its 1518 royal charter and its statutory confirmation in 1523, which also extended the College's jurisdiction to the entire kingdom. The College worked with the Crown to confirm its preeminence over the other incorporated medical practitioners in London, the barber-surgeons and apothecaries, over the sixteenth and seventeenth centuries, but it was impossible for what was essentially a learned society to control the provision of medicine or medical advice over this period, and the College did not obtain approval over medical publishing until 1687. Medical texts were thus part of the crowded and often-confusing medical "marketplace," and those physicians who chose to advertise or expand their practices via print had to convince their readers, or at least claim, that their knowledge was superior to that of their competitors. A succession of regimens, published by both practicing physicians and laymen, utilized the basic format of the non-naturals and offered suggestions for the optimal location of one's house, diet, hours of sleep and activity, "evacuations," and emotional state in accordance with dynamic variables like current epidemics or newly discovered foodstuffs or *materia medica*, occupation, age and physical health: there were regimens for university students, prospective colonists, and those in frail health or focused on attaining longevity of life in an anxious age. The adaption of the genre with particular English details and varied formats by Elyot's immediate successors, Andrew Boorde and William Bullein (both of whom practiced medicine but were not fellows of the College), combined with slim books of simple recipes like Thomas Moulton's *Myrour or glasse of helth* paved the way for the popular "every man his own doctor" texts issued throughout the seventeenth century. Regimens represent the most general and malleable of medical texts in the early modern era, and also the most practical, as they prescribed a course of behavior or conduct employed in order to achieve a desired result: the preservation of health and the extension of life. It was possible for their authors, or compilers, to integrate criticism, commentary, and new commodities to a certain extent, but the medical challenges and trends of the era provoked more focused texts as well, inspired by another late medieval genre, the plague tract. The most eminent Galenist of the sixteenth century, John Caius, took on the mysterious English Sweating Sickness, Bullein wrote on both the plague and pleurisy, Thomas Raynalde's *Byrth of mankynde*, an annotated translation of Eucharius Rösslin's pioneering *Der Rosengarten*, became the standard English midwifery text for over a century following its first illustrated edition in 1545. The preservation of eyesight was the subject of a series of treatises commencing with that of Queen Elizabeth's physician, Walter Bayley, in 1586, John Jones employed Thomas Elyot's format of branching diagrams to classify the many fevers plaguing English men and women in his *Dial for all agues*, and the newest and most threatening of diseases, syphilis, was the focus of surgeon William Clowes in *A short and profitable treatise touching the cure of the disease called (Morbus Gallicus), by unctions* (1579), who also diagnosed the "King's Evil" at the end of his career.

Medical publications were also inspired by conflict among medical practitioners: between those who were licensed and "irregular," between the College of Physicians and members of its subordinate guilds, the Barber-Surgeons and Apothecaries, who refused to behave as such, and between advocates of the new chemical medicine associated with Paracelsus and traditional Galenists. Elizabethan surgeons such as William Clowes, George Baker, and John Banister became public advocates for both a more empirical approach and the integration of Paracelsian cures into medical practice. Their battlefield and hospital experience, combined with their treatment of the topical symptoms of plague and syphilis, led them to promote more potent chemical and mineral medicines in publications such as Baker's *Newe iewell of health*, a translation of part of Conrad Gessner's *The treasure of Euonymus*. This "jewel," along with its dedications, endorsements, and companion volumes, illustrated the existence of a circle of practitioners turned knowledge-mongers focused on a practical Paracelsianism characterized primarily by the belief in the superiority of compound distillations of minerals for both "inward" and "outward" diseases: Baker asserted that "we see plainly before our eyes, that the virtues of medicines by Chemical distillation are made more valuable, better, and of more efficacy than those medicines which are in use, and accustomed."[5] Baker acknowledged the "pains" of Thomas Hyll, a prolific translator and author of England's first gardening manual, as well as the work of apothecary John Hester, another translator-practitioner who supplied distillations "to the furtherance of my patients' health." Hyll also translated a collection of distilled plague remedies by the Italian surgeon Leonardo Fioravanti as *A ioyfull iewell*, which was edited by Hester, who produced two Paracelsian translations himself. Though distilled waters, oils and quintessences proved to be no better at treating plague and other endemic diseases than the remedies of the "old physick," the focus on process in sixteenth-century distillation texts led to a more widespread application of iatrochemical practices. A half century later, William London classified distillation, alchemy, and chemistry as separate arts derived from physick.

Distillation was a key by-product of the dynamic pattern of publications relating to the preservation and restoration of health in the sixteenth century, but even more foundational to a range of pursuits was arithmetic, the "ground" of arts according to the title of the popular textbook of Robert Recorde. *The Ground of artes* (1543) was issued in 45 editions by the end of the seventeenth century, including epitomized editions marketed to merchants. Recorde initiated a tradition of the mathematician-in-service in early modern England: he served as a public mint administrator as well as a consultant to the first joint-stock company, the Muscovy Company. Recorde also initiated a more pedagogical approach to knowledge-mongering: he followed up *The Ground of artes* with texts on geometry and spherical astronomy and intended to publish works on cartography and surveying. He utilized dialogue, a classical approach refined in myriad Renaissance texts, in a particularly accessible way and always stressed applications: a lost work, *The Gate of knowledge*, was reportedly devoted to practical geometry, which was generally perceived as the art of measuring anything and everything by contemporaries, and measurement by the quadrant, a fundamental task of navigation.[6] The famous "Mathematical Praeface" of Recorde's "augmenter" John Dee, the introduction to the first English translation of Euclid's *Elements of geometrie* by Henry Billingsley, laid out a classification based on Recorde's applications from arithmetic and geometry which became standard, and was certainly the inspiration for William London's catalogue.

Mensuration in all of its forms, surveying, dialing, gauging, navigation, was an increasingly integral part of life in early modern England, and the most practical pursuit of applied mathematics. Not only was it a commercial and consequential practice, but it generally involved the use and making of instruments as these skills evolved over the sixteenth century and into the seventeenth, merging information culture with technology. The most literal example of this merger was John Blagrave's *The mathematical ievvel* (1585), which is simultaneously a book and an instrument (a stereographic astrolabe) both of which could "lead any man practising thereon, the direct pathway (from the first step to the last) through the whole Arts of Astronomy, Cosmography, Geography, Topography, Navigation, Longitudes of Regions, Dialling, Sphericall Triangles, Setting figures, and briefly whatsoever concerns the Globe or the Sphere."[7] Blagrave was writing in the midst of an extraordinary era of convergence of mathematical practitioners and pursuits: a time when it seemed possible for both scholars and craftsmen to master measuring and its means, whether on land, at sea, or gazing up at the heavens. Measuring was the fundamental step towards the mastery of nature, and as it required observation but also artifice and interpretation it enabled mere mechanics to possess the expertise of a scholar. As the scholar and "professional reader" Gabriel Harvey wrote in the margins of his copy of Blagrave's *Jewel*: "Scholars have their books & practitioners their learning."[8] The prolific annotator Harvey praised a long list of exemplary

English artisans like Blagrave in the margins of another manuscript, and coined his own word, *polytechnoscopy*, for a novel "art" that combined theoretical and practical knowledge and book learning with craft skill. He listed English exemplars, or "polymechanists":

> Astronomical instruments made & sold in London by Humphrey Cole & M. [James] Kynvyn, artificial workmen. Geometrical tables by John Read, John Reynolds & Christopher Paine, fine artificers, John Shute a skillful architect. Matthew Baker a cunning shipwright. William Bourne & Robert Norman, artificial Navigators, Bourne, also an excellent gunner, like or beyond Tartalea [Niccolò Tartaglia, mathematician and master of its myriad applications]. M. Keymis and John Hester, fine Chemists. Some other cunning, & subtle Empirics of less fame M. [Richard] Benese, M. Digges, M. Blagrave, M. Lucar & Valentine Leigh, artificial & expert Surveyors. But most of these fine Geometricians & greater artists: especially Digges, Blagrave, Lucar. As notable mathematical practitioners and polymechanists, as the most commended beyond the sea.[9]

Among his notable masters of artifice, Harvey presented the progression of one venerable art, surveying, and the emergence of a relatively new one, ballistics: both dependent on the parallel progress of mathematical practice. It was quite a claim to proclaim William Bourne as "beyond" Niccolò Tartaglia, a pioneer in the mathematical analysis of projectiles, as most of Bourne's work on navigation (Figure 10), surveying, and artillery was derivative: his *The Arte of shooting in great Ordnaunce* (1578) was largely based on Tartaglia. Bourne possessed just enough empirical experience necessary to present himself as expert in several fields, but more important for his career as a knowledge-monger was his consistent commitment to epitomizing and illustrating technical works like that of Tartaglia for practical use. Cyprian Lucar, also referenced by Harvey twice, published *Three bookes of colloquies concerning the arte of shooting in great and small peeces of artillerie*, an augmented translation of Tartaglia's *Nuova Scienzia*, in the year of the Armada, offering up a "martial book" for "these martial times." Both Bourne and Lucar benefitted from the applied mathematical texts published by the father–son succession of Leonard and Thomas Digges, starting with the former Digges's *Tectonicon* in 1556. Like his contemporary Robert Recorde, Leonard Digges was focused on mathematical instruction for a wider audience, advertising his text as "most 'conducible' for surveyors, landemeaters, joyners, carpenters, and masons" for both its arithmetic and its direction in the construction and use of instruments such as the carpenter's rule, the square, and a cross-staff called the "profitable staff". Quite logically, Digges followed up with a geometrical treatise, or "practise" called *Pantometria* (1571), which was published posthumously with additions by his son Thomas Digges. The final text of the Digges "collaborative" trilogy, *Stratioticos* (1579), applied arithmetic

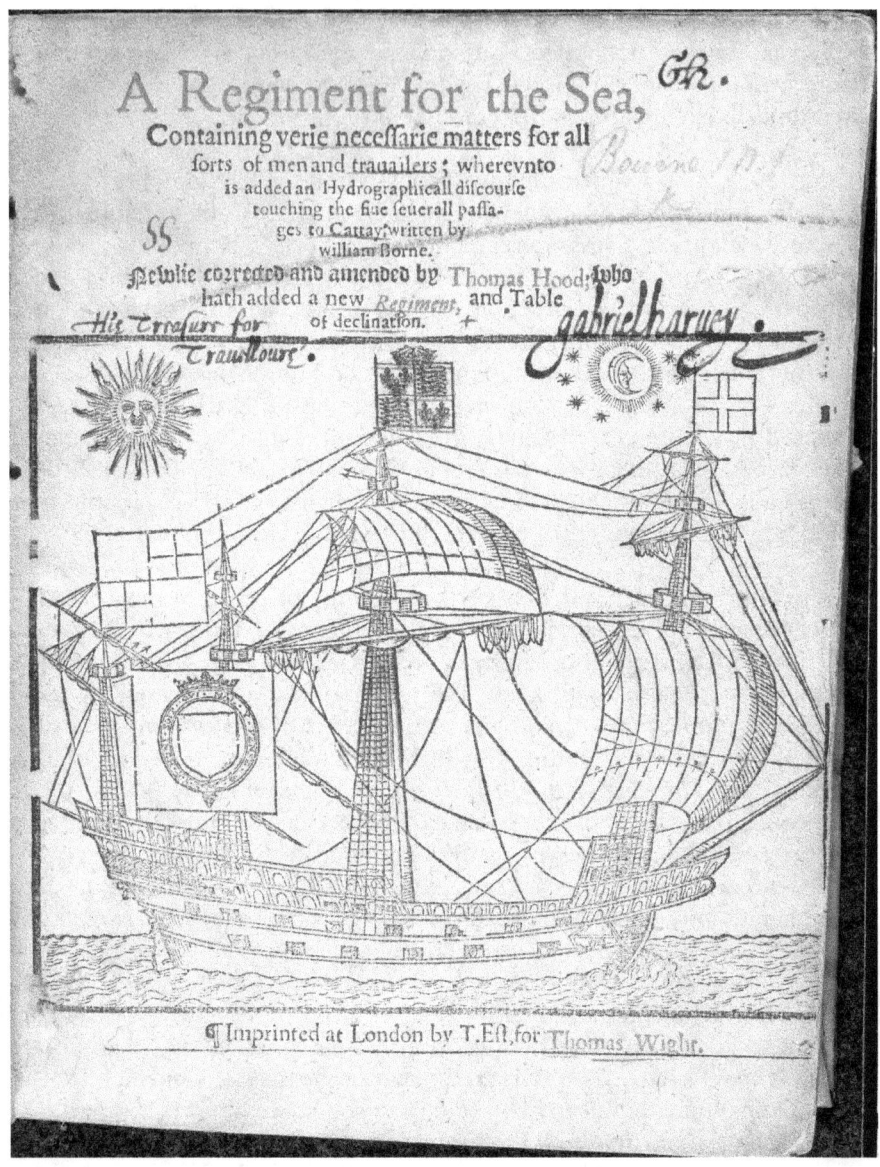

FIGURE 10 *William Bourne (c. 1535–1582), Gabriel Harvey's copy of William Bourne's* Regiment for the Sea *(London, 1592), title page.* © *British Library / Bridgeman Images.*

and algebra to military formations and expressed Thomas Digges's desire to engage "in reducing the Sciences Mathematical from Demonstrative Contemplations to Experimental Actions, for the Service of my Prince and Country," and in the public sphere.

Harvey's "polymechanists" did not really catch on but it was an apt term: it is often difficult to pin down the precise activity or discipline of mathematical practitioners: there was considerable overlap in their endeavors as they learned new skills. The ideal early Stuart surveyor was very different than his early Tudor predecessor: not only did he have to measure the parcel, with more sophisticated instruments, but he had to draw a plat, or plan, to scale. Surveyed land in the seventeenth century was not land that was merely measured and described in text and in terms of its topography and tenure; it was land that was mapped, using mathematical knowledge and instruments. The making of a land plat involved skills necessary for mapping the coastline to produce a sea chart, or a city map, or a plan for a ship or a building. John Dee expressed characteristic Renaissance respect for architecture as an art and a science in his masterful "Mathematical Praeface," given that it was both creative and mathematical and the architect was "the judge of all artificial works and all artificers." He outlined all the mathematical derivatives in text and diagram, some of which (trochilike, zogographie) seem obscure then as now, but "under the direction" of the all-encompassing architecture were the "three principal necessary Mechanical Arts. Namely Housing, Fortification, and Naupegie (shipbuilding)."[10] Carpentry remained a trade secret for most of our period, and both naval architecture and architecture in general were too rarified pursuits to generate more than a handful of instructional texts before the later seventeenth century, but John Shute, who authored England's first architectural treatise following his Italian grand tour, expressed the integration of those disciplines, including his own, grounded in mathematics when he asserted that diverse "rational" arts were bound by a "certain kindred & affinity."[11] The "kindred and affinity" between surveying and cartography was increasingly apparent throughout the sixteenth century, due not only to all those private plats, but to the major Tudor public works projects, the fortification of the southern and eastern coasts during Henry VIII's reign, and the reconstruction of Dover Harbor under Elizabeth, a project which was partially overseen by Thomas Digges after he made his "public mathematician" pledge. Several of the most active and authoritative surveyors of the sixteenth and early seventeenth centuries, Ralph Agas, John Norden and Aaron Rathborne, were all practitioners, knowledge-mongering authors very concerned with establishing standards for their profession, and cartographers, or in the case of Rathborne, a patent-holder and prospective mapmaker.[12] All three authors stressed both the geometrical foundations of their practice, Agas even going so far so say that it was a "new" profession, made new by mathematical knowledge and instruments. Once the surveyor had mastered those tools, the applications were infinite. Cyprian Lucar, the last of Gabriel Harvey's "fine geometricians and greater artists," presented a diagram-full instruction of how to measure and plat virtually any landscape in *A Treatise named Lucarsolace* (1590) and then proceeded to engage in a series of geometrical demonstrations, which led him to applications such as "how a dwelling house in the country may for the preservation of health be situated and built, and how the tunnel of a chimney may be made so no smoke shall annoy you within your house."[13] Lucar's consideration of the diverse ways to access water, including a way in which sea water "may be made fresh," led him to a brief digression into fire-fighting with "a type of a squirt which has been devised to cast much water upon a burning house" and other means of diverting or draining water. It is apparent from his fervent prose that Lucar could have gone on and on, but "for want of good health" he concluded, reiterating his belief that the reader "may learn from my four books of *Lucarsolace* to invent new works, strange engines and instruments, not only for private pleasure, but also for sundry purposes in the commonwealth & if he be an artificer, to the better maintenance of his estate." (Figure 11).[14]

Artificer was a more relevant term than "polymechanist," but "mechanic" was just as applicable. As Lucar's closing remarks indicate, however, there was a social divide between gentlemen "mechanical philosophers" who wrote about mathematics and all of its many applications "for private pleasure" and the mechanics themselves. Yet the essence of both mechanical

FIGURE 11 *Cyprian Lucar (1544–1611?), A Treatise named Lucarsolace (London, 1590), pp. 156–157. Used by permission of the Folger Shakespeare Library under a Creative Commons Attribution-ShareAlike 4.0 International License.*

philosophy and mechanical work was the alteration or manipulation of nature, rather than merely its observation or description: to reiterate Bacon's definition, it was nature "altered or wrought" by both the art and the hand of man. Decades after Bacon, both this conception and all the geometrical "grounding" texts that preceded and postceded him caused the provincial bookseller William London to place mechanics as the last derivative of geometry, and list husbandry, navigation, military discipline as its offshoots. The two most popular knowledge-mongers of our period, Thomas Tusser and Gervase Markham, became so because they were offering advice about the primary sector of the English economy in the context of rising land values, rising population, and the increasing commercialization of agriculture. Neither was offering anything new, but their success opened up opportunities for those who were, particularly during the protracted famine of the late Elizabethan era, when gentlemen experimental agronomists such as Richard Gardiner, John Taverner, and Hugh Plat advocated for enhanced kitchen gardens, more cultivation and consumption of root crops, the maintenance of fish ponds and orchards, and soil amendment and improvement. Even more so than Cyprian Lucar, Plat's many works make it difficult to categorize both the man and his pursuits: on the one hand he was very much the Elizabethan/Jacobean "projector" in the positive rather than pejorative sense and on the other merely an old-fashioned purveyor of remedies, though for distilled fragrant waters and the preservation and preparation of fruit rather than the preservation and restoration of health.[15] Plat's two most popular works, *The jewell house of art and nature* (1594) and *Delights for ladies* (1600), represent the spectrum of his interests and "inventions," including everything from dentures and toothpaste to a portable bridge and methods to preserve virtually any food or beverage for extended periods of time. The latter books of *The jewell house* contain his more serious recommendations for agricultural, chemical, and metallurgical innovations proffered for the public good and the national interest, though in a perfect illustration of the vendibility of practical knowledge he withheld some of his inventions with promises "to disclose upon reasonable considerations."[16]

Plat positioned himself between the scholars and the practitioners: as Thomas Elyot and the first generation of English knowledge-mongers were intermediaries between the ancient authorities and their readers, he was a conduit between contemporary authorities and his "studious and well-affected" readers. In his last work, the gardening treatise *Floraes paradise* (1608), he contrasted his succinct directions for the cultivation of flowers, herbs, seeds and trees with those of the unnamed Schoolmen, "who have already written many large and methodical volumes of this subject (whose labors have greatly furnished our Studies and Libraries, but little or nothing altered or graced our Gardens and Orchards)" and appealed to "those that seek out the practical, and operative part of Nature, whereunto but a few in many ages have attained, then formally and largely, to imitate her Theorists, of whom each age affords great store and plenty."[17] The preference for practice over theory was a mainstay of agricultural publications and in many ways Plat's content and range of work was previewed by that of Leonard Mascall, whose *A Booke of the art and maner, howe to plante and graffe all sortes of trees* was published in 14 editions from 1569 to 1656. Mascall was more of a translator than an experimenter but he was also an intermediary of practice: his *Booke* was based on his translations of *L'art et maniere de semer, et faire pepinieres des sauvageaux* by Davy Brossard and other continental works on arboriculture, a subject in which there was considerable interest in later Elizabethan England due to the emphasis on fruit-tree cultivation in the face of famine and general, and increasing, concerns of deforestation. Mascall followed up with books on animal husbandry, fishing, vermin-trapping, medical recipes, and, with the same ease demonstrated by Plat as he ventured into the domestic realm with *Delights for ladies*, a book on stain-removal and dyeing methods for cloth, all translations of contemporary continental authors with the exception of the fishing manual *A Booke of fishing with hooke and line* (1590), which was based on the late medieval English *Treatyse of fysshynge wyth an angle*.

Mascall's many works served as source material for the even more prolific Gervase Markham, but both authors' works, as well as those of Hugh Plat, were the basis of an expanding genre of texts for the "Countryman" published from the 1620s onward: works which emphasized "recreation" over "calling" and pleasure over profit. This was a genre largely created by Markham, but Plat's and Mascall's works were repackaged and republished long after their deaths to add to its volumes. Mascall's tree-grafting tract was republished in 1640 along with several other agricultural treatises, including Reynalde Scot's *Perfite Platform for a Hop Garden*, in *The country-mans recreation, or the art of planting, graffing, and gardening* and Plat's *Floraes Paradise* was reissued as *The Garden of Eden* in several editions beginning in 1652. Recreational texts did not cater only to country gentlemen: there were various compendia of diverse recreations encompassing everything from fireworks to waterworks published in the early seventeenth century as well, of both derivative and experimental natures. John Bate's *The mysteryes of nature, and art conteined in foure severall tretises*, including waterworks, fireworks, drawing, painting and engraving, and "extravagants," a collection of rather random recipes and tricks like "how to make birds drunk so that you may take them with your hands," and invisible ink, was "partly collected, and partly of the author's Peculiar Practice and Invention" and published in three editions beginning in 1634.[18] The whimsical inventions of the fourth book of *The mysteryes of nature* contrast quite sharply with those of the first, including engines that could manipulate and master water in all sorts of ways, illustrated with technical detail in the book's wonderful second edition. There is an engine, similar to the fire-fighting device of Cyprian Lucar, "which being placed in water will cast the same with violence on high," and another which could force spring water up to the top of a hill. But then, without much transition, Bate proceeded to inventions that could produce sounds from water only to conclude with the more practical weather-glasses and water-clocks. Like another contemporary treatise, *A treatise of artificial fire-vvorks both for vvarres and recreation*, Bate included a useful "device to try the strength of diverse sorts of Gunpowder" in his second book on fireworks, along with instructions for creating stars, dragons, and swords in the sky. Seventeenth-century technical compendia like Bate's *Mysteryes*, along with the mathematical instrument texts that preceded them, are illustrative of the technical groundwork laid for more intensive mechanization and industrialization a century later.

"Military discipline", another derivative of mechanics according to London's catalog, was a transitional term first introduced by Thomas Digges, mathematician, astronomer, surveyor, and member of Parliament, based on his experience serving with his patron Robert Dudley, the Earl of Leicester, in the Netherlands during the Dutch Revolt. As Muster-Master from 1585–1588 he observed very disorderly and ineffective soldiers, far removed from the ideal military he envisioned in his *Stratioticos* (1579). When he returned to England he wrote several tracts about his experiences and observations and revised *Stratioticos* for a second edition (1590) but he died before he could expand upon his ideas about the reform of the military. Just as he continued his father Leonard's work, his son Dudley continued his, and the two paradoxes of *Foure paradoxes, or politique discourses 2 concerning militarie discipline, written long since by Thomas Digges Esquire* was published in 1604. While Digges the Elder acknowledged that the "late invention of Artillery, or fire-shot" had altered the nature of modern warfare altogether, he still believed that ancient authority could serve as a precedent for the "new Modern Martial Discipline" that was required in this age of "fiery wars." He admired the citizen soldiers, meritorious advancement, long training, orderly encampments, commanders on foot rather than horseback, regimented collection of the spoils of war rather than the contemporary "catch as catch can" pillaging, and soldiers-in-arms bonds of ancient armies, as opposed to the bands of mercenaries and "freebooters" he observed in his own time, asserting that "it is manifest how great a difference there is between that Ancient Discipline (whereby mean and poor Estates were advanced to mighty Monarchies) and these Modern corruptions (whereby flourishing States have been spoiled and defaced, and mighty Realms and Empires brought to ruin.)"[19] When Digges referred to "military discipline" he meant discipline in deed, but successive texts in the genre utilized the term to refer more to formations, techniques and tactics. Another veteran turned knowledge-monger, Gervase Markham, entered the field with *The souldiers accidence. Or an introduction into military discipline containing the first principles and necessary knowledge meete for captaines, muster-masters, and all young souldiers of the infantrie* in 1625, focusing primarily on action: arming, outfitting, training, marching, following directions, charging, shooting, opening and closing ranks, and all the proper postures for each soldier. This was military discipline in the seventeenth century: in the era of "fiery wars" there was enough to learn without going back into the annals of ancient generals, the examples of "the latest and best experienced armies" were more relevant.[20] The Renaissance was over, but a military "revolution" was ongoing.

A slight variation on the classifications of William London and John Dee was James Howell's assessment that "the most material and useful parts of Mathematics" were "the Art of Navigation and Fortification." Howell continued with an assertion that often surfaced in texts dedicated to the history and practice of navigation, which he deemed was "more useful and important for Englishmen, and indeed for all Islanders, than others, because their security depends upon the Sea, and upon Wooden Horses."[21] In the middle of the seventeenth century, navigation seemed so central to the kingdom's prosperity and identity, whereas a century before it was seldom referenced. England became a navigating nation in the Elizabethan era, and this relatively late entry into the open seas meant that it could profit from the Spanish experience to a certain extent: Richard Eden's translation of the *Breve compendio de la sphera y de la arte de navegar* by Martin Cortés in 1561 is generally seen as the beginning of a dynamic discourse on mathematical navigation through which English navigators chartered their own course, based with plenty of empirical experience, mathematical theory and practice, and Dutch counsel. The challenges and opportunities presented by the navigation of the northern waters, which constituted England's primary terrain, created an interdisciplinary community of scholars, sailors, and instrument-makers, along with royal courtiers, all focused on the goal of claiming, and expanding, some sovereignty over the sea.

Because it was such a collaborative and consequential endeavor, both before and especially after the Armada, navigation and its literature heightened awareness of the public utility of knowledge and expertise in unprecedented ways. The perceived value of knowledge increased, as did the focus on its dissemination and presentation: in texts, in public lectures on the theory and practice of geometry at the new Gresham College, in the form of reference tables and sea charts, both updated consistently. There was an enhanced emphasis on the currency of both data and theories: updating, augmenting, and correcting had always been processes integrated with the transmission of knowledge via print, but they became part of a consistent practice in the later sixteenth and seventeenth centuries. The concluding chapter of Louis LeRoy's *Of the interchangeable course, or variety of things in the whole world*, translated by Robert Ashley in 1594, observes that there was plenty to be said that has not been said before, and "that we must by our own Inventions, augment the Doctrine of the Ancients: not contenting ourselves only with Translations, Expositions, Corrections, and Abridgements of their Writings." While some things were perpetual, much was in flux, "as there was never an age more happy for the advancement of learning, then this present." And so much was new:

new lands, new seas, new forms of men, manners, laws and customs: new diseases, and new remedies: new ways of the Heaven, and of the Ocean, never before found out, and new stars seen? Yea, and how many remain to be known by our Posterity? That which is now hidden, with time will come to light and our successors will wonder that we were ignorant of them.[22]

The art of navigation, as it developed in later Elizabethan England, was characterized by challenges both particular and universal: the reconciliation of traditional empirical seamanship with celestial navigation and current cartography, measuring magnetic variation, the ongoing quest for longitude, the logistics of long-distance travel on the open sea, the perpetual search for better instruments. Navigational texts had to be interdisciplinary, encompassing geometry, geography and cosmography with operational instructions, and systematic in their approach. The most popular textbook of the period, *A Regiment for the sea*, was not written by a famous sea captain or esteemed mathematician, but by a Gravesend gunner, William Bourne, a man who was the beneficiary of the mathematical works published by Robert Recorde and Leonard Digges. The *Regiment* was an adaptation of Cortés's *Breve Compendio* aimed at men like himself: practical, self-taught men, eager to go to sea. It laid out in simple (a word he himself utilized often) prose and sufficient detail cosmographical definitions and descriptions, how to make observations of the sun and stars and calculate the age of the moon and the tides, how to use an astrolabe and a cross-staff as well as the other "tools" at the navigator's disposal, including declination tables for the sun and the essential diagrams of the Regiment of the North Store and the Compass Circle, and how to find the entrance to the English Channel through the only way possible at the time, by taking soundings. Bourne in no way presented himself as the expert or even an expert, but more of an intermediary between the experienced seamen in his circle and a curious readership, as well as a gatherer, of the latest information and the best practices. Nothing was set in stone with the *Regiment*: Bourne corrected and augmented it with every edition and after his death, another revised edition was published with Thomas Hood, who was appointed the first "Mathematical Lecturer to the City of London," in 1588. As Hood's approach to navigation was thoroughly grounded in cosmography and geometry and he had previously published on globes, he was well-equipped to tackle some of the pressing problems of celestial navigation, but the key contribution to the reconciliation of contemporary cartography and practical navigation was made by another mathematical "lecturer," Edward Wright. In *Certaine errors in nauigation* (1599), Wright applied the Mercator map projection to the sea chart, rendering it more usable and consequently setting "the seal on the supremacy of the English in the theory and practice of the art of navigation" at the end of the sixteenth century.[23] This was the judgement of eighteenth-century and early nineteenth-century navigation texts, looking back to the origins of this supremacy and assessing Wright's constructions and calculations as "revolutionary" in bringing about the essential transition from "plane sailing" to "Mercator's sailing," which was, of course, global sailing. Two centuries later, *The New Practical Navigator* epitomized Wright's contribution succinctly: "The difficulty in constructing a true sea-chart consists in finding a proper manner of applying the surface of a globe to a plane; which Mr. Wright, an Englishman, by an ingenious conception, happily accomplished."[24]

The "art of merchandizing" does not rate in William London's catalog of vendible books, except perhaps for a passing reference to books about the "simple profits of the world," nor does Gabriel Harvey praise the ingenuity of any merchant in late Elizabethan London. Texts about trade and commerce, generally labeled under the phrase *ars mercatoria*, as well as those focused on the legal conduct and customs of trade or the *lex mercatoria*, did not encompass the realm and roles of the early modern merchant completely, so new texts emerged, with titles as variant as mercantile practice: the merchant's *aviso, mirror, handmaid, jewel, manual* were all published in the first few three decades of the seventeenth century, capped off by the comprehensive *The merchants mappe of commerce* of Lewes Roberts in 1638. The expansion of shipping and long-distance trade, combined with the increase of both chartered and joint-stock companies, created an environment of opportunity and competition, in which many different kinds of knowledge could be employed as a tool or a skill. Numeracy remained a "ground" of this new, composite art, and Robert Recorde's "ancient, ever-famous" arithmetic textbook, *Records arithmetick containing the ground of arts*, which emphasized applications in its very first edition, was epitomized and augmented in 1615 "with most brief rules of practice and others, necessary in the trade of Merchandise" including decimals, tables for timber measure, square and cubic roots, and the valuation of coins as well as "added Rules and Tables of Brevity and Practice brought into far briefer Method, then hitherto at any time has been published in our English tongue."[25] More arithmetic and accounting manuals were published for the use of merchants, as were singular texts of interest-rate tables in an age when there was still quite a bit of ambivalence about usury. That charged term was replaced with "interest" in the legislation of Henry VIII, and all economic texts in the sixteenth and seventeenth-centuries followed suit, enabling myriad variations: an updated and Englished version of Aristotle's *Politics* published in 1598 observed that "Men have now invented interest instead of usury, which is of diverse sorts, according to diverse places: for they limit in some places five for a hundred, in other places ten or twelve upon the hundred. The bankers or Merchants set it as high as they can."[26] In the first of a succession of texts and "ready reckoners" on increasingly diverse practices, the *Arithmeticall Questions* (1613) of Richard Witt, "practitioner in the art of numbers," included instruction in calculating compound interest along with tables, essential tools for men "trading with one another."[27]

Commerce was almost all-encompassing: very precise and practical texts were directed at the broad category of mercantile practice from the 1570s through the seventeenth century: texts on penmanship, letter-writing, gauging and weights and measures, languages, descriptive and cultural geography, currency exchange, and law. As we have seen, early modern texts were varied in their topics and their approaches: there was interdependence in the knowledge basis of several pursuits and disciplinary boundaries were still evolving. The recipes of sixteenth-century collections, whether gleaned from ancient or continental authorities or from their authors' experience, were medicinal, culinary, cleansing, preserving, and refreshing, and often very mundane. Revealing such "secrets" in print necessarily made them so, but some semblance of the secretive sense of artisanal practice is evident in directions to *craft*: to build or to make essentially. Given the prescriptive nature of advice literature and the limited literacy in early modern England there are not many glimpses into the culture of craftsmen beyond instrument engineering, but just as celestial navigation required its practitioners to have the knowledge of using and *making* instruments, there was an informational subgenre, or "cross-genre" of texts aimed at those who were in the business of crafting information or presentations, dispensing "stationary secrets" about writing, drawing, and making their own instruments and inks. Copy books and texts offering instruction in "fair," chancery and court handwriting belong to the realm of courtesy literature, but Martin Billingsley, author of the popular *The pen's excellencie, or the secretaries delight* seems to imply that there was some encroachment on his Art, which has been

> somewhat shadowed by the dullness of some Mechanicall spirits, who seldome have skill in anything out of their own element, that think Writing to be only a hand-labour, and so they can write to keep a dirty shop-book, they care for no more; never esteeming the commendable manner of faire and orderly Writing, which ought in all business to be observed, as well in keeping of Books for Merchants and others, as in all kind of Engrosments, appertaining to the Law, &c.[28]

Despite his disdain for "Mechanical spirits," he still asserted that "none ought to be without some knowledge" of writing, including women, and instructed his readers how to make the perfect pen. Ink recipes, for the invisible, the indestructible, and the commonplace, were included in more egalitarian and general texts like the *Widowes treasure* and the composite compendiums of Hugh Plat and John Bate: print facilitated scribal culture even as Billingsley judged the latter more worthy as a precedent of the former: "for as we say in Arithmetic, out of the greater the lesser is deducted."[29] This facile assimilation of literacy and numeracy might have been routine for a writing-master who was perhaps in service to Prince Charles and certainly the grand-nephew of the first English translator of Euclid's *Elements*, but those who aspired to practice the art of merchandising were expected to possess such skills and knowledge as well, according to a succession of early modern merchant manuals.

The Marchants avizo (1589) of Bristol merchant John Browne reflected the author's knowledge and experience of the Iberian trade and was addressed to a young merchant-in-training serving abroad: a scenario for which written communication was key. Literacy trumped numeracy as Browne expected his young factor to inform his master of everything he was doing and provided him with letter templates for every situation he might find himself in: delay, arrival, requests, expressions of gratitude or "general remembrance." Information was nearly as important a commodity as the actual, material commodities, and everything needed to be memorialized: merchants worked as much with paper as with wares. Browne provided templates for bills and other forms: of account, of exchange, of debt, of assurance, of obligation and acquittance. The young merchant needed to be knowledgeable about prices and exchange, and reconcile his accounts, but the only thing he was expected to calculate was his commission: at 2.5 percent. While Browne included information about exchanges and commodities, his emphasis was on brevity for this slim quarto, so the descriptions of wares take the form of tips, as for example the entry on cochineal, the wondrous American insect dye and a valuable Spanish monopoly at the time: "Note, that of Cochineal the largest & brightest gray or silver colour is best, and that which doth cast the quickest & most orient red in the palm of your hand, after you have rubbed and mingled it with a little spittle." It was always necessary to handle (or taste) the merchandise, and some knowledge could only be gained by experience, as was the case with wine, for which "it cannot be set down by pen or words, the right knowledge of it, for it is perceivable only by the taste and savor."[30] Browne's brevity likely made his *Avizo* more usable, but its Iberian focus leaves one wondering about the conduct of trade during war: it was reissued relatively quickly in 1590 and 1591, and then in three editions in the seventeenth century, after the close of the Anglo–Spanish War.

So much changed in terms of expectations and opportunities in the half-century between the publication of the first edition of Browne's *Avizo* in 1589 and that of a very different merchant manual, Lewes Roberts's *The merchants mappe of commerce*, in 1638. As the title reference to a *map* indicates, the latter text aimed to provide much more than just advice for a particular trade, as this term acquired a double meaning over the sixteenth century, literal and figurative: a geographical representation and the epitome of achievements or deficiencies. The poet and historian Samuel Daniel wrote of "this mighty volume of events" which "the world the universal map of deeds, strongly controls" and "the map of change and innovation" while Thomas Dekker referenced "the Map of a Country so pitifully distracted by the horror of a change" in his *The vvonderfull yeare. 1603*.[31] Decades later, Roberts produced a comprehensive guide to the vocation of a long-distance merchant while simultaneously characterizing the "art of merchandising" as a pedigreed practice encompassing many bodies of knowledge, of the world and of man. Apparently he started collecting material for his *Mappe* early in his career, and consequently it offered not only the standard topographical information sought by English travelers abroad, but also full details of local commodities, currency, weights and measures, and rates of exchange. It was an immediate success with the mercantile community, generating revised editions in 1671, 1677, and 1700 and fashioning the image of the worldly merchant for some time to come.[32]

Browne and Roberts were operating in different worlds. Browne's *The Marchants avizo* and Richard Hakluyt's *The Principall nauigations* were first published in the same year: just as the latter's advocacy for the colonization of the New World was consequential, so too were his accounts of the adventurous merchants in the East, including the travels of the Muscovy Company's agents Anthony Jenkinson, Richard Johnson, Alexander Kitchin, and Arthur Edwards, among others, in central Asia, and the exploits of John Newberry and Ralph Fitch in Persia, India, and beyond, which were published in the 1599 edition of the *Nauigations*. The Muscovy Company was joined by a succession of chartered and joint-stock trading companies, including the Eastland Company (1579), The Levant (1592), the East India Company (1600) and the Virginia Company (1606), creating demand for more "worldly" merchants able to navigate more complicated terms of trade. In the seventeenth century, Hakluyt's successor Samuel Purchas continued the travelogue tradition and kept the discourse of discovery current, most especially with the 1625 edition of *Pvrchas his pilgrimes In five bookes*, which showcased all of the "navigations, voyages, traffic, and discoveries of the English nation" along with the "modern diversifies professions of Christianity."[33] While most English merchants were contained to the counting house and the warehouse, Roberts was assembling his definitive text, and his own travels in the east and the west and service with the Levant and East India Companies informed his perspective.

The merchants mappe of commerce is a systematic work: a seventeenth-century text built on the foundations of the previous century's pioneering works of cosmographical, geographical, and mathematical instruction, combined with the author's empirical experience. Roberts gave his Art a history, raised it to the level of artifice, codified its rules, and expanded its knowledge base dramatically. Despite its ample size, it is still somewhat of an epitome of the wealth of practical and empirical knowledge existent in its time, given Roberts' range, that of a prospective scholar who was diverted "from the study of Arts to the study of Marts."[34] He laid down a geographical and cartographical foundation, indulged in a bit of navigation (apparently he was planning to expand upon that art in a forthcoming publication, which never came), and explains that each part of the world possesses commodities, both natural and artificial, which are "found fit for commerce and traffic." These commodities, combined with man's natural inclination to enrich himself (and time) had resulted in the Art of Merchandizing, which is pursued through knowledge (of the world and its potential wares) and practice through the means of weights and measures, evaluation, currency exchange, and account-keeping. Over time, the Art evolved from barter, to bargaining, to exchange, and throughout this evolution the knowledge required of the merchant-intermediary increased to include: shipping, storage, lading, insurance, and all sorts of accounting, with its "handmaid or usher," arithmetic, "in which whosoever is ignorant may not challenge to himself the Title of a Merchant, nor be said to have any judgement in the Art of Merchandizing, nor hardly deserve the attribute of a rational man."[35] These are the bare outlines of the map, and Roberts spends the rest of his compendious manual *filling in* the details, beginning with precise demonstrations of a merchant's working tools and then proceeding to the world of wares with a handy classification: the aforesaid natural and artificial, comprising goods that the earth produces with or without the labor of man, including the products of husbandry and those goods that are "wrought or perfected by Art of Mystery," including all handicrafts. These two types of goods can be further classified according to whether or not they are "staple and lasting commodities," like gems and metals, or "impairing and decaying commodities" like fish, fruit, and wine. Roberts shared the distinct early modern English concern for spoiled wine, for which so many texts supplied remedial recipes. There was an endless diversity of these classified commodities around the world, and as "this knowledge [was] so necessary to all that profess merchandizing," Roberts took his readers on a tour of the material world, commencing with the New World and proceeding back to the Old, through Africa, Asia and Europe, in order of familiarity. This tour was merely an introduction, as there was so much yet to know: along with their fellow travelers the navigators, merchants needed to observe, take it all in, and write it all down, contributing simultaneously to their emerging art and their own knowledge.

By the time that Lewes Roberts published his manual for merchants, there were two approaches to dispensing knowledge: both a product of the first century of print. The first approach was to collect, compile, classify and compend: and then present a finished product that could serve as permanent reference or continuous tool. The seventeenth-century commercial equivalents of Thomas Elyot's *The castel of helth* were books like James Warre's *The merchants hand-maide* and Nicolas Hunt's *The merchants ievvell*: instrument-books, consisting entirely of tables for ready-reckoning of commodity values, weights, measures, and exchange rates.[36] These books were updated by their authors, or compilers, rather than their readers, or purchasers, in contrast to a "workbook" like *The mariners mirrour*, which invited its readers to utilize its text as such, filling in information and expanding geographical and navigational knowledge while also facilitating their practice. *The mariners mirrour* in particular, and navigation manuals in general, represented a pathway to a dynamic, expansive, new world of knowledge, characteristic of the second approach to information retrieval and diffusion in the early modern era, which focused on discovery and documentation. As an art, a science, and an endeavor, navigation profited from the development of mathematical knowledge and practice in the sixteenth century, but also from the assertive empiricism evident in the works of scholars like William Turner, who paid tribute to the classical authorities while at the same time professing that he did not want to be "one of them which write of things which they never saw" in the preface to his pioneering *A new herball*. There was a lot to see out there in the world, and a lot to learn, for both a sixteenth-century physician/botanist and a seventeenth-century merchant.

The knowledgeable merchant was a Renaissance Man in Roberts's estimation: his judgement, developed through experience, education, and practice, could not be limited "within the compass of any one particular trade or Vocation: for herein must his mystery, skill and art exceed all other, as requiring by necessity a more general knowledge than any other tradesman." The merchant must be on a level with the fisherman, the husbandman, and the "meanest artificer" as well as those producers of "wares of value and consequence." He must know how commodities are gathered, kept, and preserved, and if they should become defective, transform them as alchemists or "Artsmasters, who before they will throw away their goods, when either they are in part decaying, or totally perishing, will try many ways and conclusions to rectify the defaults and defects thereof; sometimes by commixtures, compositions and helps, adding excellent good to the very worst, or sweet to sour, or one colour to another."[37] Not only did merchants have to know all about their wares, they had to be able to assess the market, or "the property and fitness of the place and time," in order to attain their primary goal, which was to make their own "knowledge and skill profitable and beneficial unto them," or turn a profit. Such universal knowledge, in Roberts's opinion, made the merchant's Art comparable to that of the Poets "whose excellency must consist in a cursory judgement in all sciences, and to be learned in all professions, the difference being that the Merchants skill, must be real, solid and substantial, and the Poets may be feigned and poetical."[38] The real, solid and substantial skills of this ideal merchant made him the exemplar of a practical renaissance, in the good company of improving husbandmen, provisioning housewives, practicing mathematicians, and all those who distilled and surveyed.

NOTES

Introduction: Jewels Abound

1   *The Ministers portion By William Sclater. Batchelar of Diuinity and minister of the word of God at Pitmister in Somerset* (Oxford, 1612), sig. E2r; Francis Bacon, "Of the Proficience and Advancement of Learning, Divine and Human" in *The Works of Francis Bacon, Baron of Verulam, Viscount St. Alban, and Lord High Chancellor of England*, in Ten Volumes (London: J. Johnson, 1803): Volume II, 155.

2   Lewis Bayly, *The practise of pietie directing a Christian how to walke that he may please God* (London, 1613); Henry Hammond, *A practicall catechisme* (Oxford, 1645).

3   *An epitome of Ortelivs his Theatre of the vvorld, vvherein the principal regions of the earth are described in smalle mappes. VVith a brief declaration annexed to ech mappe. And donne in more exact manner, then the lyke declarations in Latin, French, or other languages. It is also amplyfied with new mappes wanting in the Latin editions* (London, 1601).

4   Gervase Markham, *A vvay to get vvealth by approued rules of practice in good husbandry and huswiferie. Containing the foure principall offices which support and maintaine a familie. As I. The husbanding and inriching of all sorts of ground, [. . .] Also the preseruation of graine, and a computation of men and cattels labors. [. . .] II. The ordering and curing, with the natures, breeding, vse, & feeding of all sorts of cattell and fowle, fit for the vse of man: as also the riding and dieting of horses, either for warre or pleasure. III. The office of the English housewife [. . .] IIII. The office of planting and grafting, [. . .] The first three bookes gathered by G.M. The last by Mr. William Lawson, for the benefit of the empire of Great Britain* (London, 1625).

5   John Blagrave, *The mathematical ievvel shewing the making, and most excellent vse of a singuler instrument so called: in that it performeth with wonderfull dexteritie, whatsoeuer is to be done, either by quadrant, ship, circle, cylinder, ring, dyall, horoscope, astrolabe, sphere, globe, or any such like heretofore deuised* (London, 1585); one of the more spectacular jewel books was never published: George Waymouth's "Jewell of Artes," a bound manuscript of text and graphic illustrations of instruments and mathematical applications for war, navigation, and architecture presented to King James I by its author in 1604.

6   John Bate, *The mysteryes of nature, and art conteined in foure severall tretises, the first of water workes the second of fyer workes, the third of drawing,*

colouring, painting, and engrauing, the fourth of divers experiments, as wel serviceable as delightful: partly collected, and partly of the authors peculiar practice, and invention by I.B. (London, 1634).

7   Thomas Fuller, *Gnomologia: adagies and proverbs; wise sentences and witty sayings, ancient and modern, foreign and British* (London, 1732), 132.

8   Elizabeth Eisenstein, *The Printing Press as an Agent of Change: Communications and Cultural Transformations in Early Modern Europe* (Cambridge: Cambridge University Press, 1980), 243.

9   The literature on popular health, household, husbandry, horticulture and mechanical philosophy is vibrant, and includes: Rudolph Bell, *How to Do It: Guides to Good Living for Renaissance Italians* (Chicago: University of Chicago Press, 1999); Andrew McRae, *God Speed the Plough: The Representation of Agrarian England, 1500–1660* (Cambridge: Cambridge University Press, 1996); Margaret Schotte, *Sailing School: Navigating Science and Skill, 1550–800* (Baltimore: Johns Hopkins University Press, 2019); Deborah Harkness, *The Jewel House. Elizabethan London and the Scientific Revolution* (New Haven: Yale University Press, 2007); William Eamon, *Science and the Secrets of Nature: Books of Secrets in Medieval and Early Modern Culture* (Princeton: Princeton University Press, 1996); Allison B. Kavey, *Books of Secrets: Natural Philosophy in England, 1550–1600* (Champaign: University of Illinois Press, 2007); Elaine Leong and Alisha Rankin, eds., *Secrets and Knowledge in Medicine and Science, 1500–1800* (Burlington, VT: Ashgate, 2011); Michele DiMeo and Sarah Pennell, *Reading and Writing Recipe Books, 1500–1800* (Manchester: Manchester University Press, 2013); Anne Stobart, *Household Medicine in Seventeenth-century England* (London: Bloomsbury Academic, 2016); Paula Findlen, "Commerce, Art and Science in the Early Modern Cabinet of Curiosities," in *Merchants & Marvels: Commerce, Science and Art in Early Modern Europe*, ed. Pamela Smith and Paula Findlen (Abingdon, UK: Routledge, 2001): 297–323; and more recently Wendy Wall, *Recipes for Thought: Knowledge and Taste in the Early Modern English Kitchen* (Philadelphia: University of Pennsylvania Press, 2015); Elaine Leong, *Recipes and Everyday Knowledge: Medicine, Science, and the Household in Early Modern England* (Chicago: University of Chicago Press, 2018); and Frances E. Dolan, *Digging the Past: How and Why to Imagine Seventeenth-Century Agriculture* (Philadelphia: University of Pennsylvania Press, 2020).

10 See works above, and also: Charles Webster, ed., *Health, Medicine and Mortality in the Sixteenth Century* (Cambridge: Cambridge University Press, 1979); Andrew Wear, *Knowledge and Practice in English Medicine, 1550–1680* (Cambridge: Cambridge University Press, 2000); Ken Albala, *Eating Right in the Renaissance* (Berkeley: University of California Press, 2002); David Gentilcore, *Food and Health in Early Modern Europe. Diet, Medicine, and Society, 1450–1800* (London: Bloomsbury Academic, 2016); Eric Ash, *Power, Knowledge, and Expertise in Elizabethan England* (Baltimore: Johns Hopkins University Press, 2004); Pamela H. Smith and Benjamin Schmidt, eds., *Making Knowledge in Early Modern Europe: Practices, Objects, Texts, 1400–1800* (Chicago: University of Chicago Press, 2008).

11 Sebastian Brant, *The shyppe of fooles* (London, 1509), sig. B1v
12 William Eamon, "Science and Popular Culture in Sixteenth Century Italy: The 'Professors of Secrets' and Their Books," *Sixteenth Century Journal* 16, no. 4 (1985): 471–485.
13 The term is utilized by David W. Waters in his magisterial *The Art of Navigation in England in Elizabethan and Early Stuart Times* (New Haven: Yale University Press, 1958).
14 Thomas Elyot, *The castel of helth, gathered, and made by Syr Thomas Elyot knyghte, out of the chyefe authors of phisyke, wherby euerye man maye knowe the state of his owne body, the preseruation of helthe, and how to instructe wel his physytion in skynes, that he be not deceyued* (London, 1539); James Hart, *Klinikē, or The diet of the diseased. Divided into three bookes. VVherein is set downe at length the whole matter and nature of diet for those in health, but especially for the sicke; the aire, and other elements; meat and drinke, with divers other things; various controversies concerning this subject are discussed: besides many pleasant practicall and historicall relations, both of the authours owne and other mens, &c. as by the argument of each booke, the contents of the chapters, and a large table, may easily appeare* (London, 1633); The term "medical marketplace" was first used by Harold J. Cook to refer to the hierarchical and competitive medical landscape in seventeenth-century London and is now orthodoxy: *The Decline of the Old Medical Regime in Stuart London* (Ithaca, NY: Cornell University Press, 1986).
15 Thomas Moulton, *This is the myrour or glasse of helthe, necessary and nedefull for euery person to loke in, that wyll kepe theyr body from the syckenes of the pestilence* (London, 16 editions between 1531–1566); T.C., *An hospitall for the diseased. Wherein are to bee founde moste excellent and approued medicines, aswell emplasters of speciall vertue, as also notable potions or drinkes, and other comfortable receptes, bothe for the restitution and the preseruation of bodily healthe. Very necessary for this tyme of common plague and immortalitie, and for other tymes when occasion shall require* (London, 12 editions between 1579– 1638); A.T. Practitioner in Physic, *A rich store-house or treasury for the diseased. Wherein, are many approued medicines for diuers and sundry diseases, which haue been long hidden, and not come to light before this time. Now set foorth for the great benefit and comfort of the poorer sort of people that are not of abilitie to go to the physitions* (London, nine editions between 1596–1631).
16 T.C., *An hospitall for the diseased*, sig. A2r–v.
17 Thomas Elyot, *The castel of helth*; A.T, Practitioner in Physic, *A rich store-house or treasury for the diseased.*
18 Wendy Wall, "Renaissance National Husbandry: Gervase Markham and the Publication of England," *Sixteenth–century Journal* 27, no. 3 (1996): 767–785.
19 William London, *A catalogue of the most vendible books in England orderly and alphabetically digested under the heads of divinity, history, physick and chyrurgery, law, arithmetick, geometry, astrology . . .: with Hebrew, Greek and Latine for schools and scholars : the like work never yet performed by any :*

also, all sorts of globes, mapps of the world or in parts . . .: all to be sold by the author at his shop in New-Castle (London, 1657), sig. H3v.

20 Joan Thirsk, *Alternative Agriculture: A History from the Black Death to the Present Day* (New York: Oxford University Press, 1997); Hugh Plat, *Sundrie nevv and artificiall remedies against famine. Written by H.P. Esq. vppon thoccasion of this present dearth* (London, 1596), and *The nevv and admirable arte of setting of corne with all the necessarie tooles and other circumstances belonging to the same: the particular titles whereof, are set downe in the page following* (London, 1600); Richard Gardiner, *Profitable instructions for the manuring, sowing, and planting of kitchin gardens Very profitable for the commonwealth and greatly for the helpe and comfort of poore people. Gathered by Richard Gardner of Shrewsburie* (London, 1599).

21 Deborah E. Harkness. *The Jewel House: Elizabethan London and the Scientific Revolution* (New Haven: Yale University Press, 2007); Malcolm Thick, *Sir Hugh Plat: The Search for Useful Knowledge in Early Modern London* (Totnes, UK: Prospect Books, 2010).

22 *A profitable booke declaring dyuers approoued remedies, to take out spottes and staines, in silkes, veluets, linnnen [sic] and woollen clothes. With diuers colours how to die velvets and silkes, linnen and woollen, fustian and threade. Also to dresse leather, and to colour felles. How to gylde, graue, sowder and vernishe. And to harden and make softe yron and steele. : Very necessarie to all men, speciallye for those which hath or shall haue any doinges therein: with a perfite table herevnto, to fynde all things readye, not the like reuealde in English heretofore. / Taken out of Dutche, and englished by L.M.* (London, 1588).

23 Thomas Tuke, *A discourse against painting and tincturing of women Wherein the abominable sinnes of murther and poysoning, pride and ambition, adultery and witchcraft are set foorth & discouered. Whereunto is added The picture of a picture, or, the character of a painted woman* (London, 1616).

24 *The elements of geometrie of the most aunciient philosopher Euclide of Megara. Faithfully (now first) translated into the Englishe toung, by H. Billingsley, citizen of London. Whereunto are annexed certaine scholies, annotations, and inuentions, of the best mathematiciens, both of time past, and in this our age. With a very fruitfull præface made by M. I. Dee, specifying the chiefe mathematicall scie[n]ces, what they are, and wherunto commodious: where, also, are disclosed certaine new secrets mathematicall and mechanicall, vntill these our daies, greatly missed* (London, 1570).

25 *The carpenters rule, or, a booke shewing many plain waies, truly to measure ordinarie timber, and other extraordinarie sollids, or timber with a detection of sundrie great errors, generally committed by carpenters and others in measuring of timber; tending much to the buyers great losse. Published especially for the good of the Companie of Carpenters in London, and others also; . . . By Richard More carpenter* (London, 1602), sig. A4v.

26 *A boke named Tectonicon briefelye shewynge the exacte measurynge, and speady reckenynge all maner lande, squared tymber, stone, steaples, pyllers, globes. [et]c. Further, declarynge the perfecte makynge and large vse of the*

carpenters ruler, conteynynge a quadrant geometricall: comprehendynge also the rare vse of the squire. And in thende a little treatise adioyned, openinge the composition and appliancie of an instrument called the profitable staffe. With other thinges pleasant & necessary, most conducible for surueyers, landmeters, joyners, carpe[n]ters, and masons. Published by Leonarde Digges gentleman (London, 1556). *Tectonicon* was published in seven editions over the Elizabethan era, and seven more up to 1647; More, *The carpenters rule*, sig. Bv.

27 John Darling, *The carpenters rule made easie. Or, The art of measuring superficies & solids; as timber, stone, board, glasse, and the like. It being of excellent use for carpenters, joyners, masons, glasiers, painters, sawyers. Or any others that have occasion to buy or sell or make use of any such kinde of measure for themselves or others. Performed by certain tables collected for that purpose* (London, 1658).

28 William Bourne, *A regiment for the sea conteyning most profitable rules, mathematical experiences, and perfect knovvledge of nauigation, for all coastes and countreys: most needefull and necessarie for all seafaring men and trauellers, as pilotes, mariners, marchants* (11 editions between 1574–1631); *M. Blundevile his exercises containing sixe treatises, the titles wherof are set down in the next printed page: which treatises are verie necessarie to be read and learned of all yoong gentlemen that haue not bene exercised in such disciplines, and yet are desirous to haue knowledge as well in cosmographie, astronomie, and geographie, as also in the arte of navigation ... To the furtherance of which arte of navigation, the said M. Blundevile speciallie wrote the said treatises and of meere good will doth dedicate the same to all the young gentlemen of this realme* (seven editions between 1596–1638).

29 Margaret Pelling, *Medical Conflicts in Early Modern London: Patronage, Physicians, and Irregular Practitioners 1550–1640* (Oxford: Clarendon Press, 2003), 48–52.

30 Thomas Thayre, *A treatise of the pestilence vvherein is shewed all the causes thereof, with most assured preseruatiues against all infection: and lastly is taught the true and perfect cure of the pestilence, by most excellent and approued medicines. Composed by Thomas Thayre chirurgian, for the benefite of his countrie, but chiefly for the honorable city of London* (London, 1603).

31 Arthur Standish, *The commons complaint. VVherein is contained tvvo speciall grievances: The first, the generall destruction and waste of woods in this kingdome, with a remedy for the same* (London, 1611).

32 Thomas Draxe, *An alarum to the last iudgement. Or An exact discourse of the second comming of Christ and of the generall and remarkeable signes and fore-runners of it past, present, and to come; soundly and soberly handled, and wholesomely applyed. Wherein diuers deep mysteries are plainly expounded, and sundry curiosities are duely examined, answered and confuted* (London, 1615).

33 Gabriel Plattes, *A discovery of infinite treasure, hidden since the worlds beginning. Whereunto all men, of what degree so ever, are friendly invited to be sharers with the discoverer, G.P.* (London, 1639), 67.

Chapter One
Regimens and Rules: The Rudiments of Health and Husbandry

1. There is a longstanding debate as to whether *Here begynneth a newe tracte or treatyse moost profytable for all husbandmen and very frutefull for all other persons to rede* (London, 1523; alternatively titled the *Boke of husbandry*) and *Here begynneth a ryght frutefull mater: and hath to name the boke of surueyeng and improume[n]tes* (London, 1523, alternatively titled the *Boke of surueying*) were written by the jurist and legal author Sir Anthony Fitzherbert or his elder brother John, who inherited the family estate from their father Ralph Fitzherbert of Narbury around 1483. At the turn of the last century, agricultural historians settled on John, and that is the judgement of the *English Short Title Catalogue* (ESTC) as well.

2. Mary Lindemann, *Medicine and Society in Early Modern Europe* (Cambridge: Cambridge University Press, 2010), 82.

3. Andrew Maunsell's 1595 catalog of English books devotes 123 pages and the entirety of Part One to Divinity, while the 27 pages of Part Two include publications on the "Mathematical Sciences", Art of War, Navigation and Physick and Surgery, including cookery, which is "Physick for the Kitchen." A promised Part Three on the Humanities never appeared, as Maunsell died the same year: *The first part of the catalogue of English printed bookes vvhich concerneth such matters of diuinitie, as haue bin either written in our owne tongue, or translated out of anie other language: and haue bin published, to the glory of God, and edification of the Church of Christ in England. Gathered into alphabet, and such method as it is, by Andrew Maunsell, bookeseller* (London, 1595).

4. Paul Slack, "Mirrors of Health and Treasures of Poor Men: The Uses of the Vernacular Medical Literature of Tudor England" in Charles Webster, ed., *Health, Medicine and Mortality in the Sixteenth Century* (Cambridge: Cambridge University Press, 1979), 237–274.

5. Irma Taavitsainen and Päivi Patita, eds., *Early Modern English Medical Texts: Corpus Description and Studies* (John Benjamins, 2010).

6. Linda Ehrsam Voigts and Patricia Deery Kurtz, in *Scientific and Medical Writings in Old and Middle English: An Electronic Reference*, identify about 200 distinct Middle English medical texts dating from before 1400, and almost 8,000 dating to the fifteenth century. Society for Early English and Norse Electronic Texts (Ann Arbor: University of Michigan Press, 2001).

7. *In this tretyse that is cleped Gouernayle of helthe what is to be sayd wyth crystis helpe of some thynges that longen to bodily helthe* (London, 1490); *Here begynneth a lytell treatyse called the gouernall of helthe with ye medecyne of ye stomacke* (London, 1506; 1530); *Her[e be]gy[n]neth the kalender of shepherdes* (London, 1506); for the transition from script to print, see Jake Walsh Morrissey, "'To all Indifferent': The Virtues of Lydgate's Dietary," *Medium Aevum* 84 no. 2 (2015): 258–278.

8   Thomas Elyot's *The castel of helth* was published in 15 editions between 1534 and 1610; Andrew Boorde's *Compendyous regyment or dyetary of helth* in five editions between 1542 and 1576 and *The Breuiary of helthe* in seven editions from 1547 to 1598. William Bullein's *A newe booke entituled the gouernement of healthe* was issued in four editions from 1558 to 1595, and his *Bulwarke of defe[n]ce* in 1562 and 1579. Thomas Cogan's *The hauen of health* was published in eight editions from 1584 to 1636, while William Vaughan's *Naturall and artificial directions for health* was issued in eight editions from 1612 to 1633.

9   Sir John Harington, *The Englishmans doctor. Or, The Schoole of Salerne. Or, Physicall obseruations for the perfect Preseruing of the body of Man in continuall health* (London, 1607), sig. B5v.

10 *Regimen sanitatis Salerni This boke techyng al people to gouerne them in helthe, is translated out of the Latyne tonge in to englishe by Thomas Paynell. Whiche boke is as profitable [et] as nedefull to be had and redde as any can be to obserue corporall helthe* (London, 1628).

11 Sir John Harington, *A new discourse of a stale subiect, called The metamorphosis of Aiax vvritten by Misacmos to his friend and cosin Philostilpnos* (London, 1596).

12 Sir John Harrington, *The Englishmans doctor*, sig. A3r.

13 *Regimen sanitatis Salerni The schoole of Salernes most learned and iuditious directorie, or methodicall instructions, for the guide and gouerning the health of man. Dedicated, and sent by them, to the high and mighty King of England, and published (by consent of learned and skilfull physitions) for the good and benefite of all in generall. Perused, and corrected from many great and grosse imperfections, committed in former impressions: with the comment, and all the Latine verses reduced into English, and ordered in their apt and due places* (London, 1617).

14 *Here begynneth a newe boke of medecynes intytulyd or callyd the Treasure of pore men whiche sheweth many dyuerse good medicines for dyuerse certayn dysseases as in the table of this present boke more playnly shall appere. The boke of medecines* (London, 1526). The *Treasure* was reprinted in 12 editions to 1601, while other medical texts appropriated the *Treasury* title.

15 Thomas Elyot, *The castel of helth*, sig. I5r–v.

16 As visually expressed by Henry Peacham in his *Minerua Britanna or A garden of heroical deuises furnished and adorned with emblemes and impresas of sundry natures* (London, 1612), which is partially based on *Basilikon dōron* (Edinburgh, 1599), the book of advice to his young son Henry by King James VI (and I).

17 *The olde mans dietarie A worke no lesse learned then necessary for the preseruation of olde persons in perfect health and soundnesse. Englished out of Latine, and now first published by Thomas Newton* (London, 1586), sig. B2r; Newton also published *Approved medicines and cordiall receiptes with the natures, qualities, and operations of sundry samples. Very commodious and expedient for all that are studious of such knowledge* (London, 1580), the Dutch physician Levinus Lemnius's physiological text *De habitu et*

constitiontione corporis as *The touchstone of complexions* (London, 1576), and one of the Italian physician Guglielmo Gratarolo's Latin works as *A direction for the health of magistrates and students* (London, 1574).

18 See reference and page illustration of a 1610 edition in the collection of the British Library in Jennifer Richards, "Useful Books: Reading Vernacular Regimens in Sixteenth-Century England," *Journal of the History of Ideas*, 73, no. 2 (2012): 253–256; for a discussion of *The castel of helth*'s formatting, see Elizabeth Tebeaux, *The Emergence of a Tradition. Technical Writing in the English Renaissance*, 1475–1640 (Amityville, NY: Baywood, 1997), 56–58.

19 *Bulleins bulwarke of defe[n]ce against all sicknes, sornes, and woundes, that dooe daily assaulte mankinde, whiche bulwarke is kepte with Hillarius the gardiner, Health the phisician, with their chyrurgian, to helpe the wounded soldiers. Gathered and practised fro[m] the moste worthie learned, bothe old and newe: to the greate comforte of mankinde: doen by Williyam Bulleyn and ended this Marche. anno salutis. 1562* (London, 1562), sig. AA4r.

20 Thomas Cogan, *The hauen of health chiefely gathered for the comfort of students, and consequently of all those that haue a care of their health, amplified vpon fiue words of Hippocrates, written Epid. 6 Labor, cibus, potio, somnus, Venus: by Thomas Coghan master of Artes, & Bacheler of Phisicke. Hereunto is added a preseruation from the pestilence, with a short censure of the late sicknes at Oxford* (London, 1584), sig.¶¶4r.

21 Thomas Cogan, *The hauen of health*, sig. ¶¶3v.

22 *Hereafter foloweth a compendyous regyment or a dyetary of helth made in Mou[n]tpyllier, compyled by Andrew Boorde of physiycke doctour, dedycated to the armypotent prynce, and valyaunt Lorde Thomas Duke of Northfolche* (London, 1542), sigs. H1r; G1v; E3v.

23 The literature on the "medical marketplace" is vast, commencing with Harold Cook's *Decline of the Old Regime in Stuart London* and including works by: Margaret Pelling, "Medical Practice in Early Modern England: Trade or Profession?" in *The Professions in Early Modern England*, ed. W. Prest (London: Croon Helm, 1987), 90–128; *The Common Lot: Sickness, Medical Occupations and the Urban Poor in Early Modern England* (Abingdon, UK: Routledge, 1998), and *Medical Conflicts in Early Modern London: Patronage, Physicians, and Irregular Practitioners, 1550–1640*; Roy Porter, ed., *Patients and Practitioners: Lay Perceptions of Medicine in Pre–Industrial Society* (Cambridge: Cambridge University Press, 1986); and Mark S.R. Jenner and Patrick Wallis, eds., *Medicine and the Market in England and Its Colonies, c.1450–c.1850* (London: Palgrave Macmillan, 2007).

24 Elizabeth Lane Furdell, *The Royal Doctors, 1485–1714: Medical Personnel at the Tudor and Stuart Courts* (Rochester, UK: Rochester University Press, 2001).

25 Andrew Boorde, *The Breuiary of helthe* (London 1547), sig. A2r.

26 William Bullein, *Bulleins bulwark of defence*, sig. AA5v

27 Readership of the regimens has been the subject of studies by Paul Slack, "Mirrors of Health and Treasures of Poor Men: The Uses of the Vernacular Medical Literature of Tudor England"; Carol Rawcliffe, *Medicine and Society in Later Medieval England* (Stroud, UK: Sutton Publishing, 1995); Andrew

Wear, *Knowledge and Practice in English Medicine, 1550–1680* (Cambridge: Cambridge University Press, 2000); Roger French, *Medicine Before Science: the Business of Medicine from the Middle Ages to the Enlightenment* (Cambridge: Cambridge University Press, 2003); and Ken Albala, *Eating Right in the Renaissance* (Berkeley: University of California Press, 2002).

28 *The hope of health wherin is conteined a goodlie regimente of life: as medicine, good diet and the goodlie vertues of sonderie herbes, doen by Philip Moore* (London, 1564), sig. F6r.

29 Andrew Boorde, *The boke for to learne a man to be wyse in buyldyng of his howse for the helth of body [and] to holde quyetnes for the helth of his soule, and body The boke for a good husbande to lerne* (London, 1550), sig. B2v.

30 William Vaughan, *Naturall and artificial directions for health deriued from the best philosophers, as well moderne, as auncient* (London, 1600); Tobias Venner, *Via recta ad vitam longam, or A plaine philosophical discourse of the nature, faculties, and effects, of all such things, as by way of nourishments, and dieteticall obseruations, make for the preseruation of health with their iust applications vnto euery age, constitution of bodie, and time of yeare* (London, 1620), sig. B3r–v.

31 John Archer, *Every man his own doctor in two parts, shewing I. how every one may know his own constitution by certain signs, also the nature and faculties of all food as well as meats as drinks . . .: the second part shews the full knowledge and cure of the pox, running of the reins, gout, dropsie, scurvy, consumptions and obstructions, agues* (London, 1671), 2.

32 *Healths improvement: or, Rules comprizing and discovering the nature, method, and manner of preparing all sorts of food used in this nation. Written by that ever famous Thomas Muffett, Doctor in Physick: corrected and enlarged by Christopher Bennet, Doctor in Physick, and fellow of the Colledg of Physitians in London* (London, 1655), sig. B1v.

33 Thomas Elyot, *The castel of helth*, sig. F2v.

34 Phillip Moore, *The hope of health*, sig. C7r.

35 Thomas Elyot, *The castel of helth*, sig. F5v.

36 Joan Thirsk, *Alternative Agriculture. A History. From the Black Death to the Present Day* (Oxford: Oxford University Press, 1997), 32.

37 Thomas Moffatt, *Healths improvement*, sig. F1v.

38 Thomas Moffatt, *Healths improvement*, sig. GG1–2v.

39 Tobias Venner, *Via recta ad vitam longam*, sig. T3r–v. Venner's opinion of potatoes is not disputed, but Joan Thirsk believes that the Moffatt quote was likely the addition of his editor Christopher Bennett in the 1650s, as the 1590s was a bit too early for such general acceptance of the American crop.

40 William Bullein, *Bulleins bulwark of defence*, sig. B4r–B5r.

41 Louise Hill Curth and Tanya M. Cassidy, "'Health, Strength and Happiness': Medical Constructions of Wine and Beer in Early Modern England", in *A Pleasing Sinne: Drink and Conviviality in Seventeenth-century England*, ed. Adam Smyth (Martlesham, UK: Boydell and Brewer, 2004),143–159.

42 William Bullein, *Bulleins bulwark of defence*, sig. B5r.

43 William Vaughan, *Naturall and artificial directions for health*, sig. B4r.
44 William Vaughan, *Naturall and artificial directions for health*, sig. B4v–B5r.
45 Sasha Handley, *Sleep in Early Modern England* (New Haven: Yale University Press, 2016).
46 Andrew Boorde, *Hereafter foloweth a compendyous regyment or a dyetary of helth made in Mou[n]tpyllier, compyled by Andrew Boorde of physiycke doctour, dedycated to the armypotent prynce, and valyaunt Lorde Thomas Duke of Northfolche* (London, 1542), sig. D3r.
47 A. Roger Ekirch, *At Day's Close: Night in Times Past* (New York: W.W. Norton, 2006).
48 *An introduction into phisycke wyth an vniuersal dyet, gathered by Christofer Langton* (London, 1545), sig. L1r–v.
49 *The garden of health conteyning the sundry rare and hidden vertues and properties of all kindes of simples and plants, together with the maner how they are to be vsed and applyed in medicine for the health of mans body, against diuers diseases and infirmities most common amongst men. Gathered by the long experience and industrie of William Langham, practitioner in phisicke* (London, 1597).
50 Thomas Cogan, *The hauen of health*, sig. A1v.
51 Thomas Cogan, *The hauen of health*, sig. A1v.
52 *De arte natandi libri duo quorum prior regulas ipsius artis, posterior verò praxin demonstrationemque continet. Authore Euerardo Dygbeio Anglo in artibus Magistro* (London, 1587); Christopher Middleton, *A Short introduction for to learne to Swimme. Gathered out of Master Digbies Booke of the Art of Swimming. And translated into English for the better instruction of those who vnderstand not the Latine tongue. By Christofer Middleton* (London, 1595). In his entry on Digby in the *Oxford Dictionary of National Biography*, Nicholas Orme notes that Digby's original text was a "landmark in the use of pictures to convey techniques" and that "Digby may be said to have influenced the understanding and teaching of swimming for the next 200 years." Nicholas Orme, "Digby, Everard (d. 1605)" *Oxford Dictionary of National Biography*.
53 Humphrey Brooke, *Ugieine or A conservatory of health*, 144–145.
54 Humphrey Brooke, *Ugieine or A conservatory of health. Comprized in a plain and practicall discourse upon the six particulars necessary to mans life, viz. 1. Aire. 2. Meat and drink. 3. Motion and rest. 4. Sleep and wakefulness. 5. The excrements. 6. The passions of the mind. With the discussion of divers questions pertinent thereunto. Compiled and published for the prevention of sickness, and prolongation of life* (London, 1650), 144–145.
55 *The castel of health. Corrected and in some place augmented, by the fyrst author therof, syr Thomas Elyot, knighyt* (London, 1561), 64.
56 Everard Maynwaring, *Tutela sanitatis sive Vita protracta. The protection of long life, and detection of its brevity, from diætetic causes and common customs. Hygiastic præcautions and rules appropriate to the constitutions of bodyes; and various discrasyes or passions of minde; dayly to be observed for the preservation of health and prolongation of life* (London, 1664), 39.

57 James Hart, *Klinikē, or The diet of the diseased*, sig. Bbb3r.
58 James Hart, *Klinikē, or The diet of the diseased*, sig. Eee1r–v.
59 *The castel of helth corrected and in some places augmented, by the first author therof, syr Thomas Elyot knight* (London, 1541), sig. A2v.
60 John Fitzherbert, *Here begynneth a ryght frutefull mater: and hath to name the boke of surueyeng and improume[n]tes* (London, 1523), sig. a4v.
61 John Fitzherbert, *The boke of husbandry* (London, 1540), sig. J7v.
62 John Fitzherbert, *Here begynneth a newe tracte or treatyse moost profytable for all husbandmen and very frutefull for all other persons to rede* (London, 1543), fol. vii.
63 Fitzherbert's emphasis on the diversity of local conditions and practices is in accordance with current analyses of agricultural trends in the early modern era. While there may be disagreements about the degrees and chronology of agrarian capitalism and the agricultural "revolution," the preponderance of locality is beyond question. In the words of Joan Thirsk, who dominated the field of agrarian history for the entire second half of the twentieth century and into the twenty-first, "When one has grasped the full diversity of England as a whole, then much of the dynamism in the kingdom's economic and social development in the sixteenth and seventeenth centuries may be seen to have come from localized changes, setting up a chain of reactions and interactions between neighboring, varied but closely-interdependent, regions and communities." Preface to *The Rural Economy of England* (London: Hambledon Press, 1984), ix–x.
64 John Fitzherbert, *The boke of husbandry* (London, 1540), sig. a6r.
65 "Corn" and "cattle" are utilized here in the general sense, as grain and livestock. An anonymous pamphlet issued at mid-century entitled *Certayne causes gathered together, wherein is showed the decaye of England, only by the great multitude of sheep* (London, 1552) makes that connection in several ways, through proverbs like "the more sheep, the dearer the corn." The author dates the decline of "tillage" and the rise of sheep pastures all the way back to the beginning of Henry VII's reign, a notable association of political and economic history. Of course, the claim is not new, having been expressed decades earlier by a member of the entourage of the Venetian ambassador to Henry VII's court and most famously by Sir Thomas More in *Utopia* (1516). The first observer had the benefit of his continental (or more precisely Italian) perspective, as he ascribed the wealth of England to "the extraordinary abundance of wool which bears such a high price and reputation throughout Europe," while the latter warned of English sheep which have "become so great devourers and so wild, that they eat up and swallow down the very men themselves. They consume, destroy, and devour whole fields, houses and cities. For look in what part of the realm doth grow the finest and therefore dearest wool, there noblemen and gentlemen—yes, and certain Abbots, holy men no doubt—not contenting themselves with the yearly profits and revenues that were wont to grow to their forefathers and predecessors of their lands, nor being content that they live in rest and pleasure, nothing profiting—yea, much annoying the weal public—leave no ground for tillage, they enclose all into pastures; they throw down houses, they pluck down towns, and leave nothing

standing, but only the church to be made a sheephouse." C.A. Sneyd, *A Relation, or Rather a True Account, of the Island of England. With Sundry Particulars of the Customs of these People, and of the Royal Revenues under King Henry the Seventh, about the year 1500* (London: Camden Sociey, 1847), 8–12.

66 *A Proclamation concernynge corne*, 11 November 1534, in *Tudor and Stuart Proclamations, 1485–1714. Calendared by Robert Steele under the Direction of the Earl of Crawford* (Oxford: Clarendon Press, 1910), no. 145, 16.

67 Thomas Elyot, *The castel of helth* (London, 1539), sig. F2r–v.

68 Anonymous [N.F.], *The husbandmans fruitfull orchard Shewing diuers care [sic] new secrets for the true ordering of all sortes of fruite in their due seasons. Also how your encrease and profite maie bee much more then heeretofore, and yet your charge and labour the same. With the manner of gathering all kindes of fruite aswel stone-fruit as other, and hovv they are to be ordered in packing, carrying, & conueying them by land or by water. Then in separating or culling them into diuers sortes, and lastlie in reseruing or laying them vp, as may be for their best lasting and continuance. Neuer before published* (London, 1608), sig. A2r–v.

Chapter Two
Measure for Measure: Mensuration and Mathematics

1 The first arithmetic book printed in England, Cuthbert Tunstall's *De arte supputandi libri quatuor* (1522), was based on the 1494 edition of Pacioli's *Summa de Arithmetica*; Pacioli's accounting instruction was translated and published by the English schoolmaster Hugh Oldcastle in 1543, and "improved" and reissued by John Mellis in 1588 under the title *A briefe instruction and maner hovv to keepe bookes of accompts after the order of debitor and creditor & as well for proper accompts partible, &c. By the three bookes named the memoriall iournall & leager, and of other necessaries appertaining to a good and diligent marchant. The which of all other reckoninges is most lawdable: for this treatise well and sufficiently knowen, all other wayes and maners may be the easier & sooner discerned, learned and knowen. Newely augmented and set forth by Iohn Mellis scholemaister* (London, 1588).

2 This transition is examined from both perspectives in Stephen Alford's *London's Triumph: Merchants, Adventurers and Money in Shakespeare's City* (London: Bloomsbury Academic, 2017).

3 *Lesclarcissement de la langue francoyse compose par maistre Iohan Palsgraue Angloyse natyf de Londres, et gradue de Paris* (London, 1530).

4 Robert Recorde's *The grou[n]d of artes teachyng the worke and practise of arithmetike, moch necessary for all states of men. After a more easyer [et] exacter sorte, then any lyke hath hytherto ben set forth: with dyuers newe additions, as by the table doth partly appeare* (London, 1543).

5   Richard Benese, *This boke sheweth the maner of measurynge of all maner of lande as well of woodlande, as of lande in the felde, and comptynge the true nombre of acres of the-same. Newlye inuented and compyled by Syr Rycharde Benese Chanon of Marton Abbay besyde London* (Southwark, 1537): five more editions were issued to 1651.

6   *The compleat surveyor containing the whole art of surveying of land by the plain table, theodolite, circumferentor, and peractor . . .: together with the taking of all manner of heights and distances, either by William Leybourn* (London, 1653): 275.

7   *A boke named Tectonicon* (London, 1566).

8   Leonard Digges, *A geometrical practise: named pantometria, diuided into three bookes, longimetra, planimetra, and stereometria, containing rules manifolde for mensuration of all lines, superficies and solides; with sundry straunge conclusions, both by instrument and without, and also by perspectiue glasses, to set forth the true description of exact plat of an whole region. Framed by Leonard Digges . . . lately finished by Thomas Digges, his sonne. Who hath also thereunto adioyned a Mathematicall treatise of the fiue regulare Platonicall bodies, and their metamorphosis or transformation into fiue other eqiulater uniforme solides geometricall, of his owne inuention* (London, 1571).

9   Leonard Digges, *A geometrical practise: named pantometria*, sig. A3v.

10 Leonard Digges, *A geometrical practise: named pantometria*, sig. R4v.

11 Valentine Leigh, *The moste profitable and commendable science, of surueying of landes, tenementes, and hereditamentes: drawen and collected by the industrie of Valentyne Leigh. Whereunto is also annexed by the same authour, a right necessarie treatise, of the measuryng of all kyndes of lande, be it meadow, pasture, errable, wood, hill, or dale, and that aswell by certaine easie, and compendious rules, as also by an exact and beneficiall table, purposely drawen and deuised for that behalfe* (London, 1577), and five more editions to 1596.

12 Valentine Leigh, *The moste profitable and commendable science*, sig. A2v. A "terrier" is "a register of landed property" (*OED*) or simply acreage.

13 James Peele, *The maner and fourme how to kepe a perfecte reconyng after the order of the moste worthie and notable accompte, of debitour and creditour, set foorthe in certain tables, with a declaration thereunto belongyng, verie easie to be learned, and also profitable, not onely vnto suche, that trade in the facte of marchaundise, but also vnto any other estate, that will learne the same* (London, 1553); John Weddington, *A breffe instruction, and manner, howe to kepe, marchantes bokes, of accomptes. After the order of debitor and creditor, as vvell for proper accomptes, partable, factory, and other, &c. : Verry nedefull to be knovven and vsid of all men, in the feattis of marchandize. : Novve of late nevvly, set forthe, and practisyd, / By Iohan VVeddington cyttizen of London. MDLXVII* (Antwerp, 1567); John Mellis, *A briefe instruction and maner hovv to keepe bookes of accompts after the order of debitor and creditor & as well for proper accompts partible, &c. By the three bookes named the memoriall iournall & leager, and of other necessaries appertaining to a good and diligent marchant. The which of all other reckoninges is most lawdable: for this treatise well and sufficiently knowen, all other wayes and*

maners may be the easier & sooner discerned, learned and knowen. Newely augmented and set forth by Iohn Mellis scholemaister (London, 1588).

14 Essential studies of the history of mathematics in theory and practice in early modern England include E.G.R. Taylor's classic *The Mathematical Practitioners of Tudor & Stuart England 1485–1714* (Cambridge: Cambridge University Press, 1967); Stephen Johnston, "Making Mathematical Practice: Gentlemen, Practitioners and Artisans in Elizabethan England" (Ph.D. Diss., Cambridge University, 1994); available at http://www.mhs.ox.ac.uk/staff/saj/thesis/); Deborah Harkness, *The Jewel House: Elizabethan London and the Scientific Revolution*; Robert Fox, ed., *Thomas Harriot and His World: Mathematics, Exploration, and Natural Philosophy in Early Modern England* (Abingdon, UK: Routledge, 2017); Lesley B. Cormack, Steven A. Walter, and John A. Schusters, eds., *Mathematical Practitioners and the Transformation of Natural Knowledge in Early Modern Europe* (New York: Springer, 2017).

15 *The elements of geometrie of the most auncient philosopher Euclide of Megara. Faithfully (now first) translated into the Englishe toung, by H. Billingsley, citizen of London. Whereunto are annexed certaine scholies, annotations, and inuentions, of the best mathematiciens, both of time past, and in this our age. With a very fruitfull præface made by M. I. Dee, specifying the chiefe mathematicall scie[n]ces, what they are, and wherunto commodious: where, also, are disclosed certaine new secrets mathematicall and mechanicall, vntill these our daies, greatly missed* (London, 1570).

16 John Dee, "Mathematicall praeface," to *The elements of geometrie of the most auncient philosopher Euclide of Megara. Faithfully (now first) translated into the Englishe toung, by H. Billingsley, citizen of London*, sig. iiv; sig. A.iiijr–v.

17 Anonymous, *An introduction for to lerne to recken with the pen or with the counters accordynge to the trewe cast of algorysme, in hole nombers or in broken, newly corrected. And certayne notable and goodlye rules of false posytions thereunto added, not before sene in oure Englyshe tonge by the whiche all maner of difficyle questyons may easily be dissolued and assoylyd* (London, 1539).

18 Anonymous, *An introduction for to lerne to recken with the pen or with the counters*. According to a modern-day expert, the original author's methodology is flawed. Apparently, the answer is 35 days: Travis D. Williams, "Procrustean Marxism and Subjective Rigor: Early Modern Arithmetic and Its Readers," in *"Raw Data" Is an Oxymoron*, ed. Lisa Gitelman (Cambridge, MA: MIT Press, 2013), 41–59.

19 Recorde's *The grou[n]d of artes teachyng the worke and practise of arithmetike, moch necessary for all states of men* was published in at least 27 editions prior to 1640 and issued as *Recorde's Arithmetick* for much of the rest of the seventeenth century; *The pathewaie to knowledge, containyng the first principles of geometrie, as thei maie moste aptly bee applied vnto practise, bothe for vse of instrumentes geometricall, and astronomicall: and also for proiection of plattes in euery kinde, and therefore muche necessarie for all sortes of menne* was first issued in 1551, 1574 and 1602, and its title appropriated by John Tapp for his arithmetic manuals thereafter; *The castle of knowledge* was issued in 1556 and 1596; *The whetstone of witte, whiche is the*

seconde parte of Arithmetike: containyng the extraction of rootes: the cossike practise, with the rule of equation: and the woorkes of surde nombers was published in 1557, the year before Recorde's death. Studies of Recorde's life and work include A.G. Howson's *History of Mathematics Education in England* (Cambridge: Cambridge University Press, 1982); Jack Williams, *Robert Recorde: Tudor Polymath, Expositor and Practitioner of Computation* (New York: Springer, 2011); and Gareth Roberts and Fenny Smith, eds, *Robert Recorde: The Life and Times of a Tudor Mathematician* (Cardiff: University of Wales Press, 2012).

20 Robert Recorde, *The whetstone of witte*, sig. FF1v.
21 *Bulleins bulwark of defence*, sig. AA4r–v.
22 *A discouerie of sundrie errours and faults daily committed by lande-meaters, ignorant of arithmetike and geometrie, to the damage, and preiudice of many her Maiesties subiects with manifest proofe that none ought to be admitted to that function, but the learned practisioners of those sciences: written dialoguewise, according to a certaine communication had of that matter. By Edward Worsop, Londoner* (London, 1582), sig. F3r–v.
23 John Norden, *The surueyors dialogue Diuided into fiue bookes: very profitable for all men to peruse, that haue to do with the reuenues of land, or the manurance, vse, or occupation thereof, both lords and tenants: as also and especially for such as indeuor to be seene in the faculty of surueying of mannors, lands, tenements* (London, 1607); *Feudigraphia. The synopsis or epitome of surueying methodized. Anatomizing the whole corps of the facultie; viz. The materiall, mathematicall, mechanicall and legall parts, intimating all the incidents to fees and possessions, and whatsoeuer may be comprized vnder their matter, forme, proprietie, and valuation. Very pertinent to be perused of all those, whom the right, reuenewe, estimation, farming, occupation, manurance, subduing, preparing and imploying of arable, medow, pasture, and all other plots doe concerne. And no lesse remarkable for all vnder-takers in the plantation of Ireland or Virginia, . . . / Composed in a compendious digest by W. Folkingham* (London, 1610); Aaron Rathborne, *The svrveyor in foure bookes* (London, 1616).
24 *Three bookes of colloquies concerning the arte of shooting in great and small peeces of artillerie, variable randges, measure, and waight of leaden, yron, and marble stone pellets, minerall saltepeeter, gunpowder of diuers sortes, and the cause why some sortes of gunpower are corned, and some sortes of gunpowder are not corned: written in Italian, and dedicated by Nicholas Tartaglia vnto the Royall Prince of most famous memorie Henrie the eight, late King of England, Fraunce, and Ireland, defender of the faith &c. And now translated into English by Cyprian Lucar Gent. who hath also augmented the volume of the saide colloquies with the contents of euery colloquie, and with all the corollaries and tables, that are in the same volume. Also the said Cyprian Lucar hath annexed vnto the same three books of colloquies a treatise named Lucar Appendix* (London, 1588).
25 Cyprian Lucar, *Lucar Appendix*, sig. H1v.
26 *The first and chief groundes of architecture vsed in all the auncient and famous monymentes with a farther & more ample defense vppon the same, than*

hitherto hath been set out by any other. Published by Iohn Shute, paynter and archytecte (London, 1563), sig. A2v.

27 Humfrey Baker, *The welspring of sciences, which teacheth the perfecte worke and practise of arithmeticke both in vvhole numbers & fractions, with such easie and compendious instruction into the saide art, as hath not heretofore been by any set out nor laboured, : Beautified vvith most necessary rules and questions, not onely profitable for marchauntes, but also for all artificers, as in the table doth plainely appere* (London, 1562).

28 The *Cosmographicus liber* of Peter Apian was first published in 1524 and reprinted more than 30 times and translated into 14 languages in the sixteenth century. For more on this "book-instrument hybrid," see Margaret Gaida, "Reading Cosmographia: Peter Apian's Book-Instrument Hybrid and the Rise of the Mathematical Amateur in the Sixteenth Century," *Early Sci Med.* 21, no. 4 (2016): 277–302.

29 Richard Eden, *A treatyse of the newe India with other new founde landes and islandes, aswell eastwarde as westwarde, as they are knowen and found in these oure dayes, after the description of Sebastian Munster in his boke of universall cosmographie: wherin the diligent reader may see the good successe and rewarde of noble and honeste enterpryses, by the which not only worldly ryches are obtayned, but also God is glorified, [and] the Christian faythe enlarged. Translated out of Latin into Englishe* (London, 1553).

30 John Dee, "Mathematicall praeface" to *The elements of geometrie of the most auncient philosopher Euclide of Megara*, sig. b3r.

31 For a comprehensive discussion of *The Ambassadors*' instruments, see Elly Dekker and Kristen Lippincott, "The Scientific Instruments in Holbein's Ambassadors: A Re-Examination," *Journal of the Warburg and Courtauld Institutes.* 62 (1999): 93–125.

32 Robert Recorde, *The castle of knowledge*, sig. G5r–v.

33 William Cunningham, *The cosmographical glasse conteinyng the pleasant principles of cosmographie, geographie, hydrographie, or nauigation. Compiled by VVilliam Cuningham Doctor in Physicke* (London, 1559).

34 *The rutter of the sea, w[ith] the hauo[n]s, rodes, soundinges, kennynges, wyndes, floudes and ebbes, daungers and costes of dyuers regions wyth the lawes of the yle of auleron and the iudgementes of the sea. with [sic] a rutter of the northe added to the same* (London, 1557).

Chapter Three
Elizabethan Alterations: Continuity and Crisis

1 Thomas Lupton, *A thousand notable things, of sundry sortes. whereof [sic] some are wonderfull, some straunge, some pleasant, diuers necessary, a great sort profitable, and many very precious* (London, 1579).

2 Charles Estienne, *Maison Rustique, or The covntrey farme. Compiled in the French tongue by Charles Steuens and Iohn Liebault doctors of physicke. And*

translated into English by Richard Surflet practitioner in physicke (London, 1600), sig. B4r.

3   Nancy Siraisi, *Medieval and Early Renaissance Medicine. An Introduction to Knowledge and Practice* (Chicago: University of Chicago Press, 1990), 128; Paul Slack, *The Impact of Plague in Tudor and Stuart England* (Oxford: Oxford University Press, 1991); The "Little Book", the first English printed book with a title page, was published under variant titles and is derived from a Latin translation by Bengt Knutsson of "*Régime de l'épidémie*" by Joannes Jacobi.

4   Jean Goeurot, *The regiment of life, whereunto is added a treatise of the pestilence, with the boke of children, newly corrected and enlarged by T. Phayre* (London, 1550); Thomas Cogan, *The haven of health* (London, 1584).

5   Thomas Dekker, *London looke backe at that yeare of yeares 1625 and looke forvvard, vpon this yeare 1630 / written not to terrifie, but to comfort* (London, 1630).

6   As epidemics offer unique insights into global history, world historians have been particularly effective in highlighting pandemic patterns following the pioneering work of William McNeill's *Plagues and Peoples* (New York: Anchor, 1976). Consequently, the global First Pandemic (the "Plague of Justinian," sixth century), Second Pandemic ("Black Death", fourteenth century and after) and Third Pandemic (East Asian and Pacific plagues, nineteenth and twentieth centuries) have been generally accepted as the primary cycles of bubonic plague. More recent work by historians and biologists have called into question whether the Second Pandemic was in fact the bubonic plague identified in the Third: see Samuel Kline Cohn, Jr., *The Black Death Transformed. Disease and Culture in Early Renaissance Europe* (London: Bloomsbury Academic, 2003), and "Epidemiology of the Black Death and Successive Waves of Plague," *Med. Hist. Suppl.* 27 (2008): 74–100; John Theillman and Francis Cate, "A Plague of Plagues: The Problem of Plague Diagnosis in Medieval England," *Journal of Interdisciplinary History* Vol. 37, no. 3 (Winter, 2007): 371–393.

7   William Bullein, *A Dialogvue bothe pleasaunte and pietifull, wherein is a goodly regimente against the feuer Pestilence with a consolacion and comfort against death* (London, 1564); *A defensatiue against the plague contayning two partes or treatises: the first, shewing the meanes how to preserue vs from the dangerous contagion thereof: the second, how to cure those that are infected therewith. Whereunto is annexed a short treatise of the small poxe: shewing how to gouerne and helpe those that are infected therewith. Published for the loue and benefit of his countrie by Simon Kellwaye Gentleman* (London, 1594).

8   Thomas Moulton, *This is the myrour or glasse of helthe* (London, 1566); *A worthy practise of the moste learned phisition Maister Leonerd Fuchsius, Doctor in phisicke, moste necessary in this needfull tyme of our visitation, for the comforte of all good and faythfull people, both olde and yonge, bothe for the sicke and for them that woulde auoyde the daunger of the contagion* (London, 1563); Andreas Osiander, *How and whither a Chrysten man ought to flye the horryble plague of the pestilence A sermon out of the Psalme. Qui habitat in adiutorio altissimi. Translated out of hie Almaine into Englishe* (London, 1563).

9   *The gouerance and preseruation of them that feare the plage* (London, 1563); Margaret Pelling and Frances White. "VANDERNOTE, John," in *Physicians and Irregular Medical Practitioners in London 1550–1640 Database* (London: Centre for Metropolitan History, 2004), *British History Online*, accessed February 27, 2021, https://www.british-history.ac.uk/no-series/london-physicians/1550-1640/vandernote-john. Margaret Pelling and Frances White, 'VANDERNOTE, John', *Physicians and Irregular Medical Practitioners in London 1550–1640 Database* (London, 2004): https://www.british-history.ac.uk/no-series/london-physicians/1550-1640.

10 *A dial for all agues conteininge the names in Greeke, Latten, and Englyshe, with the diuersities of them, symple and compounde, proper and accident, definitions, deuisions, causes, and signes, comenly hetherto knowen: very profitable for al men, compendiously compiled (and confirmed as may appeare out of the auctors following) by Iohn Iones phisitio[n]* (London, 1566).

11 Thomas Brasbridge, *The poore mans iewell, that is to say, a treatise of the pestilence Vnto the which is annexed a declaration of the vertues of the hearbes carduus benedictus, and angelica: whiche are verie medicinable, both against the plague, & also against many other diseases. Gathered out of the bookes of diuers learned physicians* (London, 1578).

12 Conrad Gessner, *The newe iewell of health, wherein is contayned the most excellent secretes of phisicke and philosophie, deuided into fower bookes. In the which are the best approued remedies for the diseases as well inwarde as outwarde, of all the partes of mans bodie: treating very amplye of all dystillations of waters, of oyles, balmes, quintessences, with the extraction of artificiall saltes, the vse and preparation of antimonie, and potable gold. Gathered out of the best and most approued authors, by that excellent doctor Gesnerus. Also the pictures, and maner to make the vessels, furnaces, and other instrumentes thereunto belonging. Faithfully corrected and published in Englishe, by George Baker, chirurgian* (London, 1576); Leonardo Fioravanti, *A ioyfull iewell. Contayning aswell such excellent orders, preseruatiues and precious practises for the plague, as also such meruelous medcins for diuers maladies, as hitherto haue not beene published in the English tung. First made and written in the Italian tung by the famous, and learned knight and doctor M. Leonardo Fiorouantie, of his owne ingenious inuentions. And now for the carefull commoditie of his natiue countrey, translated out of the Italian by TH* (London, 1579).

13 Richard Bostocke, *The difference betwene the auncient phisicke, first taught by the godly forefathers, consisting in vnitie peace and concord: and the latter phisicke proceeding from idolaters, ethnickes, and heathen: as Gallen, and such other consisting in dualitie, discorde, and contrarietie And wherein the naturall philosophie of Aristotle doth differ from the trueth of Gods worde, and is iniurious to Christianitie and sounde doctrine* (London, 1585).

14 John Hester, *These oils, waters, extractions, or essences, salts and compositions* (1585); *The pearle of practise, or Practisers pearle, for phisicke and chirurgerie. Found out by I. H. (a spagericke or distiller) amongst the learned obseruations and prooued practises of many expert men in both faculties. Since his death it is garnished and brought into some methode by a welwiller of his* (London: James Forestier, 1594).

15 Conrad Gessner, *The newe iewell of health*, sig. *iijv.

16 Conrad Gessner, *The newe iewell of health*, sig. P3–4v.

17 The classification of Dr. Peter Turner in *The opinion of Peter Turner Doct: in physicke, concerning amulets or plague cakes whereof perhaps some holde too much, and some too little* (London 1603).

18 Ulrich von Hutten's text was translated and published by Thomas Paynell as *De Morbo Gallico* in 1533, with three other editions to 1540.

19 *A short and profitable treatise touching the cure of the disease called (Morbus Gallicus) by unctions, set forth by William Clowes, of London, chirurgion* (London, 1579), sig. D5r; *A Brief and Necessary Treatise, touching the cure of the disease called morbus Gallicus, or lues venerea* (London, 1585); for more context on Clowes, see Celeste Chamberland, "Between the Hall and the Market: William Clowes and Surgical Self-Fashioning in Elizabethan London," *Sixteenth Century Journal* 41, no. 1 (2010): 69–89.

20 Banister's "Epologue", sig. O4v; Banister also recommended tamer treatments for the various symptoms of syphilis in his *An antidotarie chyrurgicall containing great varietie and choice of all sorts of medicines that commonly fal into the chyrurgions vse: partlie taken out of authors, olde and new, printed or written: partlie obtained by free gifte of sundrie worthie men of this profession within this land* (London, 1589).

21 Lawrence M. Principe, *The Secrets of Alchemy* (Chicago: University of Chicago Press, 2013): 108.

22 John Banister, "Epilogue" to Clowes, *A Brief and Necessary Treatise*, sig. N4v.

23 *The naturall and morall historie of the East and West Indies Intreating of the remarkable things of heaven, of the elements, mettalls, plants and beasts which are proper to that country: together with the manners, ceremonies, lawes, governments, and warres of the Indians. Written in Spanish by the R.F. Ioseph Acosta, and translated into English by E.G.* (London, 1604), sig. P1v.

24 Anthony Chute, *Tabacco* (London, 1595). Alternate title: *Destinct and seuerall opinions of the late, and best phisitions that haue written of the nature of tabacco*; James I, King of England, *A counterblaste to tobacco* (London, 1604).

25 Philaretes, *VVork for chimny-sweepers: or A warning for tabacconists. Describing the pernicious vse of tabacco, no lesse pleasant then profitable for all sorts to reade* (London, 1602); Roger Marbeck, *A defence of tabacco: vvith a friendly answer to the late printed booke called Worke for chimny-sweepers, &c* (London, 1602); John Beaumont, *The metamorphosis of tabacco* (London, 1602).

26 Roger Marbeck, *A defence of tabacco* (London, 1602), sig. H3v.

27 John Clarke, *The trumpet of Apollo sounding out the sweete blast of recouerie, in diuers dangerous and desperate diseases* (London, 1602).

28 William Turner, *A new herball wherein are conteyned the names of herbes in Greke, Latin, Englysh, Duch [sic] Frenche, and in the potecaries and herbaries Latin, with the properties degrees and naturall places of the same, gathered and made by Wyllium Turner, physicion vnto the Duke of Somersettes Grace* (London, 1551). *The first and seconde partes of the herbal of William Turner*

Doctor in Phisick, lately ouersene, corrected and enlarged with the thirde parte, lately gathered, and nowe set oute with the names of the herbes, in Greke Latin, English, Duche, Frenche, and in the apothecaries and herbaries Latin, with the properties, degrees, and naturall places of the same. Here vnto is ioyned also a booke of the bath of Baeth in England, and of the vertues of the same with diuerse other bathes, moste holsom and effectuall, both in Almanye and England (Cologne, 1568)

29 John Maplet, *A greene forest, or A naturall historie vvherein may bee seene first the most sufferaigne vertues in all the whole kinde of stones & mettals: next of plants, as of herbes, trees, [and] shrubs, lastly of brute beastes, foules, fishes, creeping wormes [and] serpents, and that alphabetically: so that a table shall not neede. Compiled by Iohn Maplet, M. of Arte, and student in Cambridge: entending hereby yt God might especially be glorified: and the people furdered* (London, 1567).

30 William Turner, *The first and second partes of the herbal*, sig. U2v.

31 William Turner, *The first and second partes of the herbal*, sig. W4r.

32 Thomas Hyll, *The profitable Arte of Gardening, now the third tyme set fourth: to whiche is added muche necessary matter, and a number of secrettes with the phisick helpes belonging to eche herbe, and that easie prepared. To this annexed, two propre treatises, the one entituled The marueilous gouernment, propertie, and benefite of the bées, with the rare secrets of the honny and waxe. And the other, The yerely coniectures, méete for husbandme[n] to knowe* (London, 1568). It first appeared as *A most briefe and pleasaunte treatise, teachyng how to dresse, sowe, and set a garden* in 1558: it was published in six more additions up to 1608. Following his death c. 1574–76, the essential text was published as *The gardeners labyrinth: containing a discourse of the gardeners life, in the yearly trauels to be bestovved on his plot of earth, for the vse of a garden: with instructions for the choise of seedes, apte times for sowing, setting, planting, [and] watering, and the vessels and instruments seruing to that vse and purpose: wherein are set forth diuers herbers, knottes and mazes, cunningly handled for the beautifying of gardens. Also the physike benefit of eche herbe, plant, and floure, with the vertues of the distilled waters of euery of them, as by the sequele may further appeare. Gathered out of the best approued writers of gardening, husbandrie, and physicke* by "Dvdymus Mountaine" in 1577 and issued in eight more editions up to 1660. Rebecca Bushnell's *Green Desire: Imagining Early Modern English Gardens* (Ithaca, NY: Cornell University Press, 2003) presents an extended survey and analysis of English gardening manuals from the sixteenth to the eighteenth centuries, and Martin Hoyles surveys an even longer period in *Gardener's Delight: Gardening Books from 1560 to 1960* (London: Pluto Press, 1994).

33 William Harrison, *The Description of England*, ed. Georges Edelen (Ithaca, NY: Published for the Folger Shakespeare Library by Cornell University Press, 1968), Chapter XX.

34 *The newe iewell of health*, sig. *iiijr; *A ioyfull iewell*, sig. A1r.

35 Richard Arnold, *In this boke is conteined ye names of the baylyfs custose mayers and sherefs of ye cyte of london from the tyme of kynge Richard the fyrst* (London, c. 1525).

36 Thomas Hyll (Didymus Mountain), *The gardeners labyrinth*, sig. C2v.
37 Thomas Hyll, *The gardeners labyrinth*, sig. F4v–G3v; sig N1v–N2v.
38 Thomas Hyll, *The gardeners labyrinth*, Second Part.
39 *A booke of the arte and maner, howe to plant and graffe all sortes of trees howe to set stones, and sowe pepines to make wylde trees to graffe on, as also remedies and mediicnes [sic]. VVith diuers other newe practise, by one of the Abbey of Saint Vincent in Fraunce, practised with his owne handes, deuided into seauen chapters, as hereafter more plainely shall appeare, with an addition in the ende of this booke, of certaine Dutch practises, set forth and Englished, by Leonard Mascall* (London, 1572) was issued in seven editions up to 1652. Mascall also published: *The husbandlye ordring and gouernement of poultrie Practised by the learnedste, and suche as haue bene knowne skilfullest in that arte, and in our tyme* (London, 1581); *A profitable booke declaring dyuers approoued remedies, to take out spottes and staines* (London, 1583); *The first booke of cattell wherein is shewed the gouernment of oxen, kine, calues, and how to vse bulles and other cattell to the yoake, and fell. With diuers approued remedies, to helpe most diseases among cattell: most necessarie for all, especially for husband men, hauing the gouernment of any such cattell. Gathered and set forth by Leonard Mascall* (London, 1587); *Prepositus his Practise, a Worke . . . for the better preservation of the Health of Man. Wherein are approved Medicines, Receiptes and Ointmentes* (London, 1588); *A booke of fishing with hooke & line, and of all other instruments thereunto belonging. Another of sundrie engines and trappes to take polcats, buzards, rattes, mice and all other kindes of vermine & beasts whatsoeuer, most profitable for all warriners, and such as delight in this kinde of sport and pastime. Made by L.M* (London, 1590).
40 William Harrison, *The Description of England* (1968), 269.
41 Historians of the English landscape have cast considerable doubt on the validity of the contemporary perception that England's woodlands were "exhausted "in the early modern era: Oliver Rackham states that "the greatest threats to ancient woodland for a thousand years came from the destructive courses which both agriculture and forestry took in Britain after 1945" in *The History of the Countryside* (London: Phoenix, 2000), 93; See Keith Thomas, *Man and the Natural World: Changing Attitudes in England, 1500–1800* (Oxford: Oxford University Press, 1983), 192–223.
42 *The Statutes at Large, from the First Year of Q. Mary, to the Thirty-fifth Year of Q. Elizabeth, inclusive* (Vol. 6), ed. D. Pickering (London: C. Eyre and A. Strahan, 1763), 1 Eliz. c. 15; 27 Eliz. c. 19.
43 *Foure bookes of husbandry, collected by M. Conradus Heresbachius, counseller to the hygh and mighty prince, the Duke of Cleue: conteyning the whole arte and trade of husbandry, vvith the antiquitie, and commendation thereof. Nevvely Englished, and increased, by Barnabe Googe, Esquire* (London, 1577), Second Book; Charles Estienne, *Maison rustique, or The covntrey farme* (London, 1600): Third Book.
44 *Tudor and Stuart proclamations 1485–1714*, 7 James I, No. 1072.
45 Arthur Standish, *The commons complaint. VVherein is contained tvvo speciall grieuances. The first is, the generall destruction and waste of woods in this*

kingdome, with a remedy for the same: . . . The second grieuance is, the extreame dearth of victuals. Foure remedies for the same: 1. By a generall planting of fruit-trees, with the charge and profite. 2. By an extraordinarie breeding of fowle and pullen . . . 3. By a general destroying of all king [sic] of vermine, . . . 4. Prouing the abundance of corne, that is yearely deuoured and destroyed by the infinite number of pidgeons, kept and maintained in this kingdome (London, 1611); *Nevv directions of experience by the authour for the planting of timber and firevvood. With a neere estimation what millions of acres the kingdome doth containe; what acres is waste ground, whereon little profite for this purpose wil arise. : What millions hath been woods, and bush-grounds, what acres is woods, and in how many acres so much timber will bee contained, as will maintaine the kingdome for all vses for euer. And how as great store of fire-wood may be raised, as may plentifully mainetaine the kingdome for all purposes, without losse of ground; so as within thirty yeares all spring-woods may be conuerted to tillage and pasture* (London, 1613).

46 *Dyets dry dinner consisting of eight seuerall courses: 1. Fruites 2. Hearbes. 3. Flesh. 4. Fish. 5. whitmeats. 6. Spice. 7. Sauce. 8. Tabacco. All serued in after the order of time vniuersall. By Henry Buttes, Maister of Artes, and fellowe of C.C.C. in C* (London, 1599), sig. G4r. This rhyme influenced others involving more notable English imports: Richard Baker identified 1524 as the year that "it happened that divers things were newly brought into England, whereupon this Rime was made: 'Turke[y]s, Carps, Hoppes, Piccarell [young pike], and Beere, Came into England all in one yeere'" in *The Chronicle of the Kings of England from the Time of the Romans' Government unto the Death of King James* (London, 1643), the basis of Rudyard Kipling's more clean-cut proverb "We say—'Turkey, Heresy, Hops, and Beer Came into England all in one year," from *Puck of Pook's Hill* (1906).

47 Reginald Scot, *A perfite platforme of a hoppe garden : and necessarie instructions for the making and mayntenaunce thereof : with notes and rules for reformation of all abuses, commonly practised therein, very necessarie and expedient for all men to haue, which in any wise haue to doe with hops* (London, 1574–78).

48 Joan Thirsk, *Alternative Agriculture: A History*, 72–112.

49 William Bullein, *A dialogue bothe pleasaunte and pietifull wherein is a goodly regimente against the feuer pestilence with a consolacion and comfort against death* (London, 1564), sigs. L1v–L2v.

50 *Profitable instructions for the manuring, sowing, and planting of kitchin gardens Very profitable for the commonwealth and greatly for the helpe and comfort of poore people. Gathered by Richard Gardner of Shrewsburie* (London, 1599); *Certaine experiments concerning fish and fruite: practised by Iohn Tauerner Gentleman, and by him published for the benefit of others* (London, 1600). In terms of agricultural innovations on estates in the sixteenth century, Mark Dawson's study of the Willoughby family's estates in Nottingham and Warwickshire established that "the contribution of fishponds should not be overlooked since they provided many of the more valuable species but, like deer parks and rabbit warrens, they were a social statement

rather than an economic venture." *Plenti and Grase: Food and Drink in a Sixteenth-century Household* (London: Prospect Books, 2009), 133.

51 Hugh Plat, *Sundrie nevv and Artificiall remedies against Famine. Written by H.P. Esq. upon thoccasion of this present Dearth* (London, 1596).

52 Plat's life and published and unpublished works in the context of the emerging scientific community in late Elizabethan London are examined thoroughly in Deborah Harkness's *The Jewel House: Elizabethan London and the Scientific Revolution*; see also Malcolm Thick's *Sir Hugh Plat: The Search for Useful Knowledge in Early Modern London*; Hugh Plat, *Certaine philosophical preparations of foode and beverage for sea-men, in their long voyages: with some necessary, approoued, and hermeticall medicines and antidotes, fit to be had in readinesse at sea, for preuention or cure of diuers diseases* (London, 1607).

53 Hugh Plat, *Certaine philosophical preparations of foode and beverage for sea-men* (London, 1607).

54 Hugh Plat, *The jewell house of art and nature conteining diuers rare and profitable inuentions, together with sundry new experimentes in the art of husbandry, distillation, and moulding / faithfully and familiarly set downe, according to the authors owne experience* (London, 1594), sig. M2v.

55 Hugh Plat, *A nevv, cheape and delicate fire of cole-balles wherein seacole is by the mixture of other combustible bodies, both sweetened and multiplied. Also a speedie way for the winning of any breach: with some other new and seruiceable inuentions answerable to the time* (London, 1603).

56 Hugh Plat, *The jewell house of art and nature*, sig. F3r.

57 Deborah Harkness and more recently Ayesha Mukherjee use the word "scientist" in reference to Plat, while also acknowledging that early modern science was in a formative disciplinary phase. Harkness employs the term as a more general endeavor in which the natural world is studied and manipulated "for productive and profitable ends" in *The Jewel House: Elizabethan London and the Scientific Revolution*, while Mukherjee applies the phrase "dearth science" to Plat's texts on husbandry in *Penury into Plenty: Dearth and the Making of Knowledge in Early Modern England* (Abingdon, UK: Routledge, 2014).

58 Hugh Plat, *Delights for ladies, to adorne their persons, tables, closets, and distillatories with beauties, banquets, perfumes, and waters* (London, 1600) was published in 16 editions over the first half of the seventeenth century.

59 Thomas Tusser, *A hundreth good pointes of husbandrie* (London, 1570), G2r.

60 As tutor to the Princess Mary in the 1520s, Vives wrote with considerable authority and royal approval: *A very frutefull and pleasant boke called the instructio[n] of a Christen woma[n], made fyrst in Laten, and dedicated vnto the quenes good grace, by the right famous clerke mayster Lewes Vives, and turned out of Laten into Englysshe by Rycharde Hyrd. whiche boke who so redeth diligently shal haue knowlege of many thynges, wherin he shal take great pleasure, and specially women shall take great co[m]modyte and frute towarde the[n]crease of vertue [and] good maners* was published in nine editions from 1529–1592.

61 Attesting to its popularity, Raynalde's *Byrth of mankynde, otherwyse named the womans booke* was issued fairly regularly, with corrections and additions, over the next century. For the medieval background and sources of the *Rosengarten*, see Monica H. Green, "The Sources of Eucharius Rösslin's 'Rosegarden' for Pregnant Women and Midwives' (1513)," *Med. Hist.* 53 (2009): 167–192.

62 Jacob Rüff, *The expert midwife, or An excellent and most necessary treatise of the generation and birth of man Wherein is contained many very notable and necessary particulars requisite to be knovvne and practised: with diuers apt and usefull figures appropriated to this worke. Also the causes, signes, and various cures, of the most principall maladies and infirmities incident to women* (1637); Jacques Guillemeau, *Child-birth or, The happy deliuerie of vvomen VVherein is set downe the gouernment of women. In the time of their breeding childe: of their trauaile, both naturall, and contrary to nature: and of their lying in. Together with the diseases, which happen to women in those times, and the meanes to helpe them. To which is added, a treatise of the diseases of infants, and young children: with the cure of them* (London, 1612); Thomas Chamberlayne, *The Compleat midwifes practice, in the most weighty and high concernments of the birth of man containing perfect rules for midwifes and nurses : as also for women in their conception, bearing, and nursing of children* (London, 1656).

63 Philip Barrough, *The methode of phisicke conteyning the causes, signes, and cures of invvard diseases in mans body from the head to the foote. VVhereunto is added, the forme and rule of making remedies and medicines, which our phisitians commonly vse at this day, with the proportion, quantitie, & names of ech [sic] medicine* (London, 1583).

64 *A briefe discourse of a disease called the suffocation of the mother Written vppon occasion which hath beene of late taken thereby, to suspect possesion of an euill spirit, or some such like supernaturall power. Wherin is declared that diuers strange actions and passions of the body of man, which in the common opinion, are imputed to the diuell, haue their true naturall causes, and do accompanie this disease. By Edvvard Iorden Doctor in Physicke* (London, 1603). For the Mary Glover case, see Michael MacDonald, *Witchcraft and Hysteria in Elizabethan London: Edward Jorden and the Mary Glover Case* (New York: Tavistock Press, 1991).

65 Susan W. Hull estimates that "how-to-do-it books for women appeared in approximately 290 editions, accounting for well over half of the almost 500 editions addressed to women in the 1475–1640 period" and identifies the 1570s as an "emerging era" for practical publications aimed at English women in *Chaste, Silent & Obedient: English Books for Women, 1475–1640* (San Marino, CA: Huntington Library, 1982).

66 Pamela H. Smith, *The Body of the Artisan: Art and Experience in the Scientific Revolution* (Chicago: University of Chicago Press, 2006), 8; Wendy Wall, "Literacy and the Domestic Arts," *Huntington Library Quarterly* 73 (2010): 395; Robert Applebaum, *Aguecheek's Beef, Belch's Hiccup, and Other Gastronomic Interjections. Literature, Culture, and Food among the Early Moderns* (Chicago: Chicago University Press, 2006), Chapter Three.

67 John Partridge, *The treasurie of commodious conceits, & hidden secrets and may be called, the huswiues closet, of healthfull prouision. Mete and necessarie for the profitable vse of all estates both men and women: and also pleasaunt for recreation, with a necessary table of all things herein contayned. Gathered out of sundrye experiments lately practised by men of great knowledge* (London, 1573); and *The widowes treasure plentifully furnished with sundry precious and approoued secretes in phisicke and chirurgery for the health and pleasure of mankinde : hereunto are adioyned, sundry pretie practises and conclusions of cookerie: with many profitable and holesome medicines for sundrie diseases in cattell* (London, 1588). The *Treasurie* was issued in at least 12 editions from 1573–1653, and at least ten editions of the *Widowes Treasure* were issued from 1582–1655.

68 William Turner, *The first and second partes of the herbal* (Cologne, 1568): Turner observed that the common rose is so well-known it needs no description, but "there are found diverse other kinds as Damask roses/incarnation roses/musk roses/with certain other kinds/whereof there is no mention in any old writer" sig. U2v–W4r.

69 John Partridge, *The widowes treasure* (London, 1586), sig. A2r.

70 Wendy Wall, *Recipes for Thought: Knowledge and Taste in the Early Modern English Kitchen* (Philadelphia: University of Pennsylvania Press, 2015): 7.

71 Andrew Pettegree, "Centre and Periphery in the European Book World," *Transactions of the Royal Historical Society*, Sixth Series, Vol. 18 (2008): 101–128: "All told English presses account for between 1.5 per cent of the editions published throughout Europe before 1501; and around four per cent of those published in the sixteenth century."

72 Three editions of *A proper new booke of cookery Declaring what maner of meates be best in season for al times of the yeere, and how they ought to be dressed, [and] serued at the table, both for fleshe dayes and fish daies. with a new addition, very necessary for al them that delight in cookery* were published between 1558–1576; four of *A boke of cookery* (1584–1594); six of Thomas Dawson's *The good husvvifes ievvell*, parts I and II (1587–1610), one edition of Dawson's *The Good hus-wives treasurie* (1588), two editions of his *A booke of cookerie, otherwise called the good huswiues handmaid* (1594–97), and eight editions of Hugh Plat's *Delights for ladies, to adorne their persons, tables, closets, and distillatories* (1600–1615).

73 Thomas Dawson, *The good husvvifes ievvell VVherein is to be found most excellent and rare deuises for conceits in cookerie, found out by the practise of Thomas Dawson. Whereunto is adioyned sundry approued reseits for many soueraine oyles, and the way to distill many precious waters, with diuers approued medicines for many diseases. Also certaine approued points of husbandry, very necessarie for all husbandmen to know* (London, 1587).

74 Thomas Dawson, *The good husvvifes ievvell, part 1* (London, 1587), sig. C5v.

75 Thomas Dawson, *A booke of cookerie, otherwise called the good huswiues handmaid* (London, 1597).

76 Hugh Plat, *Delights for ladies* (1600), sig. B5r.

Chapter Four
Maritime Matters

1. Anonymous (Richard Hakluyt), *Diuers voyages touching the discouerie of America, and the ilands adiacent vnto the same made first of all by our Englishmen, and afterward by the Frenchmen and Britons: and certaine notes of aduertisements for obseruations, necessarie for such as shall heereafter make the like attempt, with two mappes annexed heereunto for the plainer vnderstanding of the whole matter* (London, 1582).

2. *The arte of nauigation conteynyng a compendious description of the sphere, with the makyng of certen instrumentes and rules for nauigations: and exemplified by manye demonstrations. Wrytten in the Spanyshe tongue by Martin Cortes and directed to the emperour Charles the fyfte. Translated out of Spanyshe into Englyshe by Richard Eden* (London, 1561).

3. *Le Grand Routier* was the basis of *Ye rutter of ye see*, printed by Robert Copland and Richard Bankes in 1528 and Thomas Petyt's *The rutter of the see with the hauens/ rodes soundynges/ kennynges/ wyndes/ floodes and ebbes daungers and costes of dyuers regions with the lawes of the yle of Auleron, & the iudgementes of y[e] see* (London, 1536), while four subsequent editions to 1573 were based on *Le Routier de la mer*. See D.W. Waters, *The rutters of the sea : the sailing directions of Pierre Garcie : a study of the first English and French printed sailing directions, with facsimile reproductions* (New Haven, CT: Yale University Press, 1967).

4. John Davis, *The seamans secrets deuided into 2. partes, wherein is taught the three kindes of sayling, horizontall, peradoxall [sic], and sayling vpon a great circle : also an horizontall tyde table for the easie finding of the ebbing and flowing of the tydes, with a regiment newly calculated for the finding of the declination of the sunne, and many other most necessary rules and instruments, not heeretofore set foorth by any / newly published by Iohn Dauis of Sandrudge* (London, 1595); *M. Blundevile his exercises containing sixe treatises, the titles wherof are set down in the next printed page: which treatises are verie necessarie to be read and learned of all yoong gentlemen that haue not bene exercised in such disciplines, and yet are desirous to haue knowledge as well in cosmographie, astronomie, and geographie, as also in the arte of navigation . . . To the furtherance of which arte of navigation, the said M. Blundevile speciallie wrote the said treatises and of meere good will doth dedicate the same to all the young gentlemen of this realme* (London, 1594).

5. Thomas Blundeville, *M. Blundevile his exercises* (London, 1594), sig. Gg 3r-v.

6. Thomas Blundeville, *M. Blundevile his exercises* (London, 1594), sig. Gg 3r-v.

7. Eric Ash, *Power, Knowledge, and Expertise in Elizabethan England* (Baltimore: Johns Hopkins University Press, 2005), 178.

8. The term "mathematization" is Ash's and much of the analysis following is based on his *Power, Knowledge, and Expertise in Elizabethan England* as well as Margaret E. Schotte's *Sailing School: Navigating Science and Skill, 1550–1800* (Baltimore: Johns Hopkins University Press, 2020).

9. Eric Ash, *Power, Knowledge, and Expertise*, Chapter Three.

10 John Dee, "Mathematicall praeface" to *The elements of geometrie of the most auncient philosopher Euclide of Megara* (London, 1570), sig. d4v.

11 John Dee, *General and rare memorials pertayning to the perfect arte of nauigation annexed to the paradoxal cumpas, in playne: now first published: 24. yeres, after the first inuention thereof* (London, 1577).

12 George Best, *A true discourse of the late voyages of discouerie, for the finding of a passage to Cathaya, by the Northvveast, vnder the conduct of Martin Frobisher Generall deuided into three bookes* (London, 1578), sig b2r.

13 William Bourne's *A regiment for the sea: conteyning most profitable rules, mathematical experiences, and perfect knovvledge of nauigation, for all coastes and countreys: most needefull and necessarie for all seafaring men and trauellers, as pilotes, mariners, marchants* (London, 1574) was published in 11 English editions to 1631, including the expanded and corrected 1592 version of Thomas Hood. At least three Dutch editions were published, beginning in 1594.

14 William Bourne, *A regiment for the sea* (London, 1592).

15 Edward Wright, *Certaine errors in nauigation, arising either of the ordinarie erroneous making or using of the Sea chart, Compasse, Crosse staffe, and Tables of Declination of the Sunne, and fixed Starres detected and corrected* (London, 1599). *Certaine errors* was revised and republished by Wright in 1610, and then revised extensively and reissued by Joseph Moxon in 1657, with Moxon's own *The Haven-finding Art, or the way to find any Haven or place appoynted at Sea* (London, 1657).

16 *The pathway to perfect sayling Being a deliuerie in as breefe mannera as may bee, of the sixe principall pointes or groundes, concerning nauigation: written by Mr. Richard Polter, one of the late principall maisters of the Nauie Royall. And now published for the common good of all maisters, pilots, and other seamen whatsoeuer* (London, 1605).

17 *A booke called the treasure for traueilers deuided into fiue bookes or partes, contayning very necessary matters, for all sortes of trauailers, eyther by sea or by lande, written by William Bourne* (London, 1578); *The Arte of shooting in great Ordnaunce Contayning very necessary matters for all sortes of seruitoures eyther by sea or by lande. Written by William Bourne* (London, 1587); *Inuentions or deuises Very necessary for all generalles and captaines, or leaders of men, as wel be sea as by land: written by William Bourne. An. 1578* (London, 1590); The "Treasure" and the "Art of Shooting" were written several years earlier and exist in manuscript form as British Library Sloane MS 3651, addressed to William Cecil, Lord Burghley.

18 William Bourne, *Inuentions or deuises*, sig. O2r.

19 *The mathematical ievvel shewing the making, and most excellent vse of a singuler instrument so called: in that it performeth with wonderfull dexteritie, whatsoeuer is to be done, either by quadrant, ship, circle, cylinder, ring, dyall, horoscope, astrolabe, sphere, globe, or any such like heretofore deuised: ... The vse of which iewel, is so aboundant and ample, that it leadeth any man practising thereon, the direct pathway ... through the whole artes of astronomy, cosmography, ... and briefely of whatsoeuer concerneth the globe*

or sphere: . . . The most part newly founde out by the author, compiled and published . . . by Iohn Blagraue of Reading gentleman and well willer to the mathematickes, who hath cut all the prints or pictures of the whole worke with his owne hands* (London, 1585).

20 John Blagrave, *The mathematical ievvel*, sig. ¶iir.

21 Gabriel Harvey's copy of *The Mathematical Jewel* in the British Library (C.60.O.7.), contains copious annotations as well as a hand-drawn paper instrument; another copy of the *Jewell* (Cambridge University Library LE.28.5) has a paper "Jewell" constructed of cut-out diagrams from the text inside its front cover.

22 John Blagrave, *Baculum familliare, catholicon siue generale A booke of the making and vse of a staffe, newly inuented by the author, called the familiar staffe* (London, 1590); *A Necessary and Pleasaunt solace and recreation for Nauigators in their long Iorneying, Containing the vse of an Instrument or generall Astrolabe: Newly for them deuised by the Author, to bring them skilfully acquainted with all the Planets Starres, and constellacions of the Heauens: and their courses, mouings, and apparences, called the (Vranicall Astrolabe.)* (London, 1596); *The Art of Dyalling in two Parts. The first shewing plainly, and in a maner mechanichally to make dyals to all plaines, either Horizontall, Murall, declining, reclining or inclining, with the theoricke of the Arte. The second how to performe the selfe same, in a more artificall kinde, and without use of Arithmeticke, together with concaue and conuex Dyals, and the inserting of the 12 signes, and the howres of any other country in any dyall, with many other things to the same Art appertaining* (London, 1609).

23 *The newe attractiue Containyng a short discourse of the magnes or lodestone, and amongst other his vertues, of a newe discouered secret and subtill propertie, concerning the declinyng of the needle, touched therewith under the plaine of the horizon. Now first founde out by Robert Norman hydrographer. Heerevnto are annexed certaine necessarie rules for the art of nauigation by the same R.N.* (London, 1581). The book went through four more editions between 1585 and 1614.

24 Eric Ash, *Power, Knowledge, and Experience in Elizabethan England*, 114.

25 *Guilielmi Gilberti Colcestrensis, medici, Londinensis, De magnete, magneticisque corporibus, et de magno magnete tellure physiologia noua, plurimis & argumentis, & experimentis demonstrate* (London, 1600): Book Four.

26 William Barlow, *The nauigators supply Conteining many things of principall importance belonging to nauigation, with the description and vse of diuerse instruments framed chiefly for that purpose; but seruing also for sundry other of cosmography in generall: the particular instruments are specified on the next page* (London, 1597).

27 British Library, MS Lansdowne 101/12 (1588).

28 Thomas Hood, *A Copie of the Speache made by the Mathematicall Lecturer, unto the Worshipfull Companye present . . . in Gracious Street: the 4 of November 1588* (London, 1588), sig. A2aff.

29 Thomas Hood, *The vse of the two mathematicall instrumentes the crosse staffe, and the Jacobes staffe: set foorth dialogue wyse* (London, 1590); *The use*

of the celestial globe in plano, set foorth in two hemispheres . . . Set foorth by Thomas Hood (London, 1590); *The vse of both the globes, celestiall, and terrestriall most plainely deliuered in forme of a dialogue. Containing most pleasant, and profitable conclusions for the mariner, and generally for all those, that are addicted to these kinde of mathematicall instruments* (London, 1592); *The vse of the two mathematicall instruments the crosse staffe, (differing from that in common vse with the mariners:) and the Iacobs staffe: set foorth dialogue wise in two briefe and plaine treatises: the one most commodious for the mariner, and all such as are to deale in astronomicall matters: the other, profitable for the surueyor, to take the length, height, depth, or breadth, of any thing measurable. Set forth by Th. Hood. mathematicall lecturer in the citie of London. The staues are to be sold in Marke lane, at the house of Francis Cooke* (London, 1596); *The making and vse of the geometricall instrument, called a sector Whereby many necessarie geometricall conclusions concerning the proportionall description, and diuision of lines, and figures, the drawing of a plot of ground, the translating of it from one quantitie to another, and the casting of it vp geometrically, the measuring of heights, lengths and breadths may be mechanically perfomed with great expedition, ease, and elight to all those, which commonly follow the practise of the mathematicall arts, either in suruaying of land, or otherwise. Written by Thomas Hood, doctor in physicke. The instrument is made by Charles Whitwell dwelling without Temple Barre against S. Clements church* (London, 1598).

30 *A regiment for the sea containing verie necessarie matters for all sorts of men and trauailers; whereunto is added an hydrographicall discourse touching the fiue seuerall passages to Cattay; written by William Borne,* with Hood's "Marriner's guide" (London, 1596), sig. A3r.

31 Lucas Janszoon Waghenaer, *The mariners mirrour wherin may playnly be seen the courses, heights, distances, depths, soundings, flouds and ebs, risings of lands, rocks, sands and shoalds, with the marks for th'entrings of the harbouroughs, havens and ports of the greatest part of Europe: their seuerall traficks and commodities: together wth. the rules and instrume[n]ts of navigation. First made & set fourth in diuers exact sea-charts, by that famous nauigator Luke Wagenar of Enchuisen and now fitted with necessarie additions for the use of Englishmen by Anthony Ashley. Heerin also may be understood the exploits lately atchiued by the right Honorable the L. Admiral of Engla[n]d with her Maties. nauie and some former seruices don by that worthy knight Sr. Fra: Drake* (London, 1588).

32 *The mariners mirrour*, sig. A2r.

33 Anna Maria Crinò and Helen Wallis. "New Researches on the Molyneux Globes/Neue Forschungsarbeiten über die Molyneux-Globen," *Der Globusfreund*, no. 35/37 (1987): 11–20.

34 Robert Hues, *Tractatus de Globis Et Eorum Usu. a Treatise Descriptive of the Globes Constructed by Emery Molyneux: And Published in 1592* (i.e., 1594) *by Robert Hues,* ed. Clements R. Markham (London: Hakluyt Society, 1889), 16.

35 Anna Maria Crinò and Helen Wallis, "New Researches on the Molyneux Globes," (1987): 13.

36 Robert Hues, *Tractatu de Globis* (London: Hakluyt Society, 1889), 95; Hues's *Tractatus de globis et eorum usu* was published in at least 15 editions before 1651, including Dutch, French and English translations. The first English edition was *A Learned Treatise of Globes, both Cœlestiall and Terrestriall: With their Severall Uses. Written first in Latine, by Mr Robert Hues: And by him so Published. Afterward Illustrated with Notes, by Io. Isa. Pontanus. And now Lastly made English, for the Benefit of the Unlearned by John Chilmead MrA of Christ-Church in Oxon* (London, 1638).

37 John Davis, *The seamans secrets*, sig. K1r.

38 Jeremy Hodgkinson, *The Wealden Iron Industry* (Stroud, UK: Tempus Publishing, 2008).

39 The compilation of materials entitled "Fragments of Ancient English Shipwrightry" by Samuel Pepys when in service to the Navy Board and Admiralty Commission is a collection of notes and plans attributed to Baker from the 1570s on and continued with notes and annotations by one of his apprentices, John Wells. It is in the collection of the Pepys Library at Magdelen College, Cambridge: PL 2991; I relied on the summary of R.A. Barker and the analysis of Stephen A. Johnston for my discussion of Baker's work process: R.A. Barker, 'Fragments from the Pepysian Library,' *Revista da Universidade de Coimbra* 32 (1986): 161–178; S.A. Johnston, "Making Mathematical Practice: Gentlemen, Practitioners and Artisans in Elizabethan England", Ph.D. diss., Cambridge University, 1994): 107–165.

40 David McGee, "From Craftsmanship to Draftsmanship: Naval Architecture and the Three Traditions of Early Modern Design," *Technology and Culture*, 40, no. 2 (1999): 209–236.

41 William Borough, *A Discourse of the Variation of the Cumpas, or Magneticall Needle* (London, 1581).

42 Margarent Blatcher, "Chatham Dockyard and a Little-Known Shipwright, Matthew Baker (1530–1613)," *Archaelogia Cantiana* 107 (1989): 155–172.

43 Blatcher, "Chatham Dockyard" (1989): 163.

44 Michael Oppenheim, *A history of the administration of the Royal Navy and of merchant shipping in relation to the Navy, from MDIX to MDCLX with an introduction treating of the preceeding period* (London: The Bodley Head, 1896): 126 (citing *State Papers, Dom.*, ccxliii, 110).

45 *State Papers, Domestic*, clii, 19.

46 William Harrison, *The Description of England*, ed. by Georges Edelen (Ithaca, NY: Published for the Folger Shakespeare Library by Cornell University Press, 1968), 246

47 *A perambulation of Kent: conteining the description, hystorie, and customes of that shire. Written in the yeere 1570, by William Lambarde, of Lincolnes inne, gent: first published in the year 1576, and now increased and altered from the author's owne last copie* (Chatham: W. Burrill, 1826): 312.

48 *A sea grammar vvith the plaine exposition of Smiths Accidence for young sea-men, enlarged. Diuided into fifteene chapters: what they are you may partly conceiue by the contents. Written by Captaine Iohn Smith, sometimes gouernour of Virginia, and admirall of Nevv-England* (London, 1627).

49 The career of Thomas Digges and his role in the Dover project are discussed in two works by Eric Ash, "'A Perfect and an Absolute Work': Expertise, Authority, and the Rebuilding of Dover Harbor, 1579–1583," *Technology and Culture* 41, No. 2 (April 2000): 239–268; and *Power, Knowledge, and Expertise in Elizabethan England*, as well as in Stephen A. Johnston's Ph.D. dissertation, 'Making mathematical practice: gentlemen, practitioners and artisans in Elizabethan England' (Ph.D. Cambridge University, 1994): Chapters 2 and 5.

50 Thomas Digges, "A Briefe Discourse," c. 1582 *Archaelogia* XI (1794).

51 *An arithmeticall militare treatise, named Stratioticos: compendiously teaching the science of nu[m]bers, as vvell in fractions as integers, and so much of the rules and aequations algebraicall and arte of numbers cossicall, as are requisite for the profession of a soldiour. Together with the moderne militare discipline, offices, lawes and dueties in euery wel gouerned campe and armie to be obserued: long since atte[m]pted by Leonard Digges Gentleman, augmented, digested, and lately finished, by Thomas Digges, his sonne* (London, 1579); Thomas Digges, *An arithmeticall vvarlike treatise named Stratioticos compendiously teaching the science of nombers as well in fractions as integers, and so much of the rules and μquations algebraicall, and art of nombers cossicall, as are requisite for the profession of a soldier. Together with the moderne militare discipline, offices, lawes and orders in euery well gouerned campe and armie inuiolably to be obserued. First published by Thomas Digges Esquire anno salutis 1579. and dedicated vnto the right Honorable Earle of Leicester, lately reuiewed and corrected by the author him selfe, and also augmented with sundry additions. Aswell concerning the science or art of great artillerie, as the offices of the Sergeant Maior Generall* (London, 1590).

52 Thomas Digges, *Stratioticos* (London, 1579), sig. A4v.

53 This was the first English reference to "nautical architecture"; Digges also referenced works in progress on Copernicus, dialing, artillery and pyrotechnics, fortifications, and asserted that these treatises would have been published if not for the "Infernall Furies" that tormented him with "Lawe-Brables". Digges omitted the list of unpublished works in the 1590 edition of the *Stratioticos*.

54 Geoffrey Parker, "The 'Dreadnought Revolution' of Tudor England," *Mariner's Mirror* 82, no. 3 (August 1996): 269–300.

Chapter Five
Public Discourses; Practical Concerns

1 Gervase Markham, *The English husbandman. The first part: contayning the knowledge of the true nature of euery soyle within this kingdome: how to plow it; and the manner of the plough, and other instruments belonging thereto. Together with the art of planting, grafting, and gardening after our latest and rarest fashion. A worke neuer written before by any author: and now newly compiled for the benefit of this kingdome* (London, 1613), sig. A1v.

2   *The two books of Francis Bacon: Of the proficience and advancement of learning, divine and human* (London: Printed by J. McCreery, for T. Payne, 1808), 441–442.
3   *The two books of Francis Bacon,* 229–235.
4   Sir Geoffrey Keynes, *The Life of William Harvey* (Oxford: Clarendon Press, 1966), 142.
5   Anonymous, *Lachrymæ Londinenses: or, Londons lamentations and teares for Gods heauie visitation of the plague of pestilence. With, a map of the cities miserie: wherein may be seene, a journall of the deplorable estate of the citie, from the beginning of the visitation vnto this present. A Christian expostulation and admonition to such as fled out of the citie. . . .* (London, 1626), 10.
6   Margaret Pelling, *Medical Conflicts in Early Modern London,* 48–49.
7   *Orders thought meet by her Majesty, and her privy Council, to be executed throughout the counties of this realm, in such towns, villages, and other places, as are, or may be hereafter infected with the plague, for the stay of further increase of the same. Also, an advise set down upon her Majesties express commandment, by the best learned in physic within this realm, containing sundry good rules and easy medicines, without charge to the meaner sort of people, as well for the preservation of her good subjects from the plague before infection, as for the curing and ordering of them after they shall be infected* was reissued in 1592, 1593, 1603, 1625, 1629, 1630, 1636, 1641 and 1646 with no substantive changes, except for the alteration of "his" Majesties government. New directives were not issued until 1666.
8   *Orders heretofore conceived and agreed to be published by the Lord Mayor and Aldermen of the city of London and the justices of peace of the counties of Middlesex and Surrey, by direction from the lords of His Majesties most honorable privy council, and now thought fit to be revived, and again published* (London, 1625).
9   Stephen Greenberg, "Plague, the Printing Press, and Public Health in Seventeenth-Century London," *Huntington Library Quarterly* 67, no. 4 (2004): 508–527.
10 Harold J. Cook, "Policing the Health of London: The College of Physicians and the Early Stuart Monarchy," *Social History of Medicine,* 2, Issue 1 (1989): 1–33.
11 Margaret Pelling, *Medical Conflicts in Early Modern London,* 151.
12 C.R.B. Barrett, *The History of the Society of Apothecaries of London* (London: E. Stock, 1905), xxi–xxxiii.
13 George Urdang, ed., *Pharmacopœia londinensis of 1618* (Madison: State Historical Society of Wisconsin, 1944), 29.
14 George Urdang, ed., *Pharmacopoeia londinensis of 1618,* 31.
15 *A physical directory, or, A translation of the dispensatory made by the Colledg of Physitians of London : and by them imposed upon all the apothecaries of England to make up their medicines by : and in this third edition is added a*

key to Galen's method of physick : wherein is three sections . . . / by Nich. Culpeper, gent student in physick and astrologie (London, 1651), 9.

16 Alexander Read [Reid], *The chirurgicall lectures of tumors and vlcers Delivered on Tusedayes appointed for these exercises and keeping of their courts in the Chirurgeans Hall these three yeeres last past, viz. 1632, 1633, and 1634. By Alexander Read Doctor of Physick, and one of the fellowes of the Physitians College of London* (London, 1635), 8.

17 Alexander Read, *The chirurgicall lectures* (London, 1635), 97.

18 *The svrgions mate, or A treatise discouering faithfully and plainely the due contents of the svrgions chest the vses of the instruments, the vertues and operations of the medicines, the cures of the most frequent diseases at sea* (London, 1617); *Woodalls viaticum: the path-way to the surgions chest Containing chirurgicall instrvctions for the yonger sort of surgions now imployed in the service of His Maiestie for the intended reliefe of Rochell* (London, 1628); *The surgeons mate, or, Military & domestique surgery. Discouering faithfully & plainly ye method and order of ye surgeons chest, ye vses of the instruments, the vertues and operations of ye medicines w[ith] ye exact cures of wounds made by gun-shott, and otherwise as namely: wounds, apostumes, ulcers, fistula's fractures, dislocations, w[ith] ye most ealie & safest wayes of amputation or dismembring, the cures of the scuruey, of ye fluxes of ye belly, of ye collicke and iliaca passio, of tenasmus and exitus ani, and of the calenture, with a treatise of ye cure of ye plague. / by John Woodall* (London, 1639).

19 John Woodall, *The surgeons mate* (London, 1639), sig. B1v.

20 *To the most Honourable House of Commons, commonly called, the Lower House of Parliament. The humble petition of the masters or gouernors of the mysterie and comminaltie of barbers and chirurgions of London* (London, 1624).

21 *A short discouerie of the vnobserued dangers of seuerall sorts of ignorant and vnconsiderate practisers of physicke in England profitable not onely for the deceiued multitude, and easie for their meane capacities, but raising reformed and more aduised thoughts in the best vnderstandings: with direction for the safest election of a physition in necessitie: by Iohn Cotta of Northampton Doctor in Physicke* (London, 1612); followed up by *A true discouery of the empericke with the fugitiue, physition and quacksaluer who display their banners vpon posts: whereby his Maiesties subiects are not onely deceiued, but greatly endangered in the health of their bodies: being very profitable as well for the ignorant, as for the learned: by I.C. Doctor in Physicke* (London, 1617); and *A short discouerie of seuerall sorts of ignorant and vnconsiderate practisers of physicke in England With direction for the safest election of a physition in necessitie: by Iohn Cotta of Northampton Doctor of Physicke* (London, 1619).

22 Francis Herring, *The anatomyes of the true physition, and counterfeit mountebanke wherein both of them, are graphically described, and set out in their right, and orient colours. Published in Latin by Iohn Oberndorff, a learned German: and translated into English by F.H. fellow of the Coll. of Physitions in London. Hereunto is annexed: A short discourse, or, Discouery of certaine stratagems, whereby our London-empericks, haue bene obserued strongly to*

oppugne, and oft times to expugne their poore patients purses (London, 1602); *Bevvare of pick-purses. Or a caueat for sick folkes to take heede of vnlearned phisitions, and vnskilfull chyrurgians. By F.H. Doctor in Phisick* (London, 1605).

23 Francis Herring, *The anatomyes of the true physition* (London, 1602), sig. G1v.

24 Thomas Lodge, *A treatise of the plague containing the nature, signes, and accidents of the same, with the certaine and absolute cure of the feuers, botches and carbuncles that raigne in these times: and aboue all things most singular experiments and preseruatiues in the same, gathered by the obseruation of diuers worthy trauailers, and selected out of the writing of the best learned phisitians in this age* (London, 1603), sig. A3r–v.

25 Francis Herring, *Certaine rules, directions, or aduertisments for this time of pestilentiall contagion: with a caueat to those that weare about their neckes impoisoned amulets as a preseruatiue from the plague: / first published for the behoofe of the city of London, and all other parts of the land at this time visited; by Francis Hering, D. in physicke, and fellow of the Colledge of Physitians in London* (London, 1603) was reissued with variant titles and additions in 1625, 1636, 1641 and 1665.

26 *A modest defence of the caueat giuen to the wearers of impoisoned amulets, as preseruatiues from the plague wherein that point is somewhat more lergely reasoned and debated with an ancient physician, who hath mainteined them by publicke writing: as likewise that vnlearned and dangerous opinion, that the plague is not infectious, lately broched in London, is briefly glansed at, and refuted by way of preface, by Fr. Hering D. in Physicke. Reade without preiudice; iudge without partialitie* (London, 1604), sig. E2r. Besides Lodge's *Treatise of the Plague*, Peter Turner (son of William) weighed in in support of plague cakes in 1603: *The opinion of Peter Turner Doct: in physicke, concerning amulets or plague cakes whereof perhaps some holde too much, and some too little* (London 1603).

27 Francis Herring, *Certaine rules, directions, or aduertisments for this time of pestilentiall contagion* (London, 1625).

28 *A Direction concerning the plague, or pestilence, for poore and rich* (London: A. Mathewes, 1625).

29 Stephen Bradwell, *A vvatch-man for the pest Teaching the true rules of preservation from the pestilent contagion, at this time fearefully over-flowing this famous cittie of London. Collected out of the best authors, mixed with aunciect experience, and moulded into a new and most plaine method* (London, 1625), Afterword.

30 *A boke, or counseill against the disease commonly called the sweate, or sweatyng sicknesse. Made by Ihon Caius doctour in phisicke. Very necessary for euerye personne, and muche requisite to be had in the handes of al sortes, for their better instruction, preparacion and defence, against the soubdein comyng, and fearful assaultying of the-same [sic] disease* (London, 1552), sig. D4r.

31 Thomas Dekker, *The vvonderfull yeare. 1603 Wherein is shewed the picture of London, lying sicke of the plague. At the ende of all (like a mery epilogue to a*

dull play) certaine tales are cut out in sundry fashions, of purpose to shorten the liues of long winters nights, that lye watching in the darke for vs (London, 1603), sig. D3r–v.

32 Matthew Gwinne, *In assertorem chymicæ, sed veræ medicinæ desertorem, Fra. Anthonium, Matthæi Gwynn philiatri in medicorum Londinensium Collegio quarti censoris regestarij succincta aduersaria* (London, 1611); John Cotta, *Cotta contra Antonium: or An Ant-Antony: or An Ant-apology manifesting Doctor Antony his apologie for aurum potabile, in true and equall ballance of right reason, to be false and counterfait. By Iohn Cotta Doctor in Physicke* (London, 1623).

33 *The apologie, or defence of a verity heretofore published concerning a medicine called aurum potabile, that is, the pure substance of gold, prepared, and made potable and medicinable without corrosiues, helpfully giuen for the health of man in most diseases, but especially auaileable for the strenghning [sic] and comforting of the heart and vitall spirits the perfomers of health: as an vniversall medicine. Together with the plaine, and true reasons . . . confirming the vniversalitie thereof. And lastly, the manner and order of administration or vse of this medicine in sundrie infirmities. / By Francis Anthonie of London, doctor in physicke* was published in both English and Latin in 1616.

34 *The cure of the plague by an antidote called aurum vitae. Being well approved to be an easie safe, and perfect cure thereof; as also of contagious agues, or feavers beginning either hot or cold. The description, order and use whereof, together with the said antidote, and are to be sold at the shop of Nicholas Bourne, stationer, at the south entrance of the royal exchange. Invented and produced by John Woodall, master in surgery. Published by authority* (London, 1640).

35 Timothie Bright, *A treatise, vvherein is declared the sufficiencie of English medicines, for cure of all diseases, cured with medicines. Whereunto is added a collection of medicines growing (for the most part) within our English climat, approoued and experimented against the iaundise, dropsie, stone, fallingsicknesse, pestilence* (London, 1615).

36 *An aduice hovv to plant tobacco in England and how to bring it to colour and perfection, to whom it may be profitable, and to whom harmfull. The vertues of the hearbe in generall, as well in the outward application as taken in fume. With the danger of the Spanish tobacco. Written by C.T.* (London, 1615), sig. A4v.

37 *The herball or Generall historie of plantes. Gathered by Iohn Gerarde of London Master in Chirurgerie very much enlarged and amended by Thomas Iohnson citizen and apothecarye of London* (London, 1633), sig. ¶¶¶r.

38 John Gerard, *The herball or, Generall historie of plantes* (London, 1597), 190, 147, 389, 1120.

39 *Paradisi in sole paradisus terrestris. or A garden of all sorts of pleasant flowers which our English ayre will permitt to be noursed vp with a kitchen garden of all manner of herbes, rootes, & fruites, for meate or sause vsed with vs, and an orchard of all sorte of fruitbearing trees and shrubbes fit for our land together with the right orderinge planting & preseruing of them and their vses &*

vertues collected by Iohn Parkinson apothecary of London (London, 1629); *Theatrum botanicum: the theater of plantes. Or, an universall and compleate herball. / Composed by John Parkinson apothecarye of London and the kings herbalist* (London, 1640).

40 Parkinson, *Paradisi in sole paradisus terrestris* (London, 1629): 348; Apparently this hellebore was actually a lady's slipper (*cypripedium calceolus*) and Parkinson's precise location of it source led to its near extinction in Britian. The plant collector and author Reginal Farrer blamed Mistress Tunstall for this occurrence in his classic text, *My Rock Garden* : "O Mistress Tomasin, if only you had loved these delights a little less ruinously for future generations! Do you sleep quiet, you worthy gentlewoman, in Tunstall Church, or does your uneasy sprite still haunt the Helks Wood in vain longing to undo the wrong you did ? And after Mistress Tomasin had long been as dead as the Cypripediums she sent up to Parkinson, there came a market-gardener, a base soul, animated only by love of lucre (and thus damned to a far lower Hell than the worthy if over-zealous gentlewoman), who grubbed up all the Cypripediums that she had left, and potted them up for sale. The Helks Wood, now, is an oyster for ever robbed of its pearl—unless, unless in some unsuspected nook somewhere, one gold-and-purple flower is yearly mocking at the memories of Mistress Tomasin and the wicked gardener both." (London: E. Arnold, 1913): 33.

41 John Parkinson, *Theatrum botanicum* (London, 1640): 699.

42 The characterizing quote is that of Brian W. Ogilvie, from *The Science of Describing: Natural History in Renaissance Europe* (Chicago: University of Chicago Press, 2008): 268.

43 John Parkinson, *Theatrum Botanicum* (London, 1640): 1325.

44 Markham's enlarged edition of the French *Maison Rustique*, orginally translated by Richard Surflet, seems to have been particularly inspirational, but he also produced a "renewed" and expanded edition of Conrad Heresbach's *The vvhole art of husbandry contained in foure books*, first translated from the German by Barnaby Googe, towards the end of his career. An important article by Wendy Wall asserts that Markham's "national husbandry" was inspired by this foreign "competition," as well as his abilities to cater to a new English audience for husbandry manuals, in part by emphasizing "English thrift": Wendy Wall, "Renaissance National Husbandry: Gervase Markham and the Publication of England," *The Sixteenth Century Journal* 27, no. 3 (1996): 767–785.

45 Gervase Markham, *The English husbandman. The first part* (London, 1613), sig. A1r–v.

46 Sam White, "The Real Little Ice Age," *Journal of Inderdisciplinary History* 44, no. 3 (2014): 327–352.

47 Gervase Markham, *The second booke of the English husbandman Contayning the ordering of the kitchin-garden, and the planting of strange flowers: the breeding of all manner of cattell* (London, 1614), 14.

48 Gervase Markham, *Markhams farwell to husbandry or, The inriching of all sorts of barren and sterill grounds in our kingdome, to be as fruitfull in all manner of graine, pulse, and grasse as the best grounds whatsoeuer together*

with the anoyances, and preseruation of all graine and seede, from one yeare to many yeares (London, 1620), 9.
49 *Markham's farwell to husbandry* (London, 1620), 129; *Hungers preuention: or, The whole arte of fovvling by vvater and land Containing all the secrets belonging to that arte, and brought into a true forme or method, by which the most ignorant may know how to take any kind of fowle, either by land or water. Also, exceeding necessary and profitable for all such as trauell by sea, and come into vninhabited places: especially, all those that haue any thing to doe with new plantations.*
50 Jennifer Mylander, "Early Modern How-to Books: Impractical Manuals and the Construction of Englishness in the Atlantic World," *Journal for Early Modern Cultural Studies*, 9, no. 1 (2009): 123–156.
51 *A vvay to get vvealth* was published in at least 15 editions between 1623–1700 with varying recycled content. F.N.L. Poynter, in his *Bibliography of Gervase Markham 1568?-1637* (Oxford: Oxford Bibliographical Society, 1962), observed that "Markham's ingenuity [was] such that he could probably devise still more varieties of presentation of his subject for the use of stationers not yet involved in his publications." 23.
52 Gervase Markham, *The inrichment of the vveald of Kent: or, A direction to the husbandman, for the true ordering, manuring, and inriching of all the grounds within the wealds of Kent and Sussex and may generally serue for all the grounds in England, of that nature* (London, 1623), 3–19.
53 Gervase Markham, *Markham's Farwell to husbandry* (London, 1620), 148.
54 *The English house-vvife* first appeared as Book Two of Markham's *Covntrey contentments, in two bookes: the first, containing the whole art of riding great horses . . . with the breeding, breaking, dyeting and ordring of them . . . The second intituled The English housewife: containing the inward and outward vertues which ought to be in a compleate women: as her phisicke, cookery . . . distillation, perfumes, . . . brewing, baking, and all other things belonging to an houshold* (London, 1615); it was also published in *A vvay to get vvealth*; and it was first published as an individual title in 1637, the year of Markham's death, as well as in successive editions of 1649, 1653, 1656, 1660, 1664, and 1683.
55 Gervase Markham, *The English house-vvife, Containing the inward and outward Virtues which ought to be in a compleate woman* (London, 1637), Chapters One and Two.
56 Gervase Markham, *The English house-vvife*, 146–147.
57 Gervase Markham, *The English house-vvife*, 200.
58 Gervase Markham, *The English house-vvife*, 247.
59 Gervase Markham, *The English house-vvife*, 251.
60 Tara Hamling and Catherine Richardson, *A Day at Home in Early Modern England: Material Culture and Domestic Life, 1500–1700* (New Haven: Yale University Press, 2017), 61–62.
61 See Mark Overton, Jane Whittle, Darron Dean and Andrew Hann, *Production and Consumption in English Households, 1600–1750* (Abingdon, UK: Routledge, 2004), 57

62 Gervase Markham, *The English house-vvife*, 167.
63 Gervase Markham, *The English house-vvife*, 183.
64 Gervase Markham, *Cheape and good husbandry for the vvell-ordering of all beasts, and fowles, and for the generall cure of their diseases Contayning the natures, breeding, choyse, vse, feeding, and curing of the diseases of all manner of cattell, as horse, oxe, cow, sheepe, goates, swine, and tame-conies* (London, 1614), 2.

Chapter Six
The Knowledge-Mongers

1 William London, *A catalogue of the most vendible books in England orderly and alphabetically digested under the heads of divinity, history, physick and chyrurgery, law, arithmetick, geometry, astrology . . . : with Hebrew, Greek and Latine for schools and scholars : the like work never yet performed by any : also, all sorts of globes, mapps of the world or in parts . . . : all to be sold by the author at his shop in New-Castle* (London, 1657), 34.
2 Gabriel Plattes, *A discovery of infinite treasure, hidden since the vvorlds beginning VVhereunto all men, of what degree soever, are friendly invited to be sharers with the discoverer* (London, 1639), sig. C1r–v.
3 Gabriel Plattes, *A discovery of infinite treasure*, sig. M2r. [Latin motto: "If God is with us, who can be against us?"].
4 *New experiments physico-mechanicall, touching the spring of the air, and its effects, (made, for the most part, in a new pneumatical engine) written by way of letter to the Right Honorable Charles Lord Vicount of Dungarvan, eldest son to the Earl of Corke. / By the Honorable Robert Boyle Esq;* (London, 1660), sig. B1v.
5 Conrad Gessner, *The newe iewell of health wherein is contayned the most excellent secretes of phisicke and philosophie* (London, 1576), sig. *iiiv.
6 Stephen Johnston, "Recorde, Robert, (c. 1512–1558")" in *Oxford Dictionary of National Biography*.
7 John Blagrave, *The mathematical ievvel* (London, 1585).
8 British Library, C.60.O.7.
9 Harvey's annotations are in his edition of Luca Guarico's *Tractatus Astrologicus* (1552): Bodleian Library 4° Rawlinson 61, cited in Nicholas Popper, "The English Polydaedali: How Gabriel Harvey Read Late Tudor England," *Journal of the History of Ideas* 66, No. 3 (July 2005): 351–381.
10 John Dee, "Mathematical praeface" to *The elements of geometrie of the most auncient philosopher Euclide of Megara*, sig. d4v.
11 John Shute, *The first and chief groundes of architecture*, sig. A2v.
12 Ralph Agas, *A preparative to platting of landes and tenements for surueigh Shewing the diuersitie of sundrie instruments applyed thereunto. Patched up as plainly together, as boldly offered to the curteous view and regard of all worthie gentlemen, louers of skill. And published in stead of his flying papers,*

which cannot abide the pasting to poasts (London, 1596); John Norden, *The surueyors dialogue Diuided into fiue bookes: very profitable for all men to peruse, that haue to do with the reuenues of land, or the manurance, vse, or occupation thereof, both lords and tenants: as also and especially for such as indeuor to be seene in the faculty of surueying of mannors, lands, tenements, &c* (London, 1618); Aaron Rathborne, *The Svrveyor in Foure Bookes* (London, 1616): Two years after this publication Rathborne was granted a patent to make maps of the cities of London, Westminster, York, Bristol, Norwich, Canterbury, Bath, Oxford, Cambridge, and Windsor in 1618, but apparently the project never got off the ground.

13 Cyprian Lucar, *A Treatise named Lucarsolace : deuided into fovver bookes, which in part are collected out of diuerse authors in diuerse languages, and in part deuised / by Cyprian Lucar, gentleman*, sig. V2r.

14 Cyprian Lucar, *A Treatise named Lucarsolace*, sig. Y3r.

15 See Vera Keller and Ted McCormick, "Towards a History of Projects," *Early Science and Medicine* 21, no. 5 (2016): 423–444; and Paul Slack, *The Invention of Improvement: Information and Material Progress in Seventeenth-Century England* (Oxford: Oxford University Press, 2015) for discussions on early modern projectors.

16 Hugh Plat, *The jewell house of art and nature* (London, 1594).

17 Hugh Plat, *Floraes paradise beautified and adorned with sundry sorts of delicate fruites and flovvers, by the industrious labour of H.P.* (London, 1608), sig. A3v–A4r.

18 John Bate, *The mysteryes of nature, and art conteined in foure severall tretises* (London, 1634).

19 *Foure paradoxes, or politique discourses 2 concerning militarie discipline, written long since by Thomas Digges Esquire. 2 of the worthinesse of warre and warriors, by Dudly Digges, his sonne. All newly published to keepe those that will read them, as they did them that wrote them, from idlenesse* (London, 1604), sig. H2v.

20 Gervase Markham, *The souldiers accidence. Or an introduction into military discipline containing the first principles and necessary knowledge meete for captaines, muster-masters, and all young souldiers of the infantrie, or foote bandes. Also, the cavallarie or formes of trayning of horse-troopes, as it hath beene received from the latest and best experiences armies* (London, 1625).

21 James Howell, *Instructions for Forreine Travell, 1642. Collated with the Second Edition of 1650. English Reprints*, ed. by Edward Arber (London, 1869), 80, 41.

22 *Of the interchangeable course, or variety of things in the whole world and the concurrence of armes and learning, thorough the first and famousest nations: from the beginning of ciuility, and memory of man, to this present. Moreouer, whether it be true or no, that there can be nothing sayd, which hath not bin said heretofore: and that we ought by our owne inuentions to augment the doctrine of the aunciencts; not contenting our selues with translations, expositions, corrections, and abridgments of their writings. Written in French*

by Loys le Roy called Regius: and translated into English by R.A. (London, 1594), 128.

23 David Waters, *The Art of Navigation in England in Elizabethan and Early Stuart Times*, 219.

24 John Hamilton Moore, *The new practical navigator : being a complete epitome of navigation to which are added all the tables requisite for determining the latitude and longitude at sea* (London: Printed for J. Johnson, 1807), 87.

25 Robert Recorde, *Records Arithmetick: Contayning the Ground of Arts: In Which is taught the generall parts, rules and operations of the same in whole Numbers and Fractions, after a more easy and exact methode than ever heretofore: first written by Robert Record, Doctor in Phisicke* (London, 1615), sig. A2–A3.

26 *Aristotles politiques, or Discourses of gouernment. Translated out of Greeke into French, with expositions taken out of the best authours, specially out of Aristotle himselfe, and out of Plato, conferred together where occasion of matter treated of by them both doth offer it selfe: the obseruations and reasons whereof are illustrated and confirmed by innumerable examples, both old and new, gathered out of the most renowmed empires, kingdomes, seignories, and commonweals that euer haue bene, and wherof the knowledge could be had in writing, or by faythfull report, concerning the beginning, proceeding, and excellencie of ciuile gouernment. By Loys Le Roy, called Regius. Translated out of French into English by I.D.* (London, 1598).

27 Richard Witt, *Arithmeticall Questions, Tovching The Buying or Exchange of Annuities; Taking of Leases for Fines, or Yearly Rent; Purchase of Fee-Simples; Dealing for present or future Possessions; and other Bargaines and Accounts; wherein allowance for disbursing or forebeareance of money intended; Briefly resolued, by means of certain Breuiats* (London, 1613), sig A3v.

28 Martin Billingsley, *The pen's exellencie, or, The secretaries delight ... together with an insertion of sondrie peeces, or examples of all y[e] vsuall hands of England : as also an addition of certaine methodicall observations for writing, making of the pen, holding the pen, &c* (London, 1618), sig. C2v.

29 Billingsley, *The pen's excellencie*, sig. C1r–v.

30 John Browne, *The marchants avizo Very necessarie for their sonnes and seruants, when they first send them beyond the seas, as to Spaine and Portingale or other countreyes. Made by their hartie wellwiller in Christ. I.B. marchant* (London, 1589), sig. E–E2. *The marhcants aviso* was issued in five more editions from 1590–1640.

31 *The complete works in verse and prose of Samuel Daniel. Ed., with memorial-introduction and a glossarial index embracing notes and illustrations, by the Rev. Alexander B. Grosart* (London: Hazell, Watson and Viney, 1885–1886): Volume One, *Musophilus*, 254; Volume Three, *Tragedy of Philotus*, 124; Thomas Dekker, *The vvonderfull yeare. 1603*, sig. B2v.

32 Lewes Roberts, *The merchants mappe of commerce wherein, the universall manner and matter of trade, is compendiously handled. The standerd and currant coines of sundry princes, observed. The reall and imaginary coines of accompts and exchanges, expressed. The naturall and artificiall commodities of*

all countries for transportation declared. The weights and measures of all eminent cities and tovvnes of traffique, collected and reduced one into another; and all to the meridian of commerce practised in the famous citie of London (London, 1638). Roberts aimed his "compendious" work not only at merchants, but also diplomats (all such as shall be imployed in the publique affaires of princes in forreigne parts," in particular and all travelers in general.

33 Samuel Purchas, *Pvrchas his pilgrimes In fiue bookes. The first, contayning the voyages and peregrinations made by ancient kings, patriarkes, apostles, philosophers, and others, to and thorow the remoter parts of the knowne world: enquiries also of languages and religions, especially of the moderne diuersified professions of Christianitie. The second, a description of all the circum-nauigations of the globe. The third, nauigations and voyages of English-men, alongst the coasts of Africa . . . The fourth, English voyages beyond the East Indies, to the ilands of Iapan, China, Cauchinchina, the Philippinæ with others . . . The fifth, nauigations, voyages, traffiques, discoueries, of the English nation in the easterne parts of the world* (London, 1625).

34 Lewes Roberts, *The merchants mappe of commerce*, sig. A5r.

35 Lewes Roberts, *The merchants mappe of commerce*, sig. C4r.

36 James Warre, *The merchants hand-maide: or, a booke containing verie necessarie and compendious tables, for the speedie casting vp, and true valuing of any commoditie whatsoeuer Very behoouefull for merchants, gentle-men, trades-men, and all such as buy, sell, or deale in any manner of accounts. By I.W. gent* (London, 1622); Nicolas Hunt, *The merchants ievvell: or, A new inuention arithmeticall with a plenary description, and perfect explanation of a most rare and admirable table: resoluing with speed and pleasing facility aboue ten hundred thousand questions, in either reduction, practise, or the golden-rule. Forraine coynes, measures and weights; as Danske, Dutch, French, Portugall, Spanish, are readily reduced to ours, and the price of the one found by the other. A catalogue of wares, with their measures and weightes alphabetically digested; perspicuously explaned, for the seruice of the great table. A table and rule for the maintenance of an armie. Deuised by N.H. of Exon: in Deuon* (London, 1628).

37 Lewes Roberts, *The merchants mappe of commerce*, sig. E4v.

38 Lewes Roberts, *The merchants mappe of commerce*, sig. E3v.

SELECT BIBLIOGRAPHY

Primary Texts

(All Published in London Except Where Otherwise Noted)

Acosta, José de (1604), *The naturall and morall historie of the East and West Indies.*
Agas, Ralph (1596), *A preparative to platting of landes and tenements for surueigh.*
Anghiera, Pietro Martire d' (1555), *The decades of the newe worlde.*
Anonymous (1485), *A passing gode lityll boke necessarye [and] behouefull a[g]enst the pestilence.*
Anonymous (1490), *In this tretyse that is cleped Gouernayle of helthe.*
Anonymous (1539), *An introduction for to lerne to recken with the pen or with the counters.*
Anonymous (1545), *A propre new booke of cokery.*
Anonymous (1552), *Certayne causes gathered together wherein is shewed the dacaye of Engla[n]d.*
Anonymous (1575), *A proper newe booke of cookerye.*
Anonymous (1580), *The first parte of the key of philosophie.*
Anonymous [Mascall, Leonard] (1583), *A profitable booke declaring dyuers approoued remedies, to take out spottes and staines.*
Anonymous (1588), *Prepositas his practise a vvorke very necessary to be vsed for the better preseruation of the health of man.*
Anonymous (1596), *A booke of secrets shewing diuers waies to make and prepare all sorts of inke, and colours.*
Anonymous (1625), *A Direction concerning the plague, or pestilence, for poore and rich.*
Anonymous (1626), *Lachrymæ Londinenses.*
Anthony, Francis (1616), *The apologie, or defence of a verity heretofore published concerning a medicine called aurum potabile.*
Bacon, Francis (1808), *The two books of Francis Bacon* (London: Printed by J. McCreery, for T. Payne, 1808).
Baker, Humfrey (1562), *The welspring of sciences.*
Banister, John (1589), *An antidotarie chyrurgicall.*
Barlow, William (1597), *The nauigators supply.*
Barrough, Philip (1583), *The methode of phisicke.*
Bate, John (1634), *The mysteryes of nature, and art conteined in foure severall tretises.*
Bayley, Walter (1586), *A brief treatise touching the preseruation of the eye-sight.*

Benese, Richard (1537), *This boke sheweth the maner of measurynge of all maner of lande as well of woodlande, as of lande in the felde, and comptynge the true nombre of acres of the-same.*
Best, George (1578), *A true discourse of the late voyages of discoverie.*
Billingsley, Martin (1618), *The pen's exellencie, or, The secretaries delight.*
Blagrave, John (1585), *The mathematical ievvel.*
Blundeville, Thomas (1594), *M. Blundevile his exercises containing sixe treatises.*
Boorde, Andrew (1542), *Hereafter foloweth a compendyous regyment or a dyetary of helth.*
Boorde, Andrew (1547), *The Breuiary of helthe.*
Boorde, Andrew (1550), *The boke for to learne a man to by wyse in buyldyng of his howse.*
Boorde, Andrew (1555), *The fyrst boke of the introduction of knowledge.*
Borough, William (1581), *A Discovrs of the Variation of the Cumpas, or Magneticall Needle.*
Bostocke, Richard (1585), *The difference betwene the aunciente phisicke, first taught by the godly forefathers, consisting in vnitie peace and concord, and the latter phisicke.*
Bourne, William (1574), *A regiment for the sea.*
Bourne, William (1592), *A regiment for the sea.*
Bourne, William (1578), *A booke called the treasure for trauveilers.*
Bourne, William (1587), *The arte of shooting in great ordnaunce.*
Bourne, William (1590), *Inuentions or deuises.*
Bourne, William (1963), *A Regiment for the Sea and Other Writings on Navigation*, ed. by E.G.R. Taylor. Cambridge: University Press for the Hakluyt Society.
Bradwell, Stephen (1625), *A vvatch-man for the pest.*
Bright, Timothie (1615), *A treatise, vvherein is declared the sufficiencie of English medicines.*
Brooke, Humphrey (1650), *Ugieine or A conservatory of health.*
J.B. [Browne, John] (1589), *The marchants avizo.*
Bullein, William (1558), *A newe booke entituled the gouernement of healthe.*
Bullein, William (1562), *Bulleins bulwarke of defe[n]ce against all sicknes, sornes, and wounds.*
Bullein, William (1562), *A comfortable regiment, and a very wholsome order against the most perilouse pleurisi.*
Bullein, William (1564), *A dialogue both pleasaunte and pietifull wherein is a goodly regimente against the feuer pestilence.*
Buttes, Henry (1599), *Dyets dry dinner.*
T.C. [widely attributed to Thomas Cartwright] (1578), *An hospitall for the diseased.*
Caius, John (1552), *A boke, or counseill against the disease commonly called the sweate, or sweatyng sicknesse.*
Clarke, John (1602), *The trumpet of Apollo sounding out the sweete blast of recouerie, in diuerse dangerous and desperate diseases.*
Chute, Anthony (1595), *Tabacco.*
Clowes, William (1579), *A short and profitable treatise touching the cure of the disease called (Morbus Gallicus).*
Cogan, Thomas (1584), *The hauen of health chiefely gathered for the comfort of students.*

College of Physicians (1618), *Pharmacopœia Londinensis.*
Cortés, Martín (1561), *The arte of nauigation.*
Cotta, John (1612), *A short discouerie of the vnobserued dangers of seuerall sorts of ignorant and vnconsiderate practisers of physicke in England.*
Cotta, John (1617), *A true discouery of the empericke with the fugitiue, physition and quacksaluer.*
Culpeper, Nicholas (1649), *A physical directory.*
Cunningham, William (1559), *The cosmographicall glasse.*
Daniel, Samuel. *The complete works in verse and prose of Samuel Daniel* (London: Hazell, Watson and Viney, 1885–1886).
Davis, John (1595), *The seamans secrets deuided into 2 partes.*
Dawson, Thomas (1587), *The good husvvifes ievvell.*
Dawson, Thomas (1597), *The second part of the good hus-wiues jewell.*
Dawson, Thomas (1620), *A booke of cookerie. And the order of meates to be serued at the table, both for flesh and fish days.*
Dee, John (1570), "Mathematical Praeface" to the *Elementes of geometrie of the most aunciend philosopher Euclide of megara.*
Dee, John (1577), *General and rare memorials pertayning to the perfect arte of nauigation.*
Dekker, Thomas (1603), *The vvonderfull yeare.*
Digby, Everard (1595), *A short introduction for to learne to swimme. Gathered out of Master Digbies Booke of the Art of Swimming.*
Digges, Leonard (1556), *A boke named Tectonicon.*
Digges, Leonard (1571), *A geometrical practise, named Pantometria.*
Digges, Leonard (1579), *An arithmeticall militare treatise, named Stratioticos.*
Digges, Thomas (1587), *A briefe report of the militarie seruices done in the Low Countries, by the Erle of Leicester.*
Digges, Thomas (1604), *Foure paradoxes, or politique discourses.*
Draxe, Thomas (1615), *An alarum to the last iudgement.*
Elyot, Thomas (1539), *The castel of helth gathered and made by Syr Thomas Elyot knyghte, out of the chiefe authors of physyke.*
Euclid (1570), *The elements of geometrie of the most aunciend philosopher Euclide of Megara.*
Estienne, Charles (1600), *Maison rustique, or the covntrey farme.*
N.F. (1608), *The husbandmans fruitfull orchard.*
Fioravanti, Leonardo (1579), *A ioyfull iewell.*
Fitzherbert, John (1523), *Here begynneth a newe tracte or treatyse moost profitable for all husbandmen and very frutefull for all other persons to rede.*
Fitzherbert, John (1523), *Here begynneth a ryght frutefull mater: and hath to name the boke of surueyeng and improume[n]tes.*
Folkingham, William (1610), *Feudigraphia.*
Fuchs, Leonhart (1563), *A worthy practise of the moste learned phisition Maister Leonerd Fuchius.*
Garcie, Pierre (1528), *The rutter of ye see.*
Garcie, Pierre (1560), *The rutter of the sea.*
Garcie, Pierre (1967), *The Rutters of the Sea. The Sailing Directions of Pierre Garcie. A Study of the First English and French Printed Sailing Directions with Facsimile Reproductions,* ed. by D.W. Waters. New Haven: Yale University Press.

Gardiner, Edmund (1610), *The triall of tabacco.*
Gardiner, Richard (1599), *Profitable instructions for the manuring, sowing, and planting of kitchin gardens.*
Gerard, John (1597), *The herball or Generall historie of plantes.*
Gerard, John (1633), *The herball or Generall historie of plantes.*
Gessner, Konrad (1559), *The treasure of Euonymus.*
Gessner, Konrad (1576), *The newe iewell of health.*
Goeurot, Jean (1600), *The regiment of life, wherevnto is added a treatise of the pestilence.*
Guillemeau, Jacques (1587), *A worthy treatise of the eyes.*
Guillemeau, Jacques (1612), *Child-birth or, The happy deliuerie of vvomen.*
Hakluyt, Richard (1589), *The principall nauigations, voiages, and discoueries of the English nation.*
Harington, John (1596), *A new discourse of a stale subiect, called The metamorphosis of Aiax.*
Harrison, William (1587), *The Description of England*, ed. by Georges Edelen (Ithaca: Published for the Folger Shakespeare Library by Cornell University Press, 1968).
Hart, James, *Klinikē, or The diet of the diseased.*
Henley, Walter de (1508), *Boke of husbandry.*
Heresbach, Conrad (1577), *Foure books of husbandry.*
Herring, Francis (1603), *Certaine rules, directions, or aduertisements for this time of pestilentiall contagion.*
Herring, Francis (1604), *A modest defence of the caueat given to the wearers of impoisoned amulets.*
Herring, Francis (1605), *Beware of pick-purses.*
Herring, Francis (1625), *Certaine rules, directions, or aduertisements for this time of pestilentiall contagion.*
Hester, John (1583), *A hundred and fourtene experiments and cures of the famous phisition Philippus Aureolus Theophrastus Paracelsus.*
Hester, John (1594), *The pearle of practise, or Practisers pearle.*
Hood, Thomas (1588), *A Copie of the Speache: made by the Mathematicall Lecturer.*
Hood, Thomas (1590), *The vse of the two mathematicall instrumentes.*
Hood, Thomas (1590), *The use of the celestial globe in plano.*
Hood, Thomas (1598), *The making and vse of the geometricall instrument, called a sector.*
Howell, James (1642), *Instructions for forreine travell.*
Hues, Robert (1639), *A learned treatise of globes.*
Hunt, Nicolas (1628), *The merchants ievvell.*
Hutten, Ulrich von (1533), *De morbo Gallico.*
Hutten, Ulrich von (1536), *Of the vvood called guaiacum that healeth the Frenche pockes.*
Hyll, Thomas (1558), *A most briefe and pleasaunte treatise, teachying how to dresse, sowe, and set a garden.*
Hyll, Thomas (1568), *The profitable Arte of gardening.*
Hyll, Thomas (1577), *The gardeners labyrinth.*
Jones, John (1566), *A dial for all agues.*
Jorden, Edward (1603), *A briefe discourse of a disease called the suffocation of the mother.*

Kellwaye, Simon (1593), *A defensatiue against the plague.*
Lambarde, William (1576), *A perambulation of Kent.*
Langham, William (1597), *The garden of health.*
Langton, Christopher (1545), *An introduction into phisycke wyth an vniuersal dyet.*
Lawson, William (1618), *A nevv orchard and garden.*
Leigh, Valentine (1577), *The moste profitable and commendable science, of surueying of lands, tenementes, and hereditamentes.*
Leroy, Louis (1594), *Of the interchangeable course, or variety of things in the whole world.*
Lessius, Leonardus (1636), *Hygiasticon.*
Levens, Peter (1596), *A right profitable booke for all diseases called, The pathway to health.*
Lodge, Thomas (1603), *A treatise of the plague.*
London, William (1657), *A catalogue of the most vendible books in England.*
Lucar, Cyprian (1590), *A Treatise named Lucarsolace deuided into fovver bookes.*
Lupton, Thomas (1579), *A thousand notable things, of sundry sortes.*
Maplet, John (1567), *A greene forest.*
Marbeck, Roger (1602), *A defence of tabacco vvith a friendly answer to the late printed booke called Worke for chimny-sweepers &.*
Markham, Gervase (1613), *The English husbandman.*
Markham, Gervase (1614), *The second booke of the English husbandman.*
Markham, Gervase (1614), *Cheap and good husbandry for the vvell-ordering of all beasts, and fowles, and for the general cure of their diseases.*
Markham, Gervase (1615), *Covntrey contentments, in two bookes.*
Markham, Gervase (1620), *Markhams farwell to husbandry.*
Markham, Gervase (1621), *Hungers preuention: or The whole arte of fovvling by vvater and land.*
Markham, Gervase (1625), *A vvay to get vvealth by approued rules of practice in good husbandry and huswiferie.*
Markham, Gervase (1625), *The inrichment of the vveald of Kent.*
Markham, Gervase (1625), *The souldiers accidence.*
Mascall, Leonard (1572), *A booke of the arte and maner, howe to plant and graffe all sortes of trees.*
Mascall, Leonard (1581), *The husbandlye ordring and gouernmente of poultrie.*
Mascall, Leonard (1587), *The first booke of cattell.*
Mascall, Leonard (1590), *A booke of fishing with hooke & line.*
Mascall, Leonard (1590), *A booke of engines and traps.*
Mascall, Leonard (1651), *The country-mans new art of planting and graffing.*
Maunsell, Andrew (1595), *The first part of the catalogue of English printed bookes.*
Maynwaringe, Everard (1663), *Tutela sanitatis sive Vita protracta.*
Medina, Pedro de (1581), *The arte of nauigation.*
Medoliano, Joannes de (1528), *Regimen sanitatis Salerni.*
Medoliano, Joannes de (1607), *The Englishmans docter. Or, The schoole of Salerne.*
Medoliano, Joannes de (1617), *Regimen sanitatis Salerni.*
Middleton, Christopher (1595), *A Short introduction for to learne to Swimme.*
Moffatt, Thomas (1655), *Healths improvement.*

Monardes, Nicolás (1577), *Ioyfull newes out of the newfound world.*
Moore, Philip (1564), *The hope of health wherin is conteined a goodlie regimente.*
More, Richard (1602), *The carpenters rule.*
Moulton, Thomas (1531), *This is the myrour or glasse of helth.*
Münster, Sebastian (1553), *A treatyse of the newe India.*
Newton, Thomas (1586), *The olde mans dietarie.*
Norden, John (1607), *The surueyors dialogue. Diuided into fiue bookes.*
Norden, John (1625), *An intended guyde, for English travailers.*
Norman, Robert (1581), *The newe attractiue.*
Oldcastle, Hugh (1588), *A brief instruction and maner hovv to keepe bookes of accompts after the order of debitor and creditor.*
Osiander, Andreas (1563), *How and whither a Chrysten man ought to flye the horryble plague of the pestilence.*
Palsgrave, John (1530), *Lesclarcissement de la langue francoyse.*
Parkinson, John (1629), *Paradisi in sole paradisus terrestris.*
Parkinson, John (1640), *Theatrum botanicum: the theater of plantes.*
Paracelsus (1590), *An excellent treatise teaching howe to cure the French-pockes.*
Paracelsus (1596), *A hundred and fouretene experiments and cures of the famous physitian Philippus Aureolus Theophrastus Paracelsus.*
Partridge, John (1573), *The treasurie of commodious conceits & hidden secrets.*
Partridge, John (1586), *The widowes treasure.*
Peacham, Henry (1606), *The art of dravving vvith the pen, and limming in water colours.*
Peele, James (1554), *The maner and fourme how to kepe a perfecte reconyng after the order of the moste worthie and notable accompte.*
Peele, James (1569), *The path waye to perfectness, in th'accompes of debitour and creditour. Pharmacopœia londinensis of 1618,* ed. by George Urdang (Madison: State Historical Society of Wisconsin, 1944).
Philaretes (1602), *VVork for chimney-sweepers: or A warning for tabacconists.*
Plat, Hugh (1594), *The jewell house of art and nature.*
Plat, Hugh (1595), *A discouerie of certaine English wants.*
Plat, Hugh (1596), *Sundrie nevv and artificiall remedies against famine.*
Plat, Hugh (1600), *Delights for ladies, to adorne their persons, tables, closets and distillatories.*
Plat, Hugh (1600), *The nevv and admirable arte of setting of corne.*
Plattes, Gabriel (1639), *A discovery of infinite treasure, hidden since the vvorlds beginning.*
Plattes, Gabriel (1639), *A discovery of subterraneall treasure.*
Polter, Richard (1605), *The pathway to perfect sayling.*
Purchas, Samuel (1613), *Pvrchas his pilgrims.*
Rathborne, Aaron (1616), *The surveyor in foure bookes.*
Read, Alexander (1635), *The chirurgicall lectures of tumors and vlcers.*
Recorde, Robert (1543), *The grou[n]d of artes, teaching the worke and practyse of arithmetike.*
Recorde, Robert (1557), *The whetstone of witte.*
Recorde, Robert (1596), *The castle of knowledge.*
Recorde, Robert (1615), *Records arithmeticke: containing the ground of arts.*
Roberts, Lewes (1638), *The merchants mappe of commerce.*
Rösslin, Eucharius (1540), *The byrth of mankynde.*

Rüff, Jakob (1637), *The expert midwife.*
Ruscelli, Girolamo (1558), *The secretes of the reuerende Maister Alexis of Piemount.*
Ruscelli, Girolamo (1560), *The second part of the Secretes of Master Alexis of Piemont.*
Ruscelli, Girolamo (1562), *The thyrde and last parte of the Secretes of the reuerende Maister Alexis of Piemont.*
Scot, Reginald (1574), *A perfite platforme of a hoppe garden.*
Shute, John (1563), *The first and chief groundes of architecture.*
Smith, John (1626), *An accidence or The path-way to experience Necessary for all you sea-men.*
Standish, Arthur (1611), *The commons complaint.*
Standish, Arthur (1618), *Nevv directions of experience by the authour for the planting of timber and firevvood.*
A.T. (1596), *A rich store-house or treasury for the diseased.*
C.T. (1615), *An aduice hovv to plant tobacco in England.*
Tartaglia, Niccolò (1588), *Three bookes of colloquies concerning the arte of shooting.*
Taverner, John (1600), *Certaine experiments concerning fish and fruite.*
Thayre, Thomas (1603), *A treatise of the pestilence. Tudor and Stuart proclamations 1485-1714. Calendared by Robert Steele under the direction of the Earl of Crawford* (Oxford: Clarendon Press, 1910).
Tuke, Thomas (1619), *A discourse against painting and tincturing of women.*
Turner, William (1551), *A new herball.*
Turner, William (1562), *The seconde part of Vuilliam Turners herbal* (Cologne: Arnold Birckman).
Turner, William (1568), *A new boke of the natures and properties of all wines that are commonly vsed here in England.*
Tusser, Thomas (1557), *A hundreth good pointes of husbandrie.*
Tusser, Thomas (1573), *Five hundreth points of good husbandry.*
Vaughan, Rowland (1610), *Most approued, and long experienced vvater-vvorkes.*
Vaughan, William (1600), *Naturall and artificial directions for health.*
Vaughan, William (1612), *Approved directions for health, both natural and artificiall.*
Venner, Tobias (1620), *Via recta ad vitam longam.*
Waghenaer, Lucas Janszoon (1588), *The mariners mirrour.*
Warre, James (1622), *The merchants hand-maide.*
Weddington, John (1567), *A breffe instruction, and manner, howe to kepe, marchantes bokes, of accomptes* (Antwerp: Petter van Keerberghen).
Wirsung, Christof (1598), *Praxis medicinae vniuersalis or A general practise of physicke.*
R.W. [Witt, Richard] (1613), *Arithmeticall questions.*
Woodall, John (1617), *The svrgions mate.*
Woodall, John (1628), *Woodalls viaticum: the path-way to the surgions chest.*
Woodall, John (1639), *The surgeons mate, or Military & domestique surgery.*
Woodall, John (1640), *The cure of the plague by an antidote called aurum vitae.*
Worsop, Edward (1582), *A discouerie of sundrie errours and faults daily committed by lande-meaters.*
Wright, Edward (1599), *Certaine errors in nauigation.*
Xenophon (1532), *Xenophon's treatise of householde.*

Secondary Texts

Albala, Ken. *Eating Right in the Renaissance*. Berkeley: University of California Press, 2002.

Alford, Stephen. *London's Triumph: Merchants, Adventurers, and Money in Shakespeare's City*. London: Bloomsbury, 2017.

Appelbaum, Robert. *Aguecheek's Beef, Belch's Hiccup, and Other Gastronomic Interjections: Literature, Culture, and Food among the Early Moderns*. Chicago: the University of Chicago Press, 2006.

Ash, Eric H. *The Draining of the Fens: Projectors, Popular Politics, and State Building in Early Modern England*. Baltimore: Johns Hopkins University Press, 2017.

Ash, Eric H. *Power, Knowledge, and Expertise in Elizabethan England*. Baltimore: Johns Hopkins University Press, 2005.

Ash, Eric. H. "'A Perfect and an Absolute Work': Expertise, Authority, and the Rebuilding of Dover Harbor, 1579–1583." *Technology and Culture* 41, no. 2 (April 2000): 239–268.

Barker, R.A. "Fragments from the Pepysian Library." *Revista da Universidade de Coimbra* 32 (1986): 161–178.

Barrett, C.R.B. *The History of the Society of Apothecaries of London*. London: E. Stock, 1905.

Bell, Rudolph. *How to Do It: Guides to Good Living for Renaissance Italians*. Chicago: University of Chicago Press, 1999.

Blair, Ann. *Too Much to Know: Managing Scholarly Information before the Modern Age*. New Haven: Yale University Press.

Blatcher, Margaret. "Chatham Dockyard and a Little-Known Shipwright, Matthew Baker (1530–1613)." *Archaeologia Cantiana* 107 (1989): 155–172.

Bushnell, Rebecca. *Green Desire: Imagining Early Modern English Gardens*. Ithaca, NY: Cornell University Press, 2003.

Chamberland, Celeste. "Between the Hall and the Market: William Clowes and Surgical Self-Fashioning in Elizabethan London." *Sixteenth Century Journal*, 41, no. 1 (2010): 69–89.

Cohn, Samuel Kline, Jr. "Epidemiology of the Black Death and Successive Waves of Plague." *Med. Hist. Suppl.* 27 (2008): 74–100.

Cohn, Samual Kline, Jr. *The Black Death Transformed: Disease and Culture in Early Renaissance Europe*. London: Bloomsbury Academic, 2003.

Cook, Harold J. "Policing the Health of London: the College of Physicians and the Early Stuart Monarchy." *Social History of Medicine* 2 (1989): 1–33.

Cook, Harold J. *The Decline of the Old Medical Regime in Stuart London*. Ithaca, NY: Cornell University Press, 1986.

Crinò, Anna Maria and Helen Wallis. "New Researches on the Molyneux Globes/ Neue Forschungsarbeiten über die Molyneux-Globen." *Der Globusfreund*. 35/37 (1987): 11–20.

Curth, Louise Hill. *English Almanacs, Astrology, and Popular Medicine*. Manchester: Manchester University Press, 2007.

Davis, Ralph. *The Rise of the English Shipping Industry in the Seventeenth and Eighteenth Centuries*. London: Macmillan & Co., 1962.

Dawson, Mark. *Plenti and Grase: Food and Drink in a Sixteenth-century Household*. Totnes, UK: Prospect Books, 2009.

Debus, Allen. *Man and Nature in the Renaissance*. Cambridge: Cambridge University Press, 1978.
Debus, Allen. *The English Paracelsians*. New York: Franklin Watts, 1965.
Dekker, Elly and Kristen Lippincott. "The Scientific Instruments in Holbein's Ambassadors: A Re-Examination." *Journal of the Warburg and Courtauld Institutes* 62 (1999): 93–125.
DiMeo, Michele and Sarah Pennell. *Reading and Writing Recipe Books, 1500-1800*. Manchester: Manchester University Press, 2013.
Dolan, Frances E. *Digging the Past: How and Why to Imagine Seventeenth-Century Agriculture*. Philadelphia: University of Pennsylvania Press, 2020.
Eamon, William. *Science and the Secrets of Nature: Books of Secrets in Medieval and Early Modern Culture*. Princeton: Princeton University Press, 1996.
Eamon, William. "Science and Popular Culture in Sixteenth Century Italy: The 'Professors of Secrets' and Their Books." *Sixteenth Century Journal* 16, no. 4 (1985): 471–485.
Eisenstein, Elizabeth. *The Printing Press as an Agent of Change: Communications and Cultural Transformations in Early Modern Europe*. Cambridge: Cambridge University Press, 1980.
Ekirch, A. Roger. *At Day's Close*: *Night in Times Past*. New York: W.W. Norton & Company, 2006.
Findlen, Paula. "Commerce, Art and Science in the Early Modern Cabinet of Curiosities." In *Merchants & Marvels*: *Commerce, Science and Art in Early Modern Europe*, ed. by Pamela Smith and Paula Findlen, 297–323. Abingdon, UK: Routledge, 2001.
Fisher, F.J., ed. *Essays in the Economic and Social History of Tudor and Stuart England, in Honour of R. H. Tawney.* Cambridge: Cambridge University Press, 1961.
Fissell, Mary. "Popular Medical Writing." In *Cheap Print in Britain and Ireland to 1660,* Volume I of *The Oxford History of Popular Print Culture*, ed. by Joad Raymond, 417–430. Oxford: Oxford University Press, 2011.
Fissell, Mary, "The Marketplace of Print." In *Medicine and the Market in England and Its Colonies, c. 1450-c. 1850,* ed. by Mark Jenner and Patrick Wallis, 108–132. Basingstoke: Palgrave Macmillan, 2007.
Fox, Adam. *Oral and Literate Culture in England, 1500–1700*. Oxford: Clarendon Press, 2000.
Fox, Robert, ed. *Thomas Hariot and His World: Mathematics, Exploration, and Natural Philosophy in Early Modern England*. Abingdon, UK: Routledge, 2017.
French, Roger. *Medicine Before Science: The Business of Medicine from the Middle Ages to the Enlightenment*. Cambridge: Cambridge University Press, 2003.
Furdell, Elizabeth Lane. *Publishing and Medicine in Early Modern England*. Rochester, UK: University of Rochester Press, 2002.
Gaida, Margaret. "Reading Cosmographia: Peter Apian's Book- Instrument Hybrid and the Rise of the Mathematical Amateur in the Sixteenth Century." *Early Sci Med.* 21, no. 4 (2016): 277–302.
Gentilcore, David. *Food and Health in Early Modern Europe: Diet Medicine and Society, 1450–1800*. London: Bloomsbury, 2016.
Grafton, Anthony, and Nancy G. Siraisi, *Natural Particulars: Nature and the Disciplines in Renaissance Europe*. Cambridge, MA: MIT Press, 1999.
Green, Monica H. "The Sources of Eucharius Rösslin's 'Rosegarden for Pregnant Women and Midwives' (1513)." *Med Hist.* 53 (2009): 167–192.

Greenberg, Stephen. "Plague, the Printing Press, and Public Health in Seventeenth-Century London." *Huntington Library Quarterly* 67, no. 4 (2004): 508–527.
Griffin, Andrew. "Banister, John (1532/33–1599?)." In *Oxford Dictionary of National Biography.* Oxford: Oxford University Press, 2004. (Accessed December 4, 2020). https://doi.org/10.1093/ref:odnb/1280.
Hamling, Tara, and Catherine Richardson. *A Day at Home in Early Modern England: Material Culture and Domestic Life, 1500–1700.* New Haven: Yale University Press, 2017.
Handley, Sasha. *Sleep in Early Modern England.* New Haven: Yale University Press, 2016.
Harkness, Deborah. *The Jewel House: Elizabethan London and the Scientific Revolution.* New Haven: Yale University Press, 2007.
Hentschell, Roze. *The Culture of Cloth in Early Modern England: Textual Constructions of a National Identity.* Abingdon, UK: Routledge, 2008.
Hodgkinson, Jeremy. *The Wealden Iron Industry.* Stroud, UK: Tempus Publishing, 2008.
Howson, A.G. *History of Mathematics Education in England.* Cambridge: Cambridge University Press, 1982.
Hoyles, Martin. *Gardener's Delight: Gardening Books from 1560 to 1960.* London: Pluto Press, 1994.
Hull, Susan W. *Chaste, Silent & Obedient: English Books for Women, 1475-1640.* San Marino, CA: Huntington Library. 1982.
Jardine, Lisa, and Anthony Grafton. "'Studied for Action': How Gabriel Harvey Read His Livy." *Past and Present* 129, no. 1 (1990): 30–78.
Johnston, Stephen. "Robert Recorde (c. 1512–1558)." In *Oxford Dictionary of National Biography.* Oxford: Oxford University Press, 2004. (Accessed October 29, 2020). https://doi.org/10.1093/ref:odnb/23241.
Johnston, Stephen. "Thomas Digges (c. 1546–1595)." In *Oxford Dictionary of National Biography.* Oxford: Oxford University Press, 2004. (Accessed September 9, 2020). https://doi.org/10.1093/ref:odnb/7639.
Johnston, Stephen. 'Making Mathematical Practice: Gentlemen, Practitioners and Artisans in Elizabethan England.' Ph.D. diss., Cambridge University, 1994; http://www.mhs.ox.ac.uk/staff/saj/thesis/.
Kavey, Allison B. *Books of Secrets: Natural Philosophy in England, 1550–1600.* Urbana: University of Illinois Press, 2007.
Keller, Vera and Ted McCormick. "Towards a History of Projects." *Early Science and Medicine* 21, no. 5 (2016): 423–444.
Keynes, Sir Geoffrey. *The Life of William Harvey.* Oxford: Clarendon Press, 1966.
Klein, Ursula, and E.C. Spary. *Materials and Expertise in Early Modern Europe: Between Market and Laboratory.* Chicago: University of Chicago Press, 2010.
Knight, Leah. *Of Books and Botany in Early Modern England: Sixteenth-Century Plants and Print Culture.* Abingdon, UK: Routledge, 2009.
Leong, Elaine. *Recipes and Everyday Knowledge: Medicine, Science, and the Household in Early Modern England.* Chicago: The University of Chicago Press, 2018.
Leong, Elaine. "'Herbals She Peruseth': Reading Medicine in Early Modern England." *Renaissance Studies* 28, no. 4 (2014): 556–578.
Leong, Elaine and Alisha Rankin, eds. *Secrets and Knowledge in Medicine and Science, 1500-1800.* Burlington, VT: Ashgate, 2011.

Lindemann, Mary. *Medicine and Society in Early Modern Europe*. Cambridge: Cambridge University Press, 2010.
Long, Pamela O. *Artisan/Practitioners and the Rise of the New Sciences, 1400–1600*. Corvallis: Oregon State University Press, 2011.
MacDonald, Michael. *Witchcraft and Hysteria in Elizabethan London: Edward Jorden and the Mary Glover Case*. New York: Tavistock Press, 1991.
McGee, David. "From Craftsmanship to Draftsmanship: Naval Architecture and the Three Traditions of Early Modern Design." *Technology and Culture* 40, no. 2 (1999): 209–236.
McRae, Andrew. *God Speed the Plough: The Representation of Agrarian England, 1500–1660*. Cambridge: Cambridge University Press, 1996.
Morrissey, Jake Walsh. "'To all Indifferent': The Virtues of Lydgate's Dietary" *Medium Aevum* 84 no. 2 (2015): 258–278.
Mukherjee, Ayesha. *Penury into Plenty. Dearth and the Making of Knowledge in Early Modern England*. Abingdon, UK: Routledge, 2015.
Myers, Anne. M. *Literature and Architecture in Early Modern England*. Baltimore: Johns Hopkins University Press, 2013.
Nylander, Jennifer. "Early Modern How-to Books: Impractical Manuals and the Construction of Englishness in the Atlantic World." *Journal for Early Modern Cultural Studies* 9, no. 1 (2009): 123–156.
Ogilvie, Brian. *The Science of Describing. Natural History in Renaissance Europe*. Chicago, 2008
Oppenheim, Michael. *A History of the Administration of the Royal Navy and of Merchant shipping in relation to the Navy, from MDIX to MDCLX with an Introduction Treating of Preceding Period*. London: The Bodley Head, 1896.
Orme, Nicholas. "Everard Digby (d. 1605)." In *Oxford Dictionary of National Biography*. Oxford: Oxford University Press, 2004. (Accessed May 27, 2020). https://doi.org/10.1093/ref:odnb/7625.
Overton, Mark, Jane Whittle, Darron Dean and Andrew Hann. *Production and Consumption in English Households, 1600-1750*. Abingdon, UK: Routledge, 2004.
Overton, Mark. *Agricultural Revolution in England. The Transformation of the Agrarian Economy 1500–1850*. Cambridge: Cambridge University Press, 1996.
Parker, Geoffrey, "The 'Dreadnought Revolution' of Tudor England." *Mariner's Mirror* 82, no. 3 (August 1996): 269–300.
Parry, Glyn. *The Arch-Conjurer of England: John Dee*. New Haven: Yale University Press, 2011.
Pelling, Margaret. *Medical Conflicts in Early Modern London: Patronage, Physicians, and Irregular Practitioners, 1559–1640*. Oxford: Clarendon Press, 2003.
Pelling, Margaret. "Trade or Profession? Medical Practice in Early Modern England." In *The Common Lot: Sickness, Medical Occupations and the Urban Poor in Early Modern England*, ed. by Margaret Pelling, 230–258. London: Longman, 1998.
Peltz, Lucy. "Martin Billingsley, (1591–1622), Writing Master." *Oxford Dictionary of National Biography*. Oxford: Oxford University Press, 2004. (Accessed February 22, 2021). https://doi.org/10.1093/ref:odnb/2395.
Pettegree, Andrew. "Centre and Periphery in the European Book World." *Transactions of the Royal Historical Society*, Sixth Series, 18 (2008): 101–128.

Porter, Roy, ed. *Patients and Practitioners: Lay Perceptions of Medicine in Pre-Industrial Society*. Cambridge: Cambridge University Press, 1986.

Poynter, F.N.L. *Bibliography of Gervase Markham 1568?-1637*. Oxford: Oxford Bibliographical Society, 1962.

Principe, Lawrence M. *The Secrets of Alchemy*. Chicago and London: the University of Chicago Press, 2013.

Rackham, Oliver. *The History of the Countryside: The Classic History of Britain's Landscape, Flora and Fauna*. London: Phoenix, 2000.

Rawcliffe, Carole. *Medicine and Society in Later Medieval England*. Stroud, UK: Sutton Publishing, 1995.

Richeson, A.W. *English Land Measuring to 1800: Instruments and Practices*. Cambridge, MA: The MIT Press, 1966.

Roberts, Gareth, and Fenny Smith, eds. *Robert Recorde: The Life and Times of a Tudor Mathematician*. Cardiff: University of Wales Press, 2012.

Schotte, Margaret. *Sailing School: Navigating Science and Skill, 1550-1800*. Baltimore: Johns Hopkins University Press, 2019.

Sherman, William. *John Dee: The Politics of Reading and Writing in the English Renaissance*. Amherst: University of Massachusetts Press, 1995.

Siraisi, Nancy G. *Medieval and Early Renaissance Medicine. An Introduction to Knowledge and Practice*. Chicago: the University of Chicago Press, 1990.

Slack, Paul. *The Impact of Plague in Tudor and Stuart England*. Oxford: Oxford University Press, 1985.

Slack, Paul. "Mirrors of Health and Treasures of Poor Men: The Uses of the Vernacular Medical Literature of Tudor England." In *Health, Medicine and Mortality in the Sixteenth Century*, ed. by Margaret Pelling and Charles Webster, 237–273. Cambridge: Cambridge University Press, 1979.

Slack, Paul. *The Invention of Improvement. Information and Material Progress in Seventeenth-century England*. Oxford: Oxford University Press, 2015.

Smith, Pamela H. *The Body of the Artisan: Art and Experience in the Scientific Revolution*. Chicago: University of Chicago Press, 2006.

Smith, Pamela H. and Benjamin Schmidt, editors. *Making Knowledge in Early Modern Europe: Practices, Objects, Texts, 1400-1800*. Chicago: University of Chicago Press, 2008.

Stobart, Anne. *Household Medicine in Seventeenth-century England*. London: Bloomsbury Academic, 2016.

Taavitsainen, Irma and Päivi Patita, eds. *Early Modern English Medical Texts: Corpus Description and Studies*. Amsterdam: John Benjamins, 2010.

Tawney, R.H. *The Agrarian Problem in the Sixteenth Century*. London: Longmans, Green & Co., 1912.

Taylor, E.G.R. *The Mathematical Practitioners of Tudor and Stuart England, 1485-1714*. Cambridge: Cambridge University Press, 1967.

Tebeaux, Elizabeth. *The Emergence of a Tradition: Technical Writing in the English Renaissance, 1475-1640*. Amityville, NY: Baywood, 1997.

Theilman, John, and Francis Cate. "A Plague of Plagues: The Problem of Plague Diagnosis in Medieval England." *Journal of Interdisciplinary History* 37, no. 3 (2007): 371–393.

Thick, Malcolm. *Sir Hugh Plat: The Search for Useful Knowledge in Early Modern London*. Totnes, UK: Prospect Books, 2010.

Thirsk, Joan. *Alternative Agriculture: A History from the Black Death to the Present Day.* Oxford: Oxford University Press, 1997.
Thirsk, Joan. *Food in Early Modern England: Phases, Fads, Fashions 1500–1760.* London: Continuum, 2006.
Thomas, Keith. *Man and the Natural World. Changing Attitudes in England, 1500–1800.* Oxford: Oxford University Press, 1983.
Wall, Wendy. "Renaissance National Husbandry: Gervase Markham and the Publication of England." *Sixteenth Century Journal* 27, no. 3 (1996): 767–785.
Wall, Wendy. "Literacy and the Domestic Arts." *Huntington Library Quarterly* 73, no. 3 (2010): 383–412.
Wall, Wendy. *Recipes for Thought: Knowledge and Taste in the Early Modern English Kitchen.* Philadelphia: University of Pennsylvania Press, 2015.
Wallis, Patrick. "Consumption, Retailing and Medicine in Early-Modern London." *Economic History Review* 16 (2008): 26–53.
Waters, David. *The Art of Navigation in England in Elizabethan and Early Stuart Times.* New Haven: Yale University Press, 1958.
Wear, Andrew. *Knowledge and Practice in English Medicine, 1550–1680.* Cambridge: Cambridge University Press, 2000.
Webster, Charles, ed. *Health, Medicine and Mortality in the Sixteenth Century.* Cambridge: Cambridge University Press, 1979
White, Sam. "The Real Little Ice Age." *Journal of Interdisciplinary History* 44, no. 3 (2014): 327–352.
Whittle, Jane, ed. *Landlords and Tenants in Britain, 1440–1660: Tawney's Agrarian Problem Revisited.* Woodbridge, UK: Boydell Press, 2013.
Williams, Jack. *Robert Recorde: Tudor Polymath, Expositor, and Practitioner of Computation.* New York: Springer, 2011.
Wrightson, Keith. *Earthly Necessities: Economic Lives in Early Modern Britain.* New Haven: Yale University Press, 2000.
Wrightson, Keith. "Numeracy in Early Modern England: the Prothero Lecture." *Transactions of the Royal Historical Society* 37 (1987): 103–132.

INDEX

A boke named Tectonicon (Digges) 13, 48
A booke of the arte and manner how to plant and graffe (Mascall) 77–78, 154, 185n.39
A booke called the treasure for traueilers (Bourne) 102
A Booke of fishing with hooke and line (Plat) 154
A briefe discourse of a disease called the suffocation of the mother (Jorden) 86
A Briefe instruction and maner hovv to keepe bookes of accompts (Oldcastle) 50
A Compendyous regyment or dyetary of helth (Boorde) 25–26
A Description of the famous Kingdom of Macaria (Hartlib/Plattes) 16
A dial for all agues (Jones) 66
A discouerie of certaine English wants (Plat) 80
A discouerie of sundrie errours and faults (Worsop) 102
A discourse against painting and tincturing of women (Tuke) 11
A discovery of infinite treasure (Plattes) 15–16, 144
A discovery of subterraneall treasure (Plattes) 143
A Discovrs of the Variation of the Cumpas (Borough) 106
Agas, Ralph 151, 202–3n.12
A geometrical practise, named Pantometria (Digges) 48–49
A greene forest (Maplet) 74
agriculture 10, 16, 41, 46, 49, 153
A hundred and fourtene experiments and cures (Hester) 68

A hundreth/Five hundreth Pointes of husbandry (Tusser) 10
A ioyfull iewell (Fioravanti) 2, 68, 75, 147
Albacar, Martín Cortés de 13–14, 97
alchemy 15, 67, 69, 77, 88, 145, 147, 163
algebra 52–53, 115–16, 145, 150
Algebrae Compendiosa (Scheubel) 53
algorism(e) 45
The Ambassadors (Holbein) 59
A new herball (Turner) 32, 74, 101, 163
An intended guyde for English travailers (Norden) 117
An introduction for to lerne to recken with the pen 51–52
The Ant-Antony (Cotta) 129
Anthony, Francis 128–29
Antonine Plague 69
A passing gode lityll boke necessarye (Jacobi) 64
A perfite platforme of a hoppe garden (Scot) 79
Apian, Peter 58–59, 180n.28
apothecaries,
    Elizabethan alterations 67–68, 71–76, 81
    instruments and invention 102
    introduction 14
    knowledge-mongers 146–47
    last herbals 131–32
    public discourses 118, 121–27
    regimens and rules 21–22, 27
Approved directions for health (Vaughan) 33
A practicall catechisme (Hammond) 1
A proclamation concernynge corne 43
A proper newe booke of cokerye 89

INDEX

arboriculture 16, 41, 154
Archer, John 30, 173n.31
A Regiment for the sea (Bourne) 13, 157
A rich store-house or treasury for the diseased 9
Aristotle 20, 158
Arithmeticall Questions (Witt) 158
Arnold, Richard 76
Art de navegar (Cortés) 100
Art de navegar (Polter) 102
Arte de Navegar (Albacar) 13–14, 97
Arte of nauigation (Eden) 93–94, 108
The Arte of shooting in great Ordnaunce (Bourne) 102, 149
"artisanal literacy" 86
Art of Merchandizing 162–63
A sea grammar (Smith) 113
Ash, Eric 97
Ashley, Sir Anthony 107–8
A short discouerie of the vnobserued dangers (Cotta) 125
A short and profitable treatise (Clowes) 70, 147
astrolabes 2, 57, 94, 96, 98, 102–4, 108, 148, 157
astrology 51, 54–55, 58, 145
astronomy 2, 14, 45, 51, 58–59, 59, 103, 110
A thousand notable things, of sundry sortes (Lupton) 63
A treatise of artificial fire-vvorks (Bate) 155
A Treatise named Lucarsolace (Harvey) 151–52
A treatyse of the newe India (Eden) 58, 180n.29
aurum potabile (mineral medicine) 128
A VVatch-man for thepest (Bradwell) 127–28
A vvay to get vvealth (Markham) 2

Bacon, Francis 1, 3, 118–19, 123, 153
Bacon, Roger 20, 68
Baker, George 68–71, 75, 118–19, 147
Baker, Humfrey 56–57
Baker, Matthew 111–13, 116, 194n.39
Banister, John 70–72, 119, 127, 147, 183n.20

barber-surgeons 14, 21, 27, 71, 118, 123–24, 146–47
Barlow, William 2, 106
Barnard, William 66
Barrough, Philip 85
Bate, John 3, 15, 154–55, 159
Bayley, Walter 147
Bayly, Lewis 1
Beaumont, John 73
beer 26, 33–34, 52, 78–80, 140
Behaim, Martin 109
Bell, Rudolph 4
Benese, Richard 47, 49, 54, 117
Bennett, Christopher 26, 32
Berthelet, Thomas 39–40, 43
Best, George 100
Beware of pick-purses (Herring) 126
Billingsley, Henry 98, 148
Billingsley, Martin 159
Bills of Mortality 121
Black Death 19–20, 64 *see also* plague
Blagrave, John 2, 96, 102–4, 148–49, 165n.5, 192n.22
Blessed Thistle 67
Blundeville, Thomas 13–14, 94, 96–97, 104, 110, 135
Boke of Husbandry (Fitzherbert) 10, 17, 170n.1
Boke of husbandry (Henley) 41
The boke of keruynge 6
The boke named the gouernour (Elyot) 23
Boke of surueyeng and improume[n]tes (Fitzherbert) 17, 39, 47
Book of Calculation (Leonardo of Pisa) 45
Book of the Duchess (Chaucer) 45
Boorde, Andrew 25–29, 34, 146, 174n.46
Borde, Andrew 135, 140
Borough, Stephen 97–100, 104, 106, 107
Borough, William 104–6, 112, 114
Bostocke, Richard 68
Bourne, Nicholas 129
Bourne, William 13, 97, 100–103, 108, 112, 149, 157, 191nn.13, 17
Boyle, Robert 145
Bradwell, Stephen 127–28

Brant, Sebastian 4
Brasbridge, Thomas 2, 67–68, 182n.11
bread 22, 31, 44, 66, 80, 140
Breffe instruction, and manner, howe to kepe, marchantes bokes, of accomptes (Weddington) 50
The breuiary of helthe (Boorde) 25–26
Breve compendio de la sphera (Cortés) 93, 156
Breviary 25, 27
Bright, Timothy 130, 132
British Empire 16, 55, 99
Brooke, Humphrey 36
Brossard, Davy 154
Browne, John 160–61
Bulleins bulwarke of defe[n]ce againste all sicknes (Bullein) 26, 54
Bullein, William 25–28, 32–33, 54, 65–66, 70, 80, 146–47, 172n.19
Bulwark of defence (Bullein) 28, 33
Buttes, Henry 79
The byrth of mankynde (Jonas) 84–85, 147, 188n.61

Cabot, Sebastian 97, 99
Caius, John 128, 147
The carpenters rule made easie (Darling) 13
The carpenters rule (More) 12, 102
Casa de Contratación 93, 97–98
The castel of helth (Elyot) 20, 23, 25, 28, 38–39, 53, 117, 145, 162, 170n.8
The castle of knowledge (Recorde) 52–54, 59–60
Catalogue of the most vendible books in England (London) 10, 143
Catholicism 55
Cavendish, Thomas 110
Caxton, William 20
Cecil, Frances 138
Cecil, William 13, 103
Certaine errors in nauigation (Wright) 101, 114, 157
Certaine experiments concerning fish and fruite (Taverner) 80
Certain rules (Herring) 126–27
Chamberlayne, Thomas 85

Charles II, King 30, 111, 124
Charles I, King 132
Chatham royal shipyard 113
Chaucer, Geoffrey 45
Child-birth (Guillemeau) 85
"China-root" 72
Chronicle or Customs of London (Arnold) 786
Chute, Anthony 72–73
ciphering 46
Clarke, John 73
"Clowes in A short and profitable treatise" 147
Clowes, William 70–71, 118, 147
Cockayne project 136
Cogan, Thomas 26, 35, 65, 172n.20
"College for Inventions in Husbandry" 16
College of Physicians 9, 14, 23, 27, 66, 71, 86, 118–29, 146–47
The commons complaint (Standish) 15, 78
"Commonwealth of Learning" (Eisenstein) 3
"Company of Merchant Adventurers to New Lands" 56–57
compasses 105–6
Compleat midwifes practice (Chamberlayne) 85
Complete Gentleman (Peacham) 145
Confessio Amantis (Gower) 45
cookery 88–91
Copernican hypothesis 60, 104
Copland, Robert 61
Copland, William 61
corn 30, 40–41, 43–44, 79–80, 82, 132, 138
Cornaro, Luigi 25
Cortés, Martin 93, 100
Cosmographia (Apian) 58, 128n.80
Cosmographia (Münster) 58, 97
The cosmographical glasse (Cunningham) 60–61
cosmography 57–62, 100, 102
Cotta, John 125, 129
Counterblaste to tobacco (King James I) 72
Cromwell, Thomas 23
Culpepper, Nicholas 67, 122–23

Cunningham, William 60–61
The cure of the plague (Woodall) 129

Daniel, Samuel 160
Darling, John 13
Davis, John 94, 96, 102, 110–11, 114, 190n.4
Dawson, Mark 80, 186–87n.50
Dawson, Thomas 2, 89
de Acosta, José 72
De arte natandi (Digby) 36
Dee, John 12, 51, 53, 56, 58, 97–100, 107, 111, 114, 148–51, 156
Defensatiue against the plague (Kellwaye) 66
De Historia Stirpium (Fuchs) 74
Dekker, Thomas 65, 119, 128, 160
Delights for ladies (Plat) 11, 83, 153–54
De magnete, magneticisque corporibus (Gilbert) 105
De Orba Nova (Martyr d'Anghiera) 97
Deptford royal shipyard 113
Description of England (Harrison) 75
Description of the famous Kingdome of Macaria (Markham) 143
Dethicke, Henry 76
Dial for all agues (Jones) 147
Dialogue against the feuer pestilence (Bullein) 65–66, 80
"Didymus Mountain" 76
Digby, Everard 36, 174n.52
Digges, Leonard 13, 48–50, 53–57, 102, 114–15, 149–50, 155, 157
Digges, Thomas 48–49, 53–54, 97, 111, 114–17, 149–51, 155, 195nn.49, 53
Dinteville, Jean de 59
The discouerie of witchcraft (Scot) 79
Discourse of horsemanship (Markham) 135
Discourses (Cornaro) 25
Dodoens, Rembert 131
Dover Harbor 111, 114–17, 151
Drake, Sir Francis 81–82, 108–9
Draxe, Thomas 15
Dreadnought (Baker) 116
drink 30–34
"Dr. Stevens Water" 87

Dudley, Robert 114–15, 155
Dyets dry dinner (Buttes) 79, 186n.46
dysentery 18

Eamon, William 4
Early Modern English Text Corpus 19
East India Company 111, 123, 161
Eden, Richard 58, 93–94, 97–98, 108, 156
Eisenstein, Elizabeth 3–4
Ekirch, A. Roger 34
Elements of geometrie (Euclid) 12, 51, 98, 148, 159–60
Elizabethan alterations 62–92
Elizabeth I, Queen,
    after the Armada 106–7, 109
    alterations 73, 79–80, 89
    expansion of the royal navy 111
    maritime matters 94
    reconstruction of Dover Harbor 117, 151
    regimens and rules 18, 22, 25
Elyot, Thomas 145–47, 153, 162, 167n.14
    introduction 8–9
    knowledge mongers 145–47, 153, 162
    public discourses 117
    regimens and rules 17–18, 20, 23–26, 28, 31, 35, 38–39, 44
"English attire" 25
The English Housewife (Markham) 138–40, 201n.54
The English husbandman (Markham) 135–36
English Revolution 143
Estienne, Charles 64, 135
Euclid 12, 51, 54, 98, 148, 159–60
evacuations 8, 19, 24, 38, 70, 146
"evil diet" 65
exercise 35–36, 38
Exercises (Blundeville) 13–14, 94, 96, 104
The expert midwife (Rüff) 85

Farwell to husbandry (Markham) 138
Feudigraphia (Folkingham) 55
Fioravanti, Leonardo 2, 68, 75, 147
Fitzgerald, John 117

Fitzherbert, John 10, 17–18, 39–41, 43, 47, 170n.1, 175–76nn.63, 65
flax 41, 74, 111, 137, 141
Floraes paradise (Plat) 153
Folkingham, William 55
food 30–34, 43
Foure bookes of husbandry (Heresbach) 78
Frampton, John 72
French pox *see* syphillis
"Friendly Advertisement to the Navigators of England" (Barlow) 106
Frisius, Gemma 58, 99
Frobisher, Martin 100–101, 109
Fuchs, Leonhart 66–67, 74
Fuller, Thomas 3
The fyrst boke of the introduction of knowledge (Boorde) 27

Galen 18, 23–24, 29, 31, 35, 69, 127
Galenic theory 7, 26, 30, 35, 39, 71–75, 119, 124–26, 145–47
Galle, Philips 70
Garcie, Pierre 61, 94
The Garden of Eden (Plat) 154
The gardeners labyrinth (Hyll) 75–76
The garden of health (Langham) 35
gardening 10, 75–76, 78, 133, 147, 153–54
Gardiner, Richard 10, 80, 82, 136, 153, 186–87n.50
Gate of knowledge (Recorde) 53, 148
General practice of physick (Wirsung) 19, 85
General and rare memorials pertayning to the perfect arte of nauigation (Dee) 99
geography 2, 12, 14–15, 58–60, 97, 103, 145
geometry 51–53, 55, 153
Georgics (Virgil) 135
Gerard, John 32, 70, 131–33
Gessner, Conrad 2, 68, 147, 182n.12
Gilbert, Humphrey 63
Gilbert, William 105–6
globes
  and Blagrave 148
  English 111

the Intellectual World 118
  Molyneux 109–10
Glover, Mary 85–86
God 3, 65, 67
God Speed the Plough (McRae) 4
The good husvvifes ievvell (Dawson) 2, 6, 89
Goodyer, John 131
Googe, Barnabe 78
The Gouernayle of helthe 20, 170n.7
The Gouernement of healthe (Bullein) 26
Gower, John 45
grafting 11, 44, 76–77, 154
Grand routier (Garcie) 94, 190n.3
Gresham College 107, 156
Grocers Company of London 122
The ground of artes (Recorde) 11–12, 46, 52–53, 56, 148
Groundes (Shute) 56
Ground (Recorde) 56
guaiacum 69–70
Guillemeau, Jacques 85
Gwinne, Matthew 129

Hakluyt, Richard 60, 93, 97–98, 109–10, 161
Hammond, Henry 1
Handley, Sasha 34
Harington, Sir John 21–22
Hariot, Thomas 63
Harkness, Deborah 4
Harrison, William 75, 77, 113
Harris, Richard 44
Hart, James 8–9, 38–39
Hartlib, Samuel 16, 143
Harvey, Gabriel 104, 148–49, 151, 158, 192n.21
Hatton, Sir Christopher 108
The hauen of health (Cogan) 26
Hawkins, John 112
Healths improvement (Moffatt) 26, 30, 32
Henrietta Maria, Queen 132
Henry VIII, King 23, 27, 32, 43–47, 58, 87, 98, 111, 116–17, 151, 158
The herball or Generall historie of plants (Gerard) 32, 131

Herball (Gerard) 32, 131
Herbert, William 54
Heresbach, Conrad 78
Hermes Trismegistus 68
Herring, Francis 125–27, 197–98nn.22-7
Hester, John 68, 71, 73, 75, 119, 147
Hillier, Nicholas 111
Hindu-Arabic system 45
Hippocrates 23
Hippocratic-Galenic tradition 8, 68
Historia medicinal (Monardes) 69, 72
Hohenheim, Theophrastus von *see* Paracelsus
Holbein, Hans 58–59
Holland, Henry 23
Holland, Philemon 22
Hondius, Jodocus 111
Hood, Thomas 101–2, 107–8, 110, 157, 192–93n.29
hops 26, 79, 136, 140
horticulture 7, 75, 81
housewives 83–91
Howell, James 156
How to Do It (Bell) 4
Hues, Robert 110, 194n.36
Hull, Susan W. 86, 188n.65
"humble pie" 89
Hungers preuention (Markham) 137
Hunt, Nicolas 2, 162
The husbandmans fruitfull orchard 44
husbandry 17–18, 40–43, 78, 83, 117, 135–42, 144, 153, 175–76n.65
"huswifery" 2, 11, 40, 83–84, 135, 138–39
Hygiasticon (Lessius) 25
Hyll, Thomas 10, 75–78, 147, 184n.32

Industrial Revolution 3
influenza 18
Introduction for to lerne to reckon with a pen (Recorde) 53
Inuentions or deuises (Bourne) 102
Ioyfull newes out of the newfound world (Frampton) 72

Jackson, Elizabeth 85–86
Jacobi, Joannes 64
James I, King 72, 78–79, 83, 121, 123

The Jewel House: Elizabethan London and the Scientific Revolution (Harkness) 4
Jewel(l) 2
The jewell house of art and nature (Plat) 2–3, 80–83, 153
Johnson, Matthew 131–32
Jonas, Richard 84
Jones, John 66–67, 147
Jorden, Edward 86

The kalender of shepherdes (Pynson) 20
Kellwaye, Simon 66
"kindred and affinity" 151
"King's Evil" 147
"kitchen physic" 11
Klinike, or, The diet of the diseased (Hart) 8
knowledge-mongers 15–16, 143–63
Knutsson, Bengt 64
Kratzer, Nicholas 58–59

Lachrymæ Londinenses 119
Ladurie, Emmanuel Le Roy 6
Lambarde, William 113
Langham, William 35, 174n.49
Langton, Christopher 34–35
L'art et maniere de semer (Brossard) 154
Lawson, William 10
Leicester, Earl of *see* Dudley, Robert
Leigh, Valentine 49–50
Leonardo of Pisa 45
Le routier de la mer (Garcie) 61, 94
LeRoy, Louis 156
Les clarcissement de la langue francoyse (Palsgrave) 46
Lessius, Hygiasticon 25
Leuven University 99
Liber Abacci (Leonardo of Pisa) 45
Liebault, Jean 135
Linacre, Thomas 23, 87
Little Ice Age 136
l'Obel, Matthias 131
Lodge, Thomas 126
London, William 10, 106, 143, 145, 147–48, 153, 156, 158
Lucar, Cyprian 55, 149, 151, 153–55, 179n.24

Lupton, Thomas 63
Lydgate, John 20, 25–26

macaroni 81
Machlinia, William de 64, 181n.3
McRae, Andrew 4
magnetic variations 105
Maison Rustique, or the covntrey farme (Estienne) 64, 78, 135
The maner and fourme how to kepe a perfecte reconyng (Weddington) 50
Maner of measurynge (Benese) 47–48
Maplet, John 74, 184n.29
Marbeck, Roger 73
The Marchants avizo (Browne) 160–61
"Mariner's Guide" (Hood) 101
The mariners mirrour 107–8, 162–63
Markham, Gervase 2, 10–11, 14–15, 89, 117, 135–43, 153–55, 200nn.44, 47-9, 201n.51
Markhams farwell to husbandry (Markham) 135
Martyr d'Anghiera, Peter 97
Mary I, Queen 48
Mascall, Leonard 11, 77–79, 154, 185n.39
The mathematical ievvel (Blagrave) 2, 103–4, 148
"Mathematicall Praeface" (Dee) 12, 98, 148
mathematics 12, 45–57, 59, 97, 103–4, 107, 109–16, 157–58
Maunsell, Andrew 3, 19, 170n.3
Mayerne, Dr. Theodore de 119
Mayerne, Theodore de 122
Maynwaring, Everard 38, 174n.56
Maynwaring, Tutela 24
melancholia 23–24, 34
Mellis, John 50, 53
mensuration 45–62, 148
mercantile medicine 125–29
Mercator, Gerard 99, 101, 109, 157–58
Mercer's Company 98
Merchant Adventurers 8, 57
Merchant Adventurers in Antwerp 57
Merchant Adventurers to New Lands *see* Muscovy Company

The merchants evvell (Hunt) 162
The merchants hand-maide (Warre) 162
The merchants ievvel (Hunt) 2
The merchants mappe of commerce (Roberts) 158, 160
mercury 69–70
The method of physick (Barrough) 85
Middleton, Christopher 36
Midland Revolt (1607) 15
Mirica, Gaspar à 99
"Mirrors of Health and Treasures of Poor Men" (Slack) 19, 170n.4
Moffatt, Thomas 26, 30, 32, 173n.32
Molyneux, Emery 109–11
Monardes, Nicolás 69–70, 72
monastic dissolution 45
Moore, Phillip 28–29, 31, 33
More, Richard 12–13, 102
More, Thomas 15
The moste profitable and commendable science, of surueying of landes, tenementes, and hereditamentes (Leigh) 49–50
Moulton, Thomas 9, 66, 146, 167n.15, 181n.8
Moxon, Joseph 111
Müenster, Sebastian 58, 97
Muffet, Thomas 119
Murrell, John 88
Muscovy Company 53–54, 57, 97–98, 105, 111, 148, 161
Myrour or glasse of helthe (Moulton) 66, 146
The mysteryes of nature, and art (Bate) 3, 154–55

native soil 133, 135–42
Naturall and artificial directions for health (Vaughan) 31–32
The naturall and morall historie of the East and West Indies (de Acosta) 72
Nauigations 161
The nauigators supply (Barlow) 2, 106
navigation 100, 102, 108, 110, 114, 118, 156–57

The nevv and admirable arte of setting of corne (Plat) 80, 82
Nevv directions of experience by the authour for the planting of timber and firevvood (Standish) 78
Nevv orchard and garden (Lawson) 10
New booke of cookerie (Murrell) 88
"New Cambriol" 33
The newe attractiue Containyng a short discourse of the magnes or lodestone (Norman) 104, 192n.23
The newe iewell of health (Gessner) 2, 68–69, 75, 147
New found vvorlde (Thevet) 101–2
The New Practical Navigator (Wright) 158
Newton, Thomas 25
New World 16, 75, 144
"non-naturals" doctrine 8
Norden, John 55, 116, 117, 151, 179n.23
Norman, Robert 104–6
Northeast Passage 8
Nova Reperta (Galle) 70
Nuova Scienzia (Lucar) 149

Oeconomicus (Xenophon) 43
Of the interchangeable course (LeRoy) 156
Of the Proficience and Advancement of Learning, Divine and Human (Bacon) 1
Oldcastle, Hugh 50
The olde mans dietarie (Newton) 25, 171–72n.17
Ortelius, Abraham 1–2
Osiander, Andreas 66

Pacioli, Luca 45, 50, 53, 176n.1
Palissey, Bernard 82
Palsgrave, John 46
Pancius, Petrus 96
Pantometria (Digges) 114, 149
Paracelsus 68, 70, 74, 88, 118–19, 124–25, 127–28, 147
Paridisi in sole 132
Parker, Matthew 11

Parkinson, John 131–33, 200n.40
Partridge, John 8, 11, 86–87, 89, 138
The pathway to knowledge (Recorde) 52, 53
The pathway to perfect sayling (Polter) 102
Paynell, Austin Friar Thomas 21–23
Peacham, Henry 9, 145
The pearle of practise, or Practisers pearle (Hester) 68
Peele, James 50
The pen's excellencie (Billingsley) 159
Perfite Platform for a Hop Garden (Scot) 154
Pettegree, Andrew 88, 189n.71
Pharmacopoeia Londinensis 121–22, 131
Phayre, Thomas 65
"Philaretes" 73, 183n.25
phlegmatic 34
plague,
    Antonine 69
    Black Death 19–20, 64
    endemic threat of 64–73
    epidemic of 1625 127, 129, 196nn.7-8
    grim reaper 80–81
    pandemic patterns 181n.6
    "Plague of Galen" 69
    and public health 119–21, 123, 125
    recurrent 14–15, 18
plants 74–83
Plat, Hugh 2–4, 10–11, 15, 80–83, 89–91, 102, 135, 153–54, 159, 187n.57
Plattes, Gabriel 15–16, 143–45
Politics (Aristotle) 158
Polter, Richard 102
"polymechanists" (Harvey) 151
polytechnoscopy (Harvey) 149
Poore mans iewell (Brasbridge) 2, 67–68
"Portingalls" 60
potato-roots 32, 131
The Practical Renaissance 13, 15
"practice" 17, 49
The practise of pietie (Bayly) 1
pregnancy 84–86

INDEX

Priest, Robert 131
The Principall nauigations (Hakluyt) 60, 109, 161
Principe, Lawrence 71
Proclamation for the Preservation of Woods (James I) 78
The profitable Arte of Gardening (Hyll) 75–76
Profitable instructions for the manuring, sowing, and planting of kitchin gardens (Gardiner) 80
The profitable intelligencer (Plattes) 16
Proude, Richard 61–62
Purchas, Samuel 161
Pvrchas his pilgrimes in five bookes (Purchas) 161
Pynson, Richard 20

quadrants 57, 98, 103–4
Quesiti et inventioni diverse (Tartaglia) 55
quicksilver *see* mercury

Rackham, Oliver 77, 185n.41
Ramist table 25, 51
Rathborne, Aaron 55, 151
Raynalde, Thomas 84–85, 147
Read, Alexander 123
ready reckoning 46, 49
reckoning 46, 52–53
Recorde, Robert 11–12, 52–60, 97, 148–49, 157–58, 176n.4, 178–79n.19
Records arithmetick containing the ground of arts (Recorde) 158
Reformation 2–3, 28, 45, 47, 101
regimens 8–9, 11, 18–29, 36, 38, 64–65
Regimen sanitatis Salerni (Holland) 20–21, 23, 171n.13
Regiment for the sea (Bourne) 100–102, 108
Restoration, the 16
Robert of Normandy 20
Roberts, Lewes 158, 160–63
The Rosengarten (Rosslin) 84, 147
Rosslin, Eucharius 84, 147
Rüff, Jacob 85, 188n.62
"Rules of Practice" 56–57

Russwurin, Valentine 70
rutters 94

Sailing School (Schotte) 4
St. Sepulchre's parish 67
Salerno, School of 20, 22, 24, 31, 69
salt 2, 32, 67–68, 82, 124
Sanderson, William 109–10
sanguine 4, 23–24
sarsaparilla 72
Saxton, Christopher 116
Scheubel, Johannes 53
Schotte, Margaret 4
Science and the Secrets of Nature (Eamon) 4
Scientific Revolution 3–4
Sclater, William 1
Scot, Reginald 136
Scot, Reynolde 79, 154, 186n.47
The seamans secrets (Davis) 94, 110, 114
Secretum secretorum (Aristotle) 20
seeds of discretion 40–41, 43–44
self-preservation 18–21
Selve, Georges de 59
seven "stages" of life (Shakespeare) 24, 171n.16
Shakespeare, William 24, 171n.16
shipbuilding 8, 111–13, 151
Ship of Fools (Brant) 4
Short introduction for to learne to Swimme (Middleton) 36
Shute, John 56, 151
Sidney, Sir Philip 93
Siraisi, Nancy 64
Slack, Paul 19, 64
Smith, Sir John 113–14
Solomon's Seal 133
The souldiers accidence (Markham) 155–56
Spanish Armada 81, 106–7, 109, 113
Stadius, Johannes 94
Standish, Arthur 15, 78, 186–87n.45
"stereometria" 49
Stirpium Historiae Pemptades Sex Stirpium (Rembert) 131
Stradanus, Johannes 70
Stratioticos (Digges) 114–16, 149–50, 155, 195n.51

Sufficiencie of English medicines (Bright) 130
Summa de Arithmetica Geometria (Pacioli) 45, 53
sundials 58, 104
Sundrie nevv and and artificiall remedies against famine (Plat) 80–82
Surflet, Richard 64, 78, 135
The surueyors dialogue (Norden) 55
The svrgions mate (Woodall) 123–24
The svrveyor in foure bookes (Rathborne) 55
sweating sickness 18, 128, 147, 198n.30
syphilis 18, 69–70, 147

"Table of Timber measure" 13
Tartaglia, Niccolò 55, 149
Taverner, John 80, 136, 153
Tectonicon (Digges) 149
Thayre, Thomas 14
Theatrum orbis terrarum (Ortelius) 1–2
theodolite 48, 55, 57
The trumpet of Apollo (Clarke) 73
Thevet, André 101–2
Thirsk, Joan 31
Thirty Years' War 136
This is the myrour or glasse of helth (Moulton) 9
Three bookes of colloquies (Lucar) 149
tobacco 25, 72–73, 117, 130, 132
The treasure of Euonymus (Gessner) 68, 147
Treasure of knowledge (Recorde) 53
The Treasure of pore men 23
The treasurie of commodious conceits, & hidden secrets (Partridge) 11, 86, 88, 189n.67
Tuke, Thomas 11
Tunstall, Thomasin 133
Turner, William 7, 32, 67, 74–76, 81, 87, 101, 131, 133, 163, 184–85n.28, 189n.67, 198n.26
Tusser, Thomas 10–11, 15, 34, 40, 63, 83–84, 87, 135, 153
Tutela sanitatis sive Vita (Maynwaring) 24

Ubaldini, Petruccio 109–10
Ugieine or A conservatory of health (Brooke) 36
Urinal of physick (Recorde) 52
usus et fabra 103

vade mecums 16
Vandernote, John 66, 181n.9
Vaughan, William 29, 31–34
Venner, Tobias 24, 29, 32, 173n.39
Vespucci, Amerigo 61
veterinary medicine 41
Via recta ad vitam longam (Venner) 24, 29
Villa Nova, Arnoldus de 21
Virgil 135
Virginian potato 131
Vives, Juan Luis 84, 187n.60
volvelles 58
von Hutten, Ulrich 69–70, 183n.18
The vvonderfull yeare (Dekker) 160
VVork for chimny-sweepers (Marbeck) 73

"waggoners" 109
Waghenaer, Lucas Janszoon 107–9, 193n.31
Wall, Wendy 88
Warre, James 162
Wealden iron industry 111
Weald of Kent 137
Weddington, John 50
The welspring of sciences (Baker) 56–57
The whetstone of witte (Recorde) 52–54, 56–57
Whitwell, Charles 106
The widowes treasure (Partridge) 8, 87–88, 159
wine 22–23, 31, 33–34, 49, 66, 77–78, 83, 87
Wirsung, Christopher 19, 85
witchcraft 85–86
Witt, Richard 158
women *see* housewives
Woodall, John 123–24, 129, 197n.18
Woodalls viaticum: the path-way to the surgions chest (Woodall) 124
woodlands 77–78, 185n.41

wool 34, 97–98, 141
Woolley, Hannah 11, 140
Woolwich royal shipyard 113
Worshipful Company of Apothecaries 122, 147
Worshipful Company of Barber-Surgeons 123–24, 147
Worsop, Edward 54–55, 102, 179n.22

Wright, Edward 101, 114, 157–58
Wyatt, Thomas 48
Wynkyn de Worde 20

Xenophon 43, 135
Xenophon's treatise of householde 43

Yersinia pestis bacterium 65

www.ingramcontent.com/pod-product-compliance
Lightning Source LLC
Chambersburg PA
CBHW051809230426
43672CB00012B/2668